Party Coalitions

John R. Petrocik

Party Coalitions

Realignment and the Decline of the New Deal Party System

The University of Chicago Press
Chicago and London

The University of Chicago Press, Chicago 60637
The University of Chicago Press, Ltd., London

Library of Congress Cataloging in Publication Data

Petrocik, John R   1944–
  Party coalitions.

  Bibliography: p.
  Includes index.
  1. Political parties—United States.   2. United
States—Politics and government—1945–   I. Title.
JK2261.P49   324.273   80–22212
ISBN 0–226–66378–7

Contents

Acknowledgments

Acknowledging one's intellectual debts is a troubling task. The genesis of the inspiration for an idea is often forgotten. At other times ideas emerge out of the interaction of several minds, resulting in a paternity that is impossible to establish. So I do not propose to attempt a comprehensive list of those who have contributed to this book. Suffice it to say that I would like to think that I learned something from every author cited, and I must thank them. But there are some people to whom I owe debts that must be specifically acknowledged. The emphasis on the sociology of the parties can be traced to a passing remark by Kenneth Prewitt and a sustained campaign by Andrew M. Greeley. Andrew Greeley is a persistent and forceful man, but his influence on this matter arises out of his persuasive scholarship. My model of political conflict and party politics is a direct result of several years of listening to him, talking with him, and reading his research. Norman Nie and Sidney Verba—teachers, colleagues, and friends—have, in different ways been a major influence on me, and they deserve a great deal of credit for whatever merit this work has. Anyone who has been privileged to work with such people as Norman and Sidney knows full well that their intellectual contributions to one's development are too numerous to list.

M. Kent Jennings and Herbert Ascher were helpful critics, especially since they usually found the same faults and pointed to similar remedies. Their agreement overcame my unfortunate tendency to resist good advice. I am grateful to both of them.

Finally, I would like to thank the energetic secretaries of the UCLA political science department. At one time or another Sharon Beckom, Nancy Gusten, Becky Herrera, Lila Merritt, Claire Suen, Clare Walker, and Hei-ok Yoon typed a part of the manuscript. Becky Herrera, however, was indispensable. She typed and retyped several drafts of several chapters. Because she worked so hard, I was able to complete this in something less than a frenzy.

Part 1

Voters and Parties

1 The New Deal Party System

Indications of Realignment

The study of party realignment has been a "growth stock" since the mid-1960s and there is no immediate prospect of a downturn in the curve. It will continue to attract the research energies of scholars as long as turbulence marks the relationship of the parties of the electorate. Before scholars are satisfied that they have answered all the important questions and most of the minor ones, the study of realignment will probably produce a literature as large as did the study of political development.

The fruits of this burgeoning research enterprise have been markedly uneven, but the overall increment of knowledge is impressive. The gross findings of early research have been re-examined and fitted with other information about the parties and the behavior of voters. The "discovery" which marked early work has yielded to more systematic research on some of the initial ideas and to attempts to reconcile apparent conflicts. There are, of course, new things to discover. There is a strong element of conjecture in much of what is known about party realignment. Only additional research will resolve these matters, and it would be unfair to characterize current work as a mopping-up operation.

This book attempts to add new information and rebuild a portion of the theoretical structure. But the former is possible only because of the latter, and, of course, the debt of both to prior research is enormous. There are two major themes in these pages.

First, the generally held theories about realignment are much more disorderly than we seem to appreciate. They are so unspecific that almost any shift in party-related phenomena has been treated as evidence of a realignment. Changes in incumbency rates, electoral oscillation, defection rates, correlations between issue preferences and vote choice, and turnout, to name just a few, have served as indicators of a realignment, and even as evidence for whether the party system will survive in anything like its present form. Most students have failed to question this variety, assuming that virtually all the things that have been studied are vital signs of the state of the party system. Only a few, Flanigan and Zingale, for example, have raised an objection and indicated a need to distinguish between changes in the party system and changes that constitute realignments of the electorate.[1]

The second theme of the book is an exploration of the consequences of one particular definition of realignment both for our historical understanding of realignments and for diagnosing the meaning of contemporary indicators of party system change.The extent to which the definition permits an interweaving of other changes in an attempt to explain the shifting party coalitions is a major component of the analysis.

The theoretical argument is necessary for the empirical analysis of contemporary party changes. After a brief examination of the turbulence of the party system, the book turns to the theoretical arguments.

The Stability of the Party System

The age and apparent permanence of the Democratic and Republican parties have given them a preeminent place in American politics. They are the institutions that apprise the public of the important issues, that sponsor candidates in elections, that turn issues into an election choice, and that champion one group over another. They have monopolized political office for the past century and a half. Election rules drastically restricting the effective entry of third parties and their candidates have assured major control of the political arena.

There are several reasons for this stability. One of the most important is the flexibility of the American parties on social and economic issues. Support built up with a set of issue positions in one generation is pursued across generations by adopting positions which the new supporters of the party seem to prefer. The parties do not adopt immutable stances on immutable issues. The issues, and the relationship of the parties to them, change across generations. But, fortunately, neither changes very rapidly. Because children follow the party preference of their parents, both the social base and the issue concerns of the supporters of a party tend not to change so quickly that the parties cannot adjust, and, by adjusting, retain their clientele.[2] With every new generation, therefore, the party adopts the mix of issue positions most congenial to a large majority of the progeny of their voting members. So, although the candidates, issues, and problems facing the new generation may be completely different, the party their parents supported is still the better representative of their own position.[3]

During a period when the issue positions of groups and individuals and the role of the parties in expressing these positions are fixed, the party system will be stable at every level.

The post–World War II years seemed to be such a time in this country. Over 71 percent of the electorate sampled in the early 1950s were committed to one of the parties; only about 7 percent insisted that they held no preference for either party; and less than 30 percent did not feel positive enough about one party to offer more positive than negative evaluations of it. Most citizens voted for the candidates of the party for which they admitted a preference (only 28 percent reported ever voting for the "other" party); and the bulk of those who did not were idiosyncratically responding to the personalities of the candidates. Only about 7 percent of the variance in party defection was correlated with the voter's issue preferences.[4] Moreover, the identification with the parties was stable. Over 81 percent of those sampled had never changed party affiliation. Discounting even a fraction of this percentage to selective recall still leaves a large proportion of the population with a constant party identification.

Changes since the Early Fifties

By the end of the 1960s, however, the daily fare of American electoral politics seemed to have little in common with the images that had been constructed out of the first election studies. Intense debate over a multitude of issues produced a political rancor that had not characterized the Eisenhower years. Some of the issues were familiar, for example, the role of the government in directing social change, in determining economic policy, and in assuring the economic welfare of segments of the society, as well as the stance of the country vis-à-vis her major rivals abroad; but some others, for example, race relations and the war in Vietnam, were unfamiliar, at least in the way the public was oriented to them. But whether the issues were new or old, the public agenda was increasingly cast in terms of fundamentals.[5] The tradition of nominating candidates on the basis of their ability to attract votes and maintain party support was displaced by the nomination of such divisive candidates as Goldwater and McGovern.

Changes in the tenor of the campaigns and the nature of the candidates were matched by a metamorphosis of the electorate. The proportion of independents began to creep upward, and defection increased even as the level of turnout declined. Expressed levels of involvement with electoral campaigns waned despite a steady, albeit small, increase in the proportion of persons who expressed overall interest in politics. Evaluations of the parties became less positive. More citizens were able to distinguish parties along issue lines, and the level of issue consistency increased markedly.[6]

A decade of Realignment or Perturbation?

For some observers, these candidates and the accompanying erosion of the hold of party symbols on the electorate represent a major transformation of the party system. Others simply concede that the parties and the electorate's relationship to them have undergone some changes, many of which may not be permanent. Should the new behavior of the electorate be seen as a durable new pattern of response to candidates, parties, and elections? Or is it not a change at all, merely "sound and fury, signifying nothing"? More to the point, did the 1964, 1968, and 1972 elections mark a realignment of the parties, or were they oscillations around a basically stable trend line? Walter Dean Burnham, Everett Ladd, Charles Hadley, and Warren Miller and Teresa Levitan are prominent proponents of the first thesis, although their interpretations of the causes and final shape of the change differ. Sundquist foresees a resurgence of the old party system. Rubin predicts continued oscillation. Nie, Verba, and Petrocik end equivocally, arguing that it could go either way.[7]

Whether the past decade has witnessed a realignment depends on what is seen as required for a realignment. The concept has been used to describe a variety of changes in the electorate's relationship to the parties.

1. The Party-Plurality Conception

V.O. Key pointed to the years around 1896 and 1928–36 as times when the party system underwent a major alignment.[8] Whether one looks at the number of offices won or the party with a majority of ballots, the central feature of both periods was a change in the popular support the parties received. As a result, realignments have been identified with a change in party pluralities. Most scholars have used this identification in their attempts to analyze contemporary party patterns.[9]

It would be difficult to document a party realignment during the past decade using this definition of the concept. The Democratic majority has remained intact. It has not increased to any appreciable degree, nor has it declined. The presidential vote has shifted wildly in the last four elections. And although the Republicans have not done as well in contests for other offices, for example, the Congress, governorships, and state legislatures, their lack of success does not seem to have much to do with a clear decline in the proportion of votes cast for Republicans. The Democratic share of the total vote cast for Congress has been stable at around 53–55 percent for the past twenty years.[10] A surge in the number of gerrymandered election districts and a shift in the sectional basis of the party vote seem to be responsible for the relative Republican decline.[11]

2. The "Exciting Times" Conception

The second definition of the concept of realignment stresses the "exciting" nature of party politics during periods of electoral realignment. Some of its characteristics include a short-lived but intense disruption of traditional voting patterns, an abnormally high intensity in the conduct of party nominations and in the writing of party platforms, an ideological polarization within and between the parties, and a surge of voter participation.[12]

By this definition, the evidence for a realignment is mixed but clearly positive. It fails only at the point where it requires a surge in the size of the electorate; the proportion of the electorate which actually votes in elections has declined since 1960. Other indicators, however, point to substantial change.

Defection rates in 1964, 1968, and 1972 produced atypical winning coalitions, and there is also evidence of considerable ideological polarization between and within the parties. The average issue difference between the two parties has increased since 1960.[13] Republicans were more conservative than Democrats through 1960. In the 1968 and 1972 elections they were even more conservative. Whether this is a large shift is open to interpretation, but it certainly did occur. The increase in the interparty issue difference displayed another feature of electoral realignments, internal party polarization. Republican activists have been more politically conservative than rank-and file Republicans in every period for which data have been examined.[14] The new feature of these data is the ideological cleavage between active and inactive Democrats after 1964. By 1972, Democratic activists exhibited as extreme an ideological bias as Republican activists.

Evidence of intense conflict over the conduct of party nominations and the writing of party platforms is also clearly visible. Since 1936, the quadrennial debate in the Republican party has been whether the party should be true to itself and select a conservative or accept the argument that the country was out of sympathy with conservative principles and nominate a more liberal candidate. The expansion of conflict over nominations, therefore, was not contributed by the Republicans but by the Democrats. Costain's analysis of the nominating conventions illustrates this change.[15] For each contested nomination since 1948, an ideological cleavage was prominent in the Republican convention, with right-wing factionalism the dominant predictor of the winner's support through 1976. In the Democratic party the mainstream bloc dominated the winner's coalition until 1968. In that year, the impact of the left wing on the Democratic nomination surged dramatically. By 1976 the ideological wings of both parties put up alternatives to the candidate the parties finally selected, and in both parties there was a sharp cleavage along ideological lines.

In summary, greater political conflict has marked the period, traditional voting patterns have been disrupted, interest in political issues has surged to a higher level, and issue conflict within and between the parties is much more in evidence.

3. The "Changing Shape" Conception

A third definition, largely formulated by Burnham, conceives of electoral realignment as a change in the patterns of behavior that characterize the electorate's response to the parties.[16] This definition assumes that realignments bring new patterns of political behavior in their wake, and by this definition the recent decade has witnessed a realignment.

First, enormous variability has characterized presidential contests since 1952. They look nothing like the elections of 1932 to 1948. And they are, no matter what is said, hard to reconcile with an electorate in which 54 percent are supposed to be committed to the Democratic party.

The presidential elections are even more troublesome since in only one election, the 1952 contest, was the Republican victor able to pull a Republican majority into Congress. Democratic dominance in Congress highlights an increase in the "insularity" of congressional elections from virtually every conceivable electoral tide.[17]

Some of this "disaggregation" of the party system may reflect institutional tinkering, for example, an abundance of Democratic gerrymanders after 1964; but there is reason to believe that changes in individual behavior have also contributed, and this points to a shift in behavior patterns of the sort Burnham has used for indexing realignments.

It is not necessary to make inferences about individual behavior from aggregate data. There is an abundance of survey data which require the development of new images of the elector. The American voter is less habituated to his party preference after the mid-1960s compared with the 1950s.[18] In 1952 and 1956, 70 percent of the electorate could be categorized as supporters of the parties. By 1968 and 1972 this proportion was down to less than 53 percent. Although party preference continues to be highly correlated with the vote choice, it explains less than half of the variance of twenty years ago.

Clearly, the sixties have seen substantial changes in the role of the parties for the political orientations of the electorate. Events have altered the attentiveness of the public to politics, and they have altered the degree to which the average citizen structures political issues. Parties have become less central to the political orientations of voters. These changes are yielding a party system whose "shape" is markedly different from that of the party system discovered by the early election studies.

4. The Political-Agenda Conception

A fourth manifestation of electoral realignments is found in alterations in what has been described as the "political agenda." A party system, in this perspective, is distinguished not only by unique political leaders and a distinctive distribution of party support but also by areas of agreement and axes of cleavage which all participants understand to be the major topics of politics and interparty conflicts. Jahnige, Funston, Ginsberg, and, especially, Everett C. Ladd are associated with this approach to the study of electoral realignment.[19] By this test, the verdict on whether the United States is in the middle of a realignment is incomplete. Again, however, the data are more positive than negative.

Recent studies by Weisberg and Rusk, for example, have documented the existence of crosscutting issues and political personalities.[20] Party preference, welfare issues, and a host of prominent mainline political leaders align along a single dimension. Attitudes on race, the Vietnam war, urban disorder, and some less traditional national political leaders cut across the primary axis. A similar analysis, conducted on data collected in 1975, paralleled these results. It showed that opinions on traditional economic welfare questions, national economic problems, and partisanship were closely correlated, while racial attitudes and attitudes on several social and life-style issues were basically orthogonal.

The data in the latter study do not do justice to the complexity of the agenda concept or to the idea that a party system has changed if the agenda undergoes a transformation, but they are corroborative, and they lend credence to the argument that a change in the society's agenda is about to precipitate an electoral realignment (if one has not already occurred).

5. The Changed-Coalitions Conception

A fifth characteristic of realignments is that they appear to represent transformations in the electoral base of the parties. V. O. Key's analysis of the rise of the New Deal was cast in terms of the emergence of distinct party preferences among Catholics, urban workers, Protestants, the silk-stocking crowd, and so forth.[21] Most party histories have emphasized the extent to which our parties have been coalitions of diverse ethnic and religious groups, and changes in the parties have often been explained in terms of the capacity of the parties to appeal to new groups or to broaden their appeal to groups associated with the opposition. Although this is the least-emphasized aspect of realignments, Key paid considerable attention to it in analyzing what he described as secular realignments. MacRae and Meldrum also dealt with change in the social basis of the Democratic party in Illinois after the 1920s, and it was prominent in Lubell's discussion of the development of the New Deal.[22] By this definition, too, the evidence of realignment is positive.

The party coalitions have undergone a substantial change in the past decade. The white South, the ethnics, and the hardhats have either slipped or at least loosened their moorings in the Democratic party. Equally important though numerically smaller losses of upper-status Protestant voters, New Englanders, and mid-Westerners have appeared to change the base of the Republicans. Most commentaries have focused on these changes as indicating potential weakening of the parties. Whether the parties have been weakened by these changes is moot. What is beyond debate is that the social base of the parties has been transformed.[23]

Clearly, most of the indicators of change are positive. There is room to debate the magnitude of the changes without calling their existence into question. The only expected change that has not occurred has been in the party pluralities, for the relative dominance of the Democratic party is undisturbed. The only question that remains is whether the shifts that have taken place are indicators of a realignment. That is, can the changes be fitted into a picture which might portray neither voter oscillation nor election-specific noise but a fundamental transformation of the party system? The answer depends upon what is agreed upon as fundamental transformation and whether some relationships between the changes mentioned above can be established.

It is the thesis of this book that the party system has undergone a major realignment over the past ten or fifteen years. Its contours are not as gross as many have expected, and for that reason the change has been misidentified and even overlooked. This book attempts to describe the change and to explain why it constitutes a party transformation major enough to merit the term "realignment"—and to do both these things in a way that is consistent with the data and with our theories of party systems and individual electoral behavior.

Chapter 2 is devoted to defining *party* in terms which are sensitive to its role in mobilizing voters. That definition is woven into the concept of *party realignment* (chap. 3), and both concepts are used to develop a perspective on party realignment which might have more utility than the multiple conceptions currently used to assess party changes. These ideas are then used to account for the development of the American party system (chap. 4). The history thus drawn is used to illustrate the preceding ideas, and it is presented to explain the character of the parties as they currently exist (chap. 5). Chapters 6–9 analyze the realignment that we have witnessed in the past decade.

A Historical Note on the Study of Electoral Coalitions

In the 1787 Massachusetts gubernatorial election of John Hancock, the Revolutionary War hero, defeated incumbent James Bowdoin, the suppressor of Shay's Rebellion. A Boston newspaper published this analysis.

	For Mr B.	For Mr H.
Users	28	0
Speculators in publick securities	576	0
Stockholders and directors of		
M———s B———k	81	0
Persons under British influence	17	0
Merchants, tradesmen, and other worthy		
members of society	21	448
Friends of the Revolution	0	327
Wizards	1	0

From Mark R. Levy and Michael S. Kramer, *The Ethnic Factor: How America's Minorities Decide Elections* (New York: Simon & Schuster, 1972)

Part 2

Social Groups, Parties, and Realignments

2 Meaning and Measurement of Realignment

Realignments as Changes in Party Coalitions

This book rests on a conception of realignment that requires a change in the partisanship of population groups.[1] An issue may be the reason for the change, but the altered division along the issue cleavage is not the essential symptom of realignment. *A realignment occurs when the measurable party bias of identifiable segments of the population changes in such a way that the social group profile of the parties–the party coalitions–is altered.*[2] A realignment is not a change in how the parties relate to the "agenda issues," although that may be the cause (or consequence) of a realignment. The "organic change" that constitutes a realignment is a shift in the alignment of party divisions with social cleavages.

This definition does not require a change in the aggregate levels of party support. The critical element of the definition is the durable and distinctive change in the groups which constitute the party coalitions. If the groups whose party bias has changed are large, the result of the change may be a shift in the balance of support that the parties enjoy. But a realignment that has not had this effect simply indicates that only small changes have occurred in the party bias of different groups, or that the group changes have counteracted each other, or that the groups which changed are not large enough to alter the competitive balance of the parties. Most, perhaps all, previous realignments have resulted in a transformation of the party equilibrium over a short period of time. But the social-group definition of realignment does not require a change in the party equilibrium.

As Key pointed out, realignments that alter the party equilibrium may be followed by "aftershocks" which continue to realign some groups long after a major change has occurred in the party balance.[3] To continue the geological metaphor, this definition also permits us to think of one class of realignments as "preshocks," that is, it is possible to have an electoral realignment without a major change in the party balance. In fact, the social-group definition of realignment does not require any change in party pluralities.

15

This party-coalition definition is the core of the analysis of re-alignment presented in this book. The study examines changes in the party bias of major segments of the electorate and changes in the social-group coalitions that we identify as the Democratic and Republican parties-in-the-electorate. Because movement rather than stasis characterizes both indicators, there is a realignment to describe and, in a specific way, to explain.

Analyzing Realignments

This party-coalition definition departs from the conventional assumption that electoral realignments are synonymous with a change to a new majority party. Yet it is a particularly useful (and maybe even superior) definition because it opens up new questions for research. Notably, when do changes in the coalitions affect party pluralities? What kinds of coalition changes influence the policy orientation of the parties? What kinds of agenda changes alter the party coalitions?

First, it should be pointed out, a transformation of the party coalitions is not insignificant because the relative electoral status of the parties is stable. If the realignment sorts groups with distinctive policy preferences, the consequences of even a small shift in the coalitions can have a large effect on the policy stance of the parties. The continuing decline of the white southern component of the Democratic party illustrates this clearly. The ever clearer racial liberalism of the Democrats and the carefully phrased Republican party support for black causes reflects the greater importance of blacks for the Democrats and of southern whites for the Re-publicans.

Separating realignment processes into several distinct compo-nents also makes it possible to devise more sophisticated explana-tions of the role of issues in precipitating realignments. We have assumed that realignments are forged by the appearance of new issues which the prevailing party system is unable to incorporate in its accepted agenda.[4] But how these issues affect party alignments has not been subjected to detailed analysis; there are many things that are unknown. For example: What kinds of issues provoke the cataclysmic changes that result in a new majority party? Are they different in kind from those that precipitate a realignment of smaller segments of the electorate, or are they only different in magnitude (however defined)? Alternatively, the whole idea of realignment issues may require more subtle conceptualization. It is clear that the American party system is based on an accumulation of cleavages.[5] Characteristically Democratic and Republic groups became so at different times and for different reasons. Southern whites, blacks, Catholics, Jews, and the urban working class came by their Democratic sympathies at different times over the past 150 years or so, and the interests that held these groups to the Democrats were not equally shared.[6] Why, therefore, should the precipitant of realignment be thought of (as it implicitly is) as *a* crosscutting issue that affects all segments of the electorate?

A more subtle and fruitful approach to studying the influence of issues on the party alignment might require the analysis to concentrate on segments of the electorate. In this approach, any given crosscutting issue might disrupt the partisan proclivities of only a fraction of the electorate whose sensitivity to the issue may be forecast. The quick response of southern whites to the injection of racial issues into party politics should surprise no one. Similarly, the issues that brought on the "system of '96" and the New Deal did not affect all groups; they were, on the contrary, specific to certain segments of the populace, some of whom may have been indifferent to party politics until these matters entered the public agenda. If the social-group heterogeneity of the Democratic and Republican parties is taken seriously there is good reason to suspect that different kinds of issues affect coalition groups differently, that some may affect few groups while others would affect many—there is almost no single issue that could be expected to affect all the coalition groups equally.

A second reason for adopting this definition of realignment is that it employs a conception of party that may be more theoretically useful than the one that implicitly underpins the electoral-majority definitions. It seems reasonable to ask for some correspondence between the definition of party and the definition of party realignment. Unfortunately, devising a connotative definition of *party* that commands general assent has eluded us, with the result that definitions abound. Some "definitions" are only analytic approaches, and frankly labeled as such.[7] There is, for example, an organizational approach to the study of parties, represented in the work of Schlesinger and Eldersveld; an office-seeking or competition approach, found in the work of Sigmund Neuman, Edward M. Sait, E. Schattschneider, Leon Epstein, and, especially, Anthony Downs; a cleavage representation theory, best manifested in the work of Lipset and Rokkan, the reader edited by Richard Rose, and in the views of ethnocultural historians like Samuel P. Hays, Lee Bensen, Richard Jensen, Paul N. Kleppner, and Ronald Formisano; and, finally, an ideological or policy perspective, found in such diverse places as Burk's 1770 definition of parties, Madison's Federalist 10, the APSA "responsible party" report, Wilson's and

McCloskey's studies of political activists, and Ladd's recent books on party change.[8] Each of these approaches might be useful in studying parties longitudinally or crossnationally. They might also serve in studies of party change in general and electoral realignments in particular. but the descriptive and explanatory power of only two of these approaches has been turned to analyses of electoral realignments.

It would assume too much self-consciousness and attentiveness to the symmetry of our theoretical architecture to believe that Key and those who followed his lead in studying electoral realignments were guided by definitions like those presented above. But in a society in which the most important thing about a party (except for ideological critics) is whether it is successful at the polls, it is easy to understand why the most important thing about a party (except for ideological critics) is whether it is successful at the polls, it is easy to understand why the most important piece in the definition of realignment would deal with the change in the party's success with the electorate (the office-seeking approach). Yet studies of realignment that focus only upon changes in party dominance ignore the fact that the greatest variety among party systems and within parties over time is to be found in the types of cleavages the parties represent and the manner in which they represent them.[9] The theoretical power of this fact sustained the crossnational study of party cleavages presented by Richard Rose.[10] In that book, analyses of the relationship between the electorate and the parties is cast in terms of the social characteristics of supporters, not in terms of the numerical popularity of a particular party. Charged to present a discussion of the variables which best describe the relationship between the electorate and parties, Philip Converse concluded that the variables "most necessary to maintain any monitoring of [political party] cleavages [in twelve Euro-American societies] are sociopolitical and few in number."[11] In reviewing the country-by-country analyses, he found that social status, religion, urban-rural differences, and regional variation in places of residence distinguished party support.[12] Their importance varied considerably, but in almost no instance were they insignificant. The intuitively obvious differences in the social and economic interests of the groups that characterize the electoral base of these parties, coupled with the ubiquitous nature of the variables that define the lines of cleavage, lend considerable empirical substance to Lipset and Rokkan's view that parties are "an institutionalization of alliances in conflict over policies and value committments within the larger body politic."[13]

American Parties as Social-Group Coalitions

Almost any other model of the party-voter alignment ignores politics in the ordinary sense of the word and deals too lightly with the persistent and substantively significant sociodemographic differences between supporters of the Republican and Democratic parties. To treat the party coalitions as aggregates of social groups—as much as or more than aggregates of issue groups—provides a considerable thread of continuity with previous studies of the sources of party support.[14] It also has the advantage of applying a general commonsense perspective about "who" supports "whom," and about who is a Democratic and who is a Republican voter.

Like those in other countries, the supporters of America's political parties have been distinguished by social, economic, demographic, and religious differences. This distinctness is so strong that it is the working politician's guide to what he must do to win votes. "From the stump . . . politicians righteously deplore any suggestion that their red-blooded American constituents might be influenced by bloc-voting patterns; off the stump they find it hard to discuss strategy in any other terms."[15] For such politicians, political discussion frequently turns on the undeserved rewards of the "other" group.[16] Scholars, like politicians, have been and still are sensitive to this sociology.

Wilfred Binkley justified his effort, in part, as an attempt to identify the social groupings which have supported American parties throughout their history, and Samuel Hays and Lee Benson encouraged a small army of historians to study the religious and cultural cleavages associated with party support.[17] A recent review article by James Wright has summarized this research;[18] and Paul Kleppner captured its spirit when he wrote that "partisan affiliations were not rooted in economic class distinctions. There were political expressions of shared values derived from the voters' membership in, and commitment to, ethnic and religious groups."[19] This perspective explains why Republican supporters, on the one hand, and Whigs in the 1830s and 1840s, tended to come from pietistic and evangelical church groups and, excepting Southerners, to be immigrants of old stock. Democrats, on the other hand, were from liturgical churches, for example, Catholic and Lutheran.[20]

Political scientists have not been insensitive to the social basis of the parties. Lubell's influential *Future of American Politics* placed considerable emphasis on the party preferences of different ethnic, religious, and regional groups in the population.[21]

Using a more conventional and less religious and ethnic paradigm of American politics, Walter Dean Burnham has demographically characterized the supporters of the parties. The Democratic counties were low income, mountain, upland, and frontier countries, and from the Appalachian Mountains eastward, counties where the Scotch-Irish had settled, and counties with fewer late immigrants.[22]

To catalogue all the various sociodemographic accounts of American party history would be exhausting. Professional historical debates about whether religious and doctrinal overtones to party politics in the past century were more important than the substantive political issues are far too extensive to review, much less evaluate, here. The essential point is that there is a tradition of political history analysis in the United States in which the central terms are social and demographic groupings.[23]

Given that such differences in the social basis of the parties persist, that they help to determine the programmatic differences between the parties, that the institution undergoes significant programmatic and electoral change when the social base is transformed, and that the purpose of these parties is to serve as a vehicle for the "policies and value commitments" of some portion of the population, it seems reasonable to view parties as coalitions of social groups and to see realignments as transformations in these coalitions. Conceiving of parties and realignments in this way generates a crossnationally useful approach that can capture cross-sectional and longitudinal variation in the institution. Furthermore, it provides an explanation of policy differences between the parties (parties represent different social groups with different interest), and it gives life to the notion that realignments create new power relationships in a society since it focuses upon the specific groups and interests whose influence is altered by virtue of their committment to one of the parties. Finally, the social-group approach is more useful for elaborating upon realignments since it disaggregates the phenomenon: Realignments can be studied as (1) a change in the social base of parties that is precipitated by (2) a transformation of the agenda which, affects (3) group perceptions of the parties and which may, under some circumstances, change (4) the competitiveness of the parties.

Types of Realignment

The definition presented here does not require a shift in the relative strength of the parties, though most historical realignments in the United States have caused just such a shift. The most dramatic examples are the realignments that took place in the 1820s and the 1850s. The reshuffling of support that accompanied the decline first of the Federalists and later of the Whigs were realignments that caused the demise of these parties.

The institutional effects of the third critical alignment were less dramatic. The farm depression that began in the 1870s broadened into an economic conflict between the sections, and the financial panic of 1893 added political stress. The extent to which the Democrats under Bryan were out of step with all the groups in the industrial Eastern and Central states is reflected in the sectional realignment that emerged from the election. The Eastern states moved sharply and uniformly toward the Republicans. Democratic counties or cities in the Northeast remained Democratic, but their pluralities were markedly smaller than they had been in previous years. An opposite development characterized party change in the West and the South. The Democratic bias of the South increased considerably, and the mining states of the West responded with enduring Democratic majorities. The nationwide character of the sectional polarization magnified the slight majority status that the Republicans had enjoyed since the Civil War; it did not result in a new majority party, but in a more secure majority party.

The fourth critical realignment in American history was the realignment that created the New Deal coalitions. This realignment produced a new majority party, but did so without destroying the major party, as two of the earlier realignments had done. It altered the party-social cleavage alignment in several ways. In addition to the now almost traditional support offered by the South and the West, the Democratic party mobilized a large portion of the industrial working class and the ethnic minorities.

There is, finally, a fifth type of realignment—one the system is currently experiencing—that differs from preceeding ones in that it lacks (so far at least) an emerging new majority party, a reinforcement of the current majority party, or the demise of either the Republicans or Democrats. For the most part, even the relative strength of the two parties is unchanged, but the Democratic and Republican coalitions look very different from those of twenty years ago.

Realignments and Critical Realignments

This last type of realignment appears to require a distinction between "critical" and "noncritical" realignment. A critical realignment changes the balance of strength between the parties, whereas a noncritical realignment is one in which the relative strength of the parties is stable. The consequences of a critical realignment will almost always be more dramatic than those of a noncritical one. The demise of a major party, or a dramatic shift in its electoral strength, will produce a larger "adjustment in community power relationships" than a simple shift of the party coalitions. The changes that accompany a noncritical realignment are more gradual, possibly more acrimonious, and probably more difficult to detect. Until it is possible to identify and study a number of noncritical realignments, however, there is no need to make any assumption about them. What the consequences of noncritical party transformations might be should remain an open question. But since realignments have been conceptually and empirically distinguished from electoral outcomes, it is clear that the critical/noncritical distinction is necessary, if only to keep the phenomena separate.

Realignment: Its Measurement

The conception of realignment developed above has empirical significance only because it is possible to develop indicators which distinguish it from other kinds of electoral variability. Its utility, therefore, turns on a set of operational measures that distinguish it from competing conceptions of electoral realignment.[24]

Burnham's notion that realignments change the nature of the party *system* is made operational by his conception of a party system as a pattern of political behavior and as a period in which one of the parties is predominant, and by his ability to convert this idea into a set of measurements.[25]

MacRae and Meldrum, following Key, conceive of a realignment as a change in the partisanship of segments of the electorate and as an enduring change in the relative electoral success of the parties.[26] Their techniques for measuring these phenomena yield a set of scores which they can use to characterize the degree of change in the partisanship of the electorate and, by relating these scores to social, economic, and demographic attributes, they can identify the social characteristics of the groups whose partisanship appears to have changed the most.

Burnham's and MacRae and Meldrum's work is notable for the correspondence between their theoretical formulation of realignments and the measurements they use. Others have been less careful, particularly those who describe realignments as a change in the parties' vote shares and then examine those changes by comparing the intercorrelation of election results.

Shover's analysis of the New Deal realignment in California illustrates the problem.[27] Shover, following Key, expected a realignment to change the pattern of party dominance, and he presents data which chart the rise of the Democratic vote in California.[28] In an attempt to determine when the transformation began, he examined the correlation between the votes cast in each county for each election between 1884 and 1940. Following a well-worn path, Shover argued that a realignment occurred around the years that the correlation for the adjacent elections declined.[29] Without commenting upon the accuracy of his substantive conclusions, their correctness cannot be tested with the correlation technique presented in the paper.[30]

The problem is that the correlation analysis is not a measure of change in party pluralities, but only a measure of the relative behavior of the counties in two elections. A correlation analysis will measure a change in the composition of the electoral result because it is sensitive to the relative voting choices of the residents of a county at two points in time. A change in the outcome of the election (a change in the mean percent Democratic of California's 58 counties) in a second election compared with a prior one does not have to affect the correlation between the two.

Consider the data in figure 2.1a. Across a number of elections (designated as occurring in time period one) party A secures 49 percent of the vote. In time period two (representing some number of elections), party A secures an average of about 56 percent of the vote. The correlation between set 1 and set 2 is +1.00. By the majority-party definition of realignment, which Shover used, the party system has undergone a realignment, and yet there is a perfect correlation between the results of the elections across the five "voters." Every voting unit was equally affected by whatever forged a majority for party A and voted exactly 7 percent more for it. Figure 2.1b, by contrast, presents two electoral periods in which the voting units behaved very differently (the correlation is +.12), but in which party A enjoyed no increase in its vote. The point is very simple. The correlation analysis is not appropriate for diagnosing a change in the party plurality. If that plurality change is associated with changes in the behavior of the voting units, as in figure 2.1c, then the correlation analysis will measure the alignment, since the value of the coefficient will decline. But it declines not because the plurality has changed, but because the relative behavior of the voting units changed.

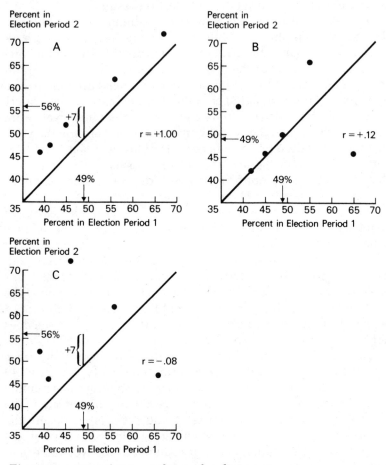

Fig. 2.1   Correlation analyses of realignments

Apparently, correlation analyses of studies of electoral change in the United States have not misled us as much as they might simply because shifts in party pluralities have been based upon social-group changes which are also related to the geographical distribution of the electorate. Yet this fortuitous relationship need not obtain at all times, and when it does not, a weak correspondence between the theory and its operationalization can be more than troublesome, as the data in figure 2.1 indicate.

So, although there seems to be nothing exceptional in observing that a close correspondence between how realignments are conceived and how they are measured is necessary, it is clear that not all studies of party-system change have taken the admonition as seriously as they should have.

Elections and Realignments

If a definition of realignment that turns on the results of an election is not adequate, there is some reason to believe that an emphasis on election statistics to identify a realignment will also not always be adequate. Not only can a concentration on election results impede an analysis of realignment, but it will frequently prove inadequate even for an analysis of its symptoms. Elections can be a poor source of data for the study of realignment for at least three reasons. One of these reasons, the conceptual restrictiveness of the majority-party definition of realignment, was discussed above. The second reason is that election results suffer from fluctuations which do not suit them to studying party realignments, whether one adopts the social-group or party-majority definition of realignments. The third reason that realignments are difficult to study through election returns is that the underlying belief that realignments are election-specific events is misleading and perhaps even wrong.[31]

Short-term fluctuations can cause elections to take on the characteristics that mistakenly lead one to believe a realignment has occurred. Worse, a realignment can occur where one might find either a maintaining or deviating election.[32] The conventional symptoms of a realignment period, high voter interest, high levels of turnout, substantial differences between candidates and parties, and perhaps active minority parties probably do indicate a period of realignment.[33] But all of these things can be found, the electorate can realign, and yet the election can result in the previously dominant party retaining its dominance.

Another problem arises from the differences that distinguish elections for local, state, and national offices. The same rules of evidence applied to presidential, congressional, and local elections frequently lead to different conclusions about outcomes. Voters seem to use different decision rules for different offices and there is no method of compensating for these differences when election results are inspected to discover a realignment.[34]

The Democrats, for example, have won only three of the last seven presidential elections, and the election-to-election swings have been dramatic. The Republicans won with large majorities in 1952 and 1956; they lost by very little in 1960; they were trounced in 1964 but returned with a narrow victory in 1968, a very large one in 1972, and then suffered a loss by a few percentage points in 1976. Post-mortems of each election have established that the explanation for such results lies in the popularity or unpopularity of the opposing presidential candidates. To the extent that personality intrudes into candidate choice, it is difficult to use the election to support a judgment about how the election relates to party align-ment. When the candidate is evaluated independent of the party banner under which he is running, there is no role that party preference can play in determining the vote. The greater the impact of candidate personality and voter idiosyncracies on an election, the less that election can serve in the study of realignment, because party preference—the variable we are interested in—is only weakly reflected in the outcome. Two decades of research have demon-strated that a person can vote for a candidate of the other party without surrendering his party preference. A candidate with a very poor image can suffer a loss even if he is the candidate of the majority party. And if the defectors return to their party in sub-sequent elections, they have not changed their party identification and no realignment has occurred. Overall, presidential elections have too many idiosyncracies to be a completely accurate index of party strength.[35]

Studying voting for lesser offices to identify realignments is not an acceptable alternative. Although one might argue that voting for lower-level offices is primarily controlled by party preference, it does not follow that returns at these levels are necessarily more useful to study realignment.[36] Although some lower-level state and local offices tend to have less of the distracting candidate emphasis of the presidency, they also suffer from several confounding fac-tors, and frequently voting for lower-level offices is as sensitive to candidate effects as the presidential vote. In small communities particularly, or for offices that have restricted constituencies, the specific candidate is more important in the voting decision than the party of the candidate, even if the election is a partisan one.

Even if it is accepted that the candidate emphasis is usually less at the local level compared with the presidential or gubernatorial level, there are still problems in using election results for lower-level offices to discover a realignment. The most important prob-lem arises out of the discrepancy between the absolute number of votes cast for candidates of lower-level offices compared with "top of the ticket" offices. Lower-level elections have fewer votes cast in them, particularly when there is no prominent office at stake. The problem with low turnout is that it increases the un-representativeness of the voters compared with the total eligible electorate. Generally, the similarity of active voters to inactive nonvoters declines, as active voters are a smaller portion of the total.[37] The participatory bias is evident in studies comparing primary votes with general election votes.[38]

Finally, aggregate election returns ignore the matter of in-cumbency. The incumbent converts familiarity into votes.[39] The low turnout and low interest that characterize elections for lesser offices provide sufficient inertia to allow incumbents to retain their office, even when their party has long since lost its dominance in the affections of the electorate.[40]

Under most conditions, therefore, one must cautiously conclude that elections for lesser offices do not necessarily reflect the distribution of party preference in the pool of available voters.

Measuring Changes in Party Coalitions

This does not mean that it is impossible to study realignments with election returns. It only indicates that election returns are a second choice since they contain numerous errors difficult to identify or eliminate. With this caution in mind, it is possible to analyze realignments with election returns, as Paul Kleppner's work demonstrates.[41] Compact and demographically homogeneous ecological units could be used to develop sociological profiles of the party coalitions with election returns. It would also be possible to estimate with confidence the degree of change in the party bias of the groups that make up the party coalitions. The estimating errors associated with using election returns could probably be accepted with small ecological units. But the effort required to collect such data is as great as that needed to collect survey responses about party identification and having collected the ecological data, one would be unable to answer the major theoretical question of the analysis, which is why the groups are changing their party bias. Whatever their utility in the study of historical realignments, election returns should not be used to study contemporary realignments.

An Alternative Index of Realignment

An alternative measure of realignment, which does not suffer the shortcomings associated with election returns and does not require shifts in the vote or in party strength, is a survey estimate of the expressed party preference of the population. Since this is the variable that should change with the realignment and since it is the variable that election returns presume to measure, the party preference reported by respondents in a survey sample is the best estimate of the distribution of party preference in the population. Group differences in partisanship allow the construction of the social-group profile of the party identifiers, and changes in the social-group profile of the parties can be measured directly. The major theoretical advantage to using reported party identification in a survey sample arises out of the ability to query respondents about opinions and attitudes toward several objects other than the party. Because it is possible to demonstrate relationships between party preference and other political attitudes and perceptions, it becomes possible to determine whether changes in the agenda or the perceptions of the parties' positions on the agenda are related, and if so, how. Only survey data hold this possibility.

Agenda and Agendas: Why Party Biases Change

Posing the question of why the partisanship of a group is changing raises the issue of the bond that connects different groups to the parties. The extent to which demography determines party preference is a feature of American party politics with which even casual observers are familiar because it is such an enduring trait of our party systems. Good analyses of the party alignment implicitly (sometimes explicitly) explain that these sociological groupings "worked" because they corresponded to differences in the social and political interests of the members of these groupings. The "ethnics," union members, and unskilled workers are Democrats in party preference because the Democratic party advocates policies that benefit them economically and extend recognition to the group. The party system is differentiated by demography, but the basis of the party alignment is not demographic differences, but issue preferences. Demography differentiates party preference because demographically defined groups are issue publics. When a Democratic candidate talks about minimum wage laws or educational financing acts and otherwise "talks to the issues," he is using information about who his constituents are, and because he knows who they are, he understands what they will generally prefer. When demography and issue preference break down and when the group lacks the expected issue preference, issues, and not social characteristics, better account for party preference and vote choice. Jews and farmers are conspicuous because of a party preference one would not expect on the basis of their status attributes. On the basis of economic characteristics, one would expect Jews to be conservative and Republican, but they are not. They are quite liberal, and they prefer the Democratic party. Farmers, in contrast, are substantially disadvantaged in economic terms. Inasmuch as the Democratic party has been the champion of the economically disadvantage since at least the New Deal, one would expect farmers to follow a "natural economic interest" and support the Democratic party, but they do not. Farmers are rather conservative, and they support the Republican party more heavily than the Democratic party.

Survey data that can be used to categorize respondents into social groups also yield information about the party identification, issue position, and party perceptions of the individuals who compose the group. Respondents can be questioned about their issue positions and their party perceptions as well as their party identification. With these data it is possible to provide a relatively complete description of changing party coalitions and the characteristics correlated with these changes.

Each of these implied relationships will be analyzed later. The next chapter will present a general analysis of the dynamics of electoral and party-system change; chapter 8 offers a brief statement on what causes them. Chapters 4 and 5 will attempt to apply this theory to the development of the current party coalitions. The remainder of the book is an analysis of the current realignment.

3 The Dynamics
of Realignment I

Fluctuations in Electoral Size

Attempts to categorize the causes of crime have neatly reduced those causes to two: the criminals and the conditions of society. Studies of realignment have likewise found two causes: either the realigners did it or the existing conditions of the society brought it about. Burnham, Ladd, and Jahnige have sought to account for realignments as an outcome of major social, economic, or political events, while Butler and Stokes have viewed realignments in terms of the changing political behavior of segments of the electorate.[1] Neither perspective offers a comprehensive explanation. Indeed, most analysts of party transformation have used both explanations even when they have concentrated on one of them, as Converse did.[2]

This chapter establishes the theoretical groundwork for understanding the historical answer to the "who" part of the question dealt with in the next chapter. The central thesis is that realignments result from the mobilization of previously inactive citizens. The nature of this mobilization is substantially similar to the mobilization that occurs in elections generally. The processes that underlie interelection variation also underlie party-voter realignments, and since there are more elections than realignments, we will use the former to elucidate the dynamics of the latter.

Fluctuations in the Size of the Electorate

The essential ingredient in the impact of irregular voters or previous nonvoters of any election is that they are not the image of regular voters but differ in many ways: social class, political interest, party affiliation, and political and social policy preferences, to name only a few.[3] The most important feature of these voters, however, is that their relative disinterest and lack of information about politics increase their vulnerability to the prevailing political winds. Simply because they are not consumers of political news, they are poorly informed and they are likely to lack strong political commitments. The tug of an election deals them a mighty blow.[4] The effect of this bias among nonvoters can be illustrated by comparing the preferences of nonvoters with the choices reported by voters (fig. 1). In 1956 the preference for Eisenhower among nonvoters was 16 points larger than that among voters; in 1964 the preference for Goldwater among nonvoters was 16 points less than that among voters; in 1968 Wallace did 12 percentage points better among nonvoters than among voters. In 1960, a more balanced election year, nonvoters chose to support Nixon in almost the same proportion as voters. No candidate was overwhelmingly preferred, and there were no unsettling third-party candidates with a significant following. As the 1956 and 1964 elections show, nonvoters lead the crowd; and, as the Wallace vote shows, they are also more responsive to deviant candidates.

There are four kinds of voter responses that constitute the dynamics of electoral oscillation. The first is loyalty; it is essential to be aware of the role of the committed and unwavering partisan in the shaping of an election. The second response is "switching,"

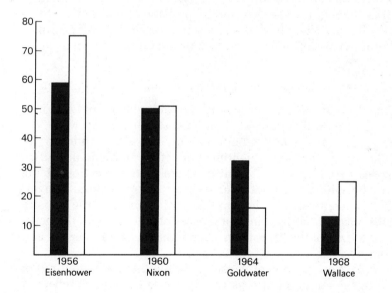

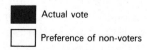 Actual vote

☐ Preference of non-voters

Fig. 3.1   Comparison of the preferences of voters and nonvoters in different presidential elections

or changing from the candidate of one party to the candidate of the other by those who vote in most elections. The size of this group varies in a comparison of any two consecutive elections, but it is always large enough to determine the outcome of an election. The third response is entrance. Entering voters are those who did not vote in the previous election, either because they were not eligible (for any reason), because they are irregular voters, or because they were chronic nonvoters. When a high turnout election follows a low turnout contest, interelection shifts will be larger because the fraction of the electorate that is especially susceptible to the pull of electoral tides is larger. Inactivity is the last response that a voter might make to an election. Voters might remain inactive or become inactive. Becoming inactive might be thought of as a process of exit. Whether exit has a significant influence on the election outcome will depend on the magnitude of the decline in turnout. However, since exiting voters are like entering voters in their low level of psychological involvement in politics there is always a substantial probability that a sharp turnout decline will help to shape an election result that will be different from what would be found in a normal turnout contest.

Realignments: Conversion, Mobilization, and Demobilization

The election response of loyalty, switching, exit, and entrance have analogs in realignment situations: stability, conversion, demobilization, and mobilization. Stability refers to a condition of no change in the party identification of an individual; and in analyses of realignment stability points to that fraction of the electorate which does not alter its party identification. Conversion, by contrast, is the process of changing one's party identification. Mobilization is a process of entering into the partisan fray. Demobilization is an abandonment of the parties and politics.

Mobilization has two dimensions. In the first instance it might point to the adoption of a party preference by large numbers of voters who had previously considered themselves independents. By adopting partisanship, these individuals alter the normal party vote. At times this mobilization will result in proportionate increases in all parties, or it might increase the size of only one of the parties. Whether either result is described as a realignment depends upon whether the social-group composition of the parties is altered. When the party coalitions do not change, there has simply been an increase in the fraction of the electorate whose vote is committed. There are, however, two reasons for thinking that any substantial mobilization of the electorate will take on the qualities of a realignment. First, independence is not uniformly distributed among segments of the population. Any decrease in independence should alter the party coalitions simply because there are proportionately more of some types of voters (sociologically defined) available to the parties.[5] Second, even if the mobilization were evenly distributed, the kinds of social events that galvanize populations and might cause some to adopt party loyalties also pull voters in different ways. To take a historical example: The night-watchman attitude of the Republicans at the start of the Depression worked a particular hardship on the less fortunate who were also predominantly Catholic and blue-collar workers. The Democratic party that emerged from the New Deal was a coalition that was noticeably more Catholic, working class, and ethnic than twenty years earlier.

Another way to understand the process of mobilization is to concentrate on levels of turnout rather than rates of identification and nominal support of the parties.[6] The effective meaning of majority support turns on the voting rates of the population. The Democratic party can enjoy greater support among the potential electorate than the Republican party, but if that support is never brought to the polls, the Republicans may be the effectively dominant party. Nominal identifiers with an anemic turnout rate are less weighty in party councils and a less significant factor in the party coalition as a result. On that ground alone it would be reasonable to consider an abrupt increase in turnout significant for the party coalitions.

Demobilization, the equivalent in a realignment context to exit in the study in interelection oscillation, is the last response needed to study the behavior of voters during realignments. Demobilization, like mobilization, is a concept which describes two different processes. It can be used to describe a drop in turnout or on the abandonment of a party preference in segments of the population. If this abandonment or turnout decline occurs at the same rate for both parties, the result might be a simple dealignment of the electorate.[7] Even when the rate is equal, however, demobilization might constitute a realignment of the parties because of the way it affects their partisans. If the shift were concentrated among one or only two groups among the Democrats, and then among a different one or two groups among the Republicans, the group coalitions that constitute the electoral base of the parties would be altered. In short, any demobilization of the electorate which did not equally affect most groups in either party would be a change tending toward a realignment of the electorate, and not just a dealignment.

Mobilization, Demobilization, and Party Coalitions

Conversion, mobilization, and demobilization represent alternative and often competing explanations of realignments. The conversion explanation has clearly dominated accounts of historical realignments. In writing that "a realignment requires that the switching voters (in an election) remain "switched," Sundquist summarized this conviction.[8] By continuing to devote valuable space to asking respondents if they have ever changed their party identification, and when, the periodic election studies of the University of Michigan's Center for Political Studies testify to the belief that conversion is a principal element of re-alignments. The mobilization explanation is not new. Almost thirty years ago, Eldersveld and then Lubell charged the New Deal to the coming-of-age and activation of the immigrant masses of the big cities.[9] A few years later, Key also noted that the New Deal realignment rested upon "the *activation* by the Democratic candidate of low-income, Catholic, urban voters of recent immigrant stock" (my emphasis).[10] Shortly after that *The American Voter* demonstrated that some of the new Democrats of the 1930s may have been former Republicans but "a larger component of the gain came from young voters entering the electorate and older people who had previously failed to vote."[11] Burnham traced the changing shape of American party politics to the *demobilization* of large numbers of voters after about 1900; Cameron, Inglehart, and Hochstein attributed the rise of the Gaullists to the mobilization of new or unattached voters; Paul Allen Beck developed a socialization theory of realignments which allocated most of the influence to new voters; and Kristi Andersen definitively analyzed the role of mobilization in the New Deal realignment.[12]

The history of the transformation of the American party system, as the preceding work clearly documents, is interwined with the mobilization and demobilization of the electorate. The growth of the American party system paralleled the expansion of the franchise, and, generally, changes in the party system are coincidental with the expansion of the electorate. Consider figure 3.2., which shows the percentage increase in turnout for adjacent presidential elections between 1840 and 1940. A line extending up indicates an increase in the number of votes cast, for example, the 12 percent increase in 1840 over 1836. A line extending down indicates

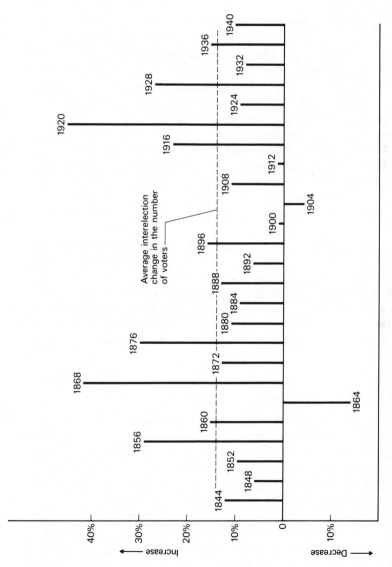

Fig. 3.2   Percentage change in the number of votes cast for successive presidential elections, 1840–1940

that fewer votes were cast in that election compared with the preceding one, for example, 1864 compared with 1860. The feature of the graph to be noted is that virtually every realignment is associated with a large, absolute increase in the number of voters. Only the years 1876 and 1920 are troublesome since they show a surge in the absence of a realignment; while 1864 and 1904 show decline in the absolute size of the electorate; but each anomaly is explicable.

The return of the Southern states is responsible for the 1876 surge; 1920 reflects the enfranchisement of women; the Civil War was responsible for the 1864 decline. The 4 percent drop in 1904, more difficult to explain, is extensively analyzed in the next chapter. But this decline is less important than one might assume since even the "system of '96" involved some electoral expansion. The small decline in 1904 is overcome by an increase in 1908. The interesting thing about the "system of '96" electorate is how slowly it expanded. At almost no point in the history of the party system was the increase in the electorate so modest over so many elections. Between 1896 and 1912 the electorate grew less than 9 percent, or an average of 2 percent between presidential elections. This arrested development had major consequences for the "system of '96."

Demobilization, in short, appears to have had only a small effect on the party system. There is very little evidence that a large number of voters has ever permanently exited from the active electorate. The decline in turnout that marked the "system of '96" (and the increase in independence in the contemporary electorate) largely reflects a failure to mobilize newer cohorts and not an abandonment of the party system by previously active age cohorts.

The Source of New Voters

While conversion and demobilization played some part in realignments and other party-system transformations, electoral mobilization has been the principal factor. The still unanswered questions are where new voters come from and what the expansion and the new voters have to do with the coalition structure of American parties and the character of realignments.

Paul Beck's socialization theory of realignment provides part of the answer, simultaneously accounting for the apparent periodicity of American party-system transformations. In Beck's view, realignments are periodic because they depend upon political generations. Generations that come of age when the short-term forces

of realignment periods favor one of the parties are likely to develop a pronounced preference for the favored party, while generations that emerge in a period when short-term forces are more
balanced, after the galvanizing controversies of the realignment
period have been resolved, will drift into the partisanship of the
most influential socializer in their environment, usually parents.
His theory accounts for most of the data that must be explained.

It requires some amendment, however, before it will also explain the ethnic and regional coalitions that characterize the
popular support enjoyed by the parties.

Generally, the electoral success of parties depends upon their
ability to divide a finite population in which the total number of
voters is relatively fixed and can be expected to change only
slowly through population replacement. For most party systems
birth and death are the only mechanisms for replacing voters.
Perhaps the only other familiar device for changing the size of the
electorate lies in altering the rules of eligibility to vote. The expansion of the electorate through progressive extensions of the
franchise, for example, profoundly affected the party systems of
the European democracies.[13] The extension of the franchise
through a progressive reduction of property, racial, and sex re-
strictions also influenced political developments in the United
States. But in the United States after 1840, and excepting female
suffrage in 1920, the electorate was enlarged the most by successive waves of immigrants.

At the beginning of this century, 14 percent of the population
was foreign-born. The proportion of foreign-born in the industrial
North Atlantic and North Central states was even higher, ap-
proaching perhaps 20 percent. If one regards immediate children
of the foreign-born as immigrants, estimates place the immigrant
population at over a third of the total population in 1900.[14] The
importance of this foreign population for the party system is
largely unexamined.

What can be expected from voters who must choose among
parties toward which they do not have any accumulated
loyalties? Normally the voter will support the party most similar
to the one preferred in some earlier setting.[15] But for most immigrants to the United States there was no similar party. The United
States was operating a party system long before party systems
developed in Europe; most immigrants to this country had no
experience with party politics, much less with a particular kind of
political party. What was the impact of these various waves of
immigration?

Figure 3.3 shows the party bias (percent Republican minus per-

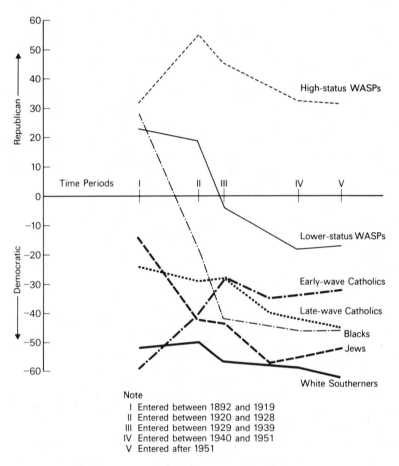

Note
I Entered between 1892 and 1919
II Entered between 1920 and 1928
III Entered between 1929 and 1939
IV Entered between 1940 and 1951
V Entered after 1951

Fig. 3.3   Shifts in the party bias of different coalition groups

cent Democratic) of seven major population groups by the period
during which the individuals came of age. The changes that
created the New Deal Democratic party of white southerners,
Jews, blacks, Catholics, and lower-status Northern whites can be
illustrated with the groups in the figure.

Figure 3.3 is based upon the electorate of the 1950s, a period of
political calm in which Democratic dominance was not in doubt.
Virtually all of this electorate came of age between 1892 and 1950
and over 60 percent of it entered after 1928. The cohort that entered between 1892 and 1919 would have reflected the partisanship of generations that entered between the middle 1860s and
1892, a largely Republican generation in a period of Republican

dominance. But as the pre-1892 cohort died off, the post-1892 electorate became numerically dominant, and in the decade of the 1950s a New Deal generation (those who entered after 1929) was the majority. Clearly generational replacement alone played a major role changing the party system from one dominated by the Republicans to one controlled by the Democrats. The question that needs answering, however, is whether this new generation is largely composed of the children of Republicans who became Democrats, as the unamended socialization theory predicts or whether it is heavily infiltrated by the children of the immigrants, most of whom were always Democrats.

The children of Republicans would have been concentrated among Northern Protestants and blacks. White Southerners, Catholics, and some lower-status Northern Protestants constituted the Democratic party.[16] Jews divided equally between them. A quick inspection of figure 3.3 indicates that the movement toward the Democrats was concentrated among lower-status Northern white Protestants, blacks, and Jews. Two of these groups, the lower-status WASPs and blacks, did not represent immigrant groups and it is reasonable to assume that the increasing Democratic identification of the generations represents an inability of Republican parents to pass their party preference on to their children. Jews represent an immigrant group in the sense that most American Jews can probably trace their residence in the United States no earlier than about 1880.

Adding some side information to the graph leads to the conclusion that immigration played a role in the transformation. Consider the effects of the size of the groups involved. By 1880 most immigration was coming from eastern and southern Europe. The British, Irish, German, and Scandinavian fraction of the total was much smaller than it had been 30 years previously. That means that late-wave Catholics, always Democratic, were becoming a larger part of the population. Keeping in mind that the Democrats could have become the larger party either by conversion or by increasing the representation of already Democratic groups in the electorate, one might look for the effect of immigrant new generations by examining whether the size of the group in figure 3.3 is changing in a manner that would benefit the Democrats.

Table 1 permits an examination of two different cohorts of the groups in figure 3.3. The first cohort entered the electorate between 1892 and 1919, well before the New Deal. The second cohort entered during the period of Democratic ascendancy, between 1929 and 1951. The proportion of Democrats in the later cohort increased 8 percentage points from 42 percent Democrat to

Table 3.1. Contribution of Groups to Changes in Rates of Democratic Identification (as of 1960)

Party Coalition Groups	Entered 1892–1919			Entered 1929–51			Contribution to Democratic Change
	Percent Democratic	× Size of Group	= Contribution to Democratic Percentage	Percent Democratic	× Size of Group	= Contribution to Democratic Percentage	
White Protestants							
Southerners	70	19	14	71	18	13	−1
upper-status Northerners	16	14	2	21	16	3	+1
lower-status Northerners	31	40	12	43	30	14	+2
Catholics							
early-wave migrants	58	7	4	51	6	3	−1
late-wave migrants	54	11	6	58	18	10	+4
Blacks	46	6	3	61	9	5	+2
Jews	66	2	1	60	3	2	+1
TOTAL			42			50	+8

50 percent Democrat. The role of migration in creating our hetero-
geneous party coalitions can be examined, though not precisely
measured, with these data. Lower-status WASPs and late-wave
Catholics are particularly important groups for studying the interaction of migration and mobilization.

Between the first and second period the proportion of Democrats among lower-status WASPs increased from 31 percent to 43
percent. At the same time, however, the lower-status WASPs became a smaller fraction of the population. Some of the decline
represents an increase in the proportion of northern WASPs with
upper-status attributes, but at least half of the decline of the group
from 40 percent to 30 percent of the population reflects the growth
of other groups through immigration and birth rates. The result of
the latter change is to reduce the contribution of the lower-status
WASPs to less than half of what it would have been had the
increase in the proportion of Democrats been sustained by a group
that was still 40 percent of the population. If the relative size of
the groups were the same in both cohorts, lower-status WASPs
would have contributed 5 points of the 8-point increase, but because they declined in size they contributed only 2 points. Late-
wave migrants, in contrast, increased their Democratic identification only slightly (to 58 percent), but the size of the group in the
cohort increased by almost 67 percent. The net result of both
effects is that late-wave Catholics, most of whom entered the
country after 1880 (and the electorate later still), contributed twice
as much as lower-status WASPs to the growth of Democratic
identification. If all northern WASPs are treated as a group, the
migrants' impact on Democratic growth relative to the natives' is
lessened, but it is still larger. Including upper-status WASPs,
however, does not change the result, only its magnitude. The
creation of Democrats among the children of likely Republicans
contributes 3 points to the 8-point increase, while the late wave
migrants add 4 percentage points. No matter how the total change
is calculated, the migration population—late-wave Catholics and
Jews—contributed at least as much to the change in the size of
the Democratic party as the "mal-socialization" of the post-1920
cohort.

These figures are, of course, rough estimates. Their value is less
important than their relative magnitude. They are important,
however, for what they offer as an insight into the inter-
dependence of immigration waves and waves of party-system
mobilization in the construction of our mosaiclike party coali-

tions. Realignments have altered the party coalitions and the party agenda because the "available" critical realignment electorate has been composed largely of new and sociologically different populations. This process will be described more fully in chapter 4.

4 The Historical Origins of the Party Coalitions

Before the transformation of the party coalitions can be studied, it is essential to identify the components of the coalitions that might change. Knowing that new voters (or a fluctuation in the size of the electorate) are basic to the process of realignment answers only a portion of the "who" part of the realignment question. The other half of the answer requires some understanding of how the coalitions are altered by electoral expansion. The preceding chapter indicated the dynamics of the process. This chapter attempts a reconstruction of historical realignments in order to show (a) how electoral expansion (a surge in the absolute number of voters) drew into the party system (b) socially distinct groups and impressed a particular party bias on the groups, and (c) how this process of mobilization of social groups fueled realignments.

The detail required for a full account of the party bias of the groups which comprise the party coalitions would yield many colorful and particularistic histories. The reasons for their partisanship are almost as numerous as the groups in question. A detailed explanation of the partisanship of each group is not the objective of this narrative; its purpose is to outline overall similarities in a way that will help to account for the development of the party coalitions.

The major thrust of the chapter is simply to point out the concurrence of political crises, electoral expansion, and the "arrival" of a new social group in the party system. In general the theoretical structure of chapter 3 is used to interpret the development of the contemporary Democratic and Republican parties.

The Mobilization of the Republican Majority: First Elements of the Coalitions

By the middle of the 1850s the country had experienced over a decade and a half of increasing conflict on the question of slavery.[1] Several movements and parties—the Free Soilers, Know-Nothings, and the African Colonization Society, for example—had considerably politicized and polarized the issue. In 1854 the

Republican party was organized as an antislavery party. While it would be inaccurate to portray the Republicans as united on every facet of the slavery question, it was clearly a party opposed to the extension of slavery in the West. Several of its spokesmen, Abraham Lincoln among them, took the very radical position that slavery was a definite evil that should be contained and eventually eradicated.[2] The Whigs, attempting to straddle the issue, lost to both the Republicans and the Democrats. In the North, in particular, the movement away from the Whigs favored the Republicans. While there was considerable conversion of Whigs to Republicans and even desertion of Democrats to Republicans, most of the success of the Republican party must be attributed to an expansion of the electorate, and not to the conversion of Democrats. The influence of the electoral expansion is shown in figure 4.1. The line labelled A represents the number of voters in the states of Connecticut, Maine, Massachusetts, New Hampshire, Rhode Island, and Vermont. Collectively these are considered the states of the Northeast. Line B is the number of voters in the Middle Atlantic states—those of New Jersey, New York, and Pennsylvania. Line C is the number of voters in the West; an area which includes the states of Illinois, Indiana, Michigan, Ohio, Wisconsin, and Iowa. The corresponding letters A^1, B^1, and C^1 are the number of Democratic votes in each of these regions.

With two exceptions, the Democratic party elected every president from 1812 through 1856. The Whigs were the minority party. If the demise of the Whigs and the desertion of Democrats was the sole explanation for the rise of the Republican party, the patterns in figure 4.1 would be different. If only Whig voters had become Republican voters, the Republicans would not have assumed the dominant position they enjoyed beginning with the election of 1860. But if the Republican success had been the result of the coalescing of Whigs and some fraction of northern Democrats, the number of Democratic votes would not have been as stable as they are in figure 4.1. The data in figure 4.1 imply that the success of the Republican party depended less on the desertion of Democrats than it did on the capture of Whigs and new voters. In the Northeast, the number of Democratic voters is fairly stable. There is a decline after 1856, but the percentage decline of the Democratic party in the Northeast after 1852 was caused less by the defection of Democrats to the new Republican party than it was by the Republicans' getting a disproportionate share of the new voters between 1852 and 1856. The Middle Atlantic states show a similar pattern, and the change is even more dramatic. Although the number of Democratic voters declined after 1852,

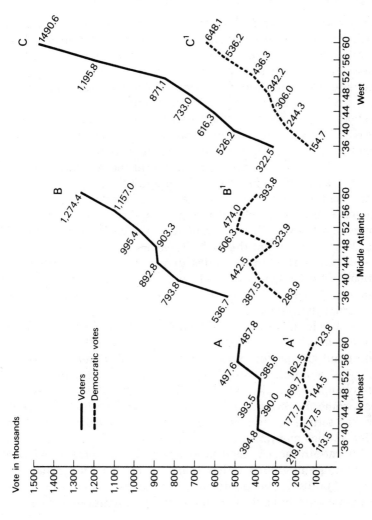

Vote in thousands

Fig. 4.1   Partisan consequences of the expansion of the electorate in the 1850s

the deline in Democratic voters is much smaller than the increase in the total number of voters. In the Middle Atlantic, as in the Northeastern states, the Democratic party simply was not gathering a share of new voters that even remotely corresponded with its previous share of the electorate. The data for the West is more dramatic still. Overall, the total number of votes cast increased markedly in the decade of the 1850s but the Democratic vote changed very little. This new electorate fueled the growth of the Republican party and placed the Democrats in the minority.

Immigrants and The New Republican Electorate

What was the source of this new electorate? The only thing that can actually be said with certainty is that a large portion of the population which had never voted cast their lot with the Republican party. Ther? is indirect evidence, however, that immigrants and their children contributed disproportionately to the increase in turnout and the changed strength of the parties.

There are certain immigrant nationalities from which the increase in the electorate did not come. The Irish, who represented about a third of all foreign-born residents in 1860, contributed only modestly to the growth in turnout or the Republican party. As early as 1790, according to Glazer and Moynihan, Irish immigrants had developed a preference for the Democratic party.[3] The general nativism of the Federalists, in addition to the Federalist opposition to extending the franchise, was partly responsible for the Democratic bias of the Irish. However, the existence of active Democratic parties in the cities in which the Irish settled was probably the indispensable element in attaching them to the Democratic party.[4] By 1840 the overwhelming majority of them supported the Democrats.

The development of political party traditions among other immigrant nationalities took much longer. Unlike the Irish, many immigrant groups, for example, Germans and Scandinavians, did not possess a culture and language that was even superficially interchangeable with that of the United States. Also unlike the Irish, some major nationalities, Germans and English, for example, had settled outside the urban centers where party activity and organizations mobilized the immigrants into party politics. In addition, certain social and cultural factors served to repel several of the immigrant groups rather than attract them to parties and electoral politics. The identification of the Irish Catholics with the Democratic party kept many non-Catholic immigrants from supporting the Democrats. At the same time the nativism and political evangelism of the Whigs (expressed through blue laws and prohibition laws) kept many, perhaps most, of these same immigrants from supporting the Whigs.[5]

In short, then, there are many reasons for believing that a large fraction of the immigrant population was not active in party politics for a long period after their numbers made them an important fraction of the total population. There are also some data that indicate that many immigrants became politically active only in the 1850s and 1860s. One of the most interesting bits of data for examining the influence of immigrants on turnout is a survey done in Lansing, Michigan.[6] In 1858 Lansing was a small town with an even smaller potential electorate. It was easy for someone in the town to know enough about his fellow residents to characterize their politics; what one did not know personally could be determined by questioning friends. In that year, a Lansing Republican politician by the name of David Marion Bagley produced a sample of 712 potential voters.[7] In an age when partisanship was valued, and freely expressed, it is surprising, that about 42 percent of his sample either lacked a party preference or had a partisanship that could not be determined. Many of these "apoliticals" were immigrants. Overall, about 22 percent of the sample was of foreign birth, but those of foreign birth constituted fully 47 percent of the group whose party preference could not be unequivocally determined. Put differently, then, almost half of the party mobilization that occurred in the 1850s and 1860s would have been contributed by individuals who were foreign born. But whether the "doubtfuls" were immigrants, their children, or apolitical native Americans, they constituted a large fraction of the age-eligible electorate. If this group was as indifferent toward voting as they were toward the parties (assuming that Bagley's inability to determine their partisanship reflects its absence), it is not difficult to understand how such a group would alter the party balance.

The most important feature of the Lansing data is the degree to which they corroborate the explanation for the aggregate totals of figure 4.1. In general, Michigan is a case through which the mobilization explanation of the Civil War realignment can be illustrated in detail.[8]

Between 1852 and 1856 the Democratic vote in Michigan increased by over 10,500 to a total of 52,139. In this same period, the Republican vote (formerly Whigs and Free Soilers) increased more than 30,000 to 71,763 in 1856. A large part of this increase came from German Protestants and, especially, "new" British, that is, recent immigrants of British extraction. The influence of the new British on the Republican surge appears in many county-level analyses of the election outcomes. In 1852, 70 percent of 358 voters in Sanilac County supported the Democratic candidate in the presidential election. In the 1856 election 1,005 votes were cast but only about 20 percent of this number was for the Democrat. In 1860, the turnout surged to 1,304 and the Democratic vote represented about 30 percent of the total.

The percentages would lead one to suspect that a shift in the voting choices of the electorate brought about the decline of the Democratic share of the vote from 70 percent in 1852 to 30 percent in 1860. But such a conclusion ignores the substantial increase in the number of voters. In a very literal sense, the electorate of 1860 was not the electorate of 1852.

The participants, the voters, were not the same people. While most of the voters in 1852 were probably also voting in 1860, most of the 1860 voters had not participated in the 1852 election. Unless one is willing to argue that the Democratic voters of eight years before had shifted to the Republicans and had their places taken by new entrants, these data suggest that the same 200 to 230 people who voted Democratic in 1852 did so in 1856. By 1860 this Democratic base had been reinforced by another 100 to 150 supporters. But the non-Democratic vote was surging from 150 or so, to over 900, with virtually all of the increase coming from the ranks of previous nonvoters. It strains credulity to believe that the 200 Democratic voters of 1852 cast Republican ballots in 1860. But even if they had, their contribution to the increase was overwhelmed by that of the 550 or so that, at a bare minimum, must have come from the 1852 inactives. The stability of the population of the county and its ethnic composition seems to eliminate any other explanation for the rise of the Republicans.

One check, although not a definitive one, on the utility of this explanation might be the social basis of Republican and Democratic partisans in the late 1800s. If the Republican bias of the events of the 1850s created the partisanship of groups that had been politically inactive, we would expect the nationality and ethnic base of the parties to reflect the changes. That is, groups that displayed low rates of involvement and commitment prior to 1860 should have been drawn to the Republicans and processes of intergenerational socialization should have assured that support across subsequent cohorts. Again, some late nineteenth-century surveys have data on this point. Table 4.1 presents some Midwest data from the 1896 election. Given the previous discussion, we

Table 4.1   Voting Patterns from Various Areas of the Midwest for Different Ethnic Groups around the Year 1890

| | Republican Percentage of the Vote in | | |
Ethnic Group	1888	1892	1896
Irish			
seven rural Iowa townships	20%		23%
Dubuque, Ward 1	21%		28%
Chicago, Wards 6 and 29		27%	38%
Bohemian			
seven Iowa wards and townships	20%		28%
twelve Chicago precincts		21%	42%
Polish			
Milwaukee, Ward 14	10%		17%
thirteen Chicago precincts		21%	33%
French Catholic			
Bourbonnais, Illinois		58%	77%
Norwegian			
eleven rural Iowa townships	77%		83%
five recent rural Wis. settlements	73%		81%
nine older rural Wis. settlements	64%		69%
six Chicago precincts			69%
Swedish			
six rural Iowa townships	72%		74%
Chicago, Ward 23		43%	59%
Rockford, Illinois		64%	89%
German			
city of Chicago			75%
Negro			
six Chicago precincts			90%

Source: Richard Jensen, *The Winning of the Midwest: Social and Political Conflict, 1888–1896* (Chicago: University of Chicago Press, 1971), pp. 297, 298.

would expect Catholics to be concentrated in the Democratic party and the early-wave Protestant immigrants (Germans, British, and others) to support the Republican party. Exactly such a pattern is found in the data. The native-born Protestants and German, Scandinavian, and British immigrants supported the Republicans, and the Catholics (and, again, especially the Irish) supported the Democrats.

How representative these limited samples are of the politics of the entire Midwest, much less the entire country, cannot be determined. Their correspondence with each other and with expectations, however, is encouraging. The fact that Republican success in the 1850s and 1860s corresponded with the size of the (non-Irish) immigrant population lends further support to the general notion that the political maturation of immigrants helped realign the parties as a response to the events of the period. In the North-east, for example, where the non-Irish immigrant population was the smallest (about 5 percent) the growth of the Republican elec-torate was least (see fig. 4.1). In the Middle Atlantic and Western states, where the non-Irish, foreign-born population was largest—averaging over 12 percent—the growth of the electorate and the Republican party was the most substantial.[9]

Finally, of course, there is evidence from survey research today that the most Republican segments of the country are Americans of German, English, and Scandinavian extraction. Americans of these diverse nationalities exhibit the party preference their an-cestors developed at the time they became politically involved. These nationalities settled in the Midwest, and the Midwest re-mained a bastion of Republican strength.

The surge of new voters in the 1850s, then, converted both an immigrant and a native "new population" to the Republican party. Individuals who had not voted before entered the party system on the side of the party favored by the flow of short-term events. As a result, from the moment of their effective political maturity, the new voters of the 1850s were Republican. The im-portance of the Civil War through the 1870s and 1880s meant that perhaps two generations of new voters were swayed by the "bloody shirt" to support the party of the Union, the party which their forebears supported at the moment of their entrance into the party system. Their political loyalties were simply reinforced by the sectionalism that characterized the parties after the war.

The Civil War was also influential for other groups. The social and political uniqueness of the South predates the Civil War, but it was the Civil War which cemented the existing party dif-ferences and guaranteed southern opposition to the Republican party.[10] Whatever success the Republicans enjoyed in the South after the Civil War depended on the presence of the federal army and the Republican sympathies of former slaves. The only reliable basis of Republican support was the black population, and much of the postwar political history of the south is a story of efforts to disenfranchise blacks and relegate them to the inferior position they held before the Civil War. Complete dominance by the Dem-ocratic party was the institutional structure through which this policy was carried out.[11] Eliminating a black electorate eliminated a Republican base in the area.

Opposition to the war within the South also found expression in postwar loyalties. The islands of Republican voting in the South correspond to the Piedmont and mountain areas where the war was opposed. Counties that voted against secession and failed to support the war with money or men are the same counties that supported the Republican party well into this century.[12]

The Depression and the New Deal Coalitions

Sectional party conflict was the earmark of party politics throughout most of the remaining decades of the nineteenth century. Differences between the industrial Northeast and the agricultural West, intensified by the general farm depression that occurred after the Civil War, resulted in some decline in the support enjoyed by the Republican party outside the South.[13] For a long time this loss was not a gain for the Democrats. It benefitted state political movements primarily. While there was some decline in Republican support as agrarian protest found a home in the Democratic party, much of the decline occurred in the South, where the Republican party gathered few votes at any time. The waxing sympathy of the urban, immigrant working class for the Democratic party made only a small contribution to the party nationally.[14] The most striking feature of the period is the near cessation of electoral growth.

This depression of normal electoral expansion is obvious in figure 4.2. Between 1880 and 1910 the age-eligible male electorate doubled. The actual number of voters, however, increased slightly more than 61 percent. This pattern of electoral expansion lagging behind the growth of the potential electorate occurs in almost every state and county in which the data have been examined. In each case the gap between the potential electorate and the number voting is greatest in those counties with large numbers of late-wave immigrants, but it occurs elsewhere, too.

Three important features of the "system of '96" are visible in figure 4.2; and one of them contradicts the prevailing image of that transformation of the party system. First, there was no decline in the size of the electorate. The actual number of voters increased over the years, albeit at a rate much smaller than was normal for the century. Between 1896 and 1912, the increase was almost imperceptible (and contained a decline between 1900 and 1904), but even in those years new voters augmented the electorate. A second feature is that the changes that yielded a larger Republican majority are remarkably similar to those from 1850 to 1860. Between 1892 and 1896, the electorate increased about 15 percent, but almost all of this expansion of the electorate appears to have fueled an increase in Republican votes. The decline of the Populists gave the Democrats another one million votes in 1896 compared with 1892, but this was not enough to counteract the

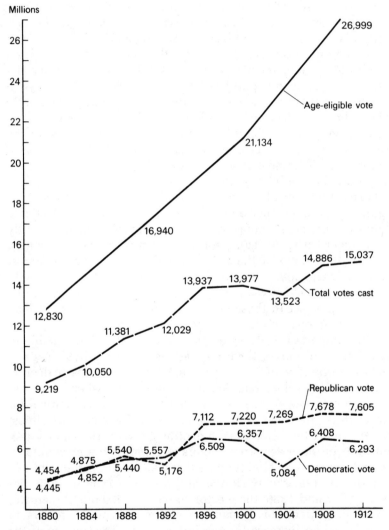

Fig. 4.2   Number of votes cast in presidential elections, 1880–1912

almost two million votes that were added by new electors to the Republicans. The "system of '96" seems to have developed out of an electoral expansion in the same manner characteristic of prior electoral realignments.

The third, and most important, feature of the "system of '96" is the growing disparity between the number of eligible voters and the number that actually took part. It seems that the decline in turnout which has been such a focus for commentaries on this period of party history did not result from a retreat from participation by large numbers of previously active voters, rather, turnout declined because the number of eligible voters changed more rapidly. The denominator (the number of eligible voters), not the numerator (the actual number who voted) caused a change in turnout. These effects are slightly exaggerated by failing to distinguish between those eligible to vote by virtue of their age and the portion of citizens in the group. The latter category defines eligibility for voting purposes.

Many different groups of voters contributed to this turnout depression; but some groups overcontributed, and their subsequent mobilization gave the New Deal parties much of their distinctive social base. There are several reasons for believing that the growing disparity between the number of voters and the number of eligible voters reflected a surge in immigration that brought millions of southern and eastern Europeans to the United States.[15]

The Immigrants as Democrats

Virtually every available history of the parties and many focused monographs have documented that these groups represented a clientele for the Democratic party, and that they had usually supported Democrats over Republicans, when they voted.[16] Not until the 1930s, however, did the Democratic sympathies of the urban working class and the recent Catholic immigrants become converted into a Democratic plurality.

There were two reasons for this considerable undermobilization of the Democratic vote in the industrial North. The first, interestingly, arose out of the success of the Progressives in combatting the urban political machines, in organizing and promoting the idea of a civil service as opposed to patronage employment in government, and, generally, promoting the Protestant, middle-class, Republican notion of what good government should look like. One of the effects of the Progressive efforts to reform politics and government was the weakening of the political organizations which were best suited to mobilize immigrants into party politics.[17]

This assumes, of course, that parties, especially the fabled urban machines of the period, were effective at mobilizing the immigrant vote. There is some reason to question whether they even made a serious attempt to draw large numbers of late-wave migrants into electoral politics.[18] A careful study is needed to assess the degree to which the Progressives did retard the mobilization of urban voters by the their open warfare on party politics; but the precipitous decline in voter turnout after the turn of the century coupled with the introduction of legislation which was intended to restrict the political activity of immigrants, makes the hypothesized relationship especially credible.[19]

The second reason for the lackadaisical response of the urban, immigrant working class to the parties arises out of posture of the parties, especially the Democrats, toward them. The Democratic party, from the end of the Civil War, was dominated by groups no more sympathetic to the urban and immigrant working class than the middle-class Protestants of the Republican party. The history of the Democratic party throughout the first decades of the twentieth century is one of warfare among its constituent elements. The immigrant, "wet," industrial-urban working class elements of the Democratic party in the north were divided from the native Protestant, agrarian, and Southern and Western elements by almost as many questions as they were united. Southern and Western Democrats looked as unfamiliar and unfriendly to the Northern urban Democrats as the Protestant, prohibitionist, and often nativist middle-class Republican.[20] Until the New Deal, the Western and Southern Democrats were the essential Democrats. Bryan was not an aberration. He represented the dominant faction within the party and he contributed to the conflict between the Western agrarian and industrial-urban groups through the 1920s.[21] By exhibiting as much hostility toward the urban, immigrant, industrial Democrats as did the nativist element of the Republican party, the Western agrarian Democrats were probably responsible for the fact that the Democratic party did not mobilize enough of these potential Democrats in the East to replace the Republican party. Most of the immigrant and industrial urban working class had nothing to choose between the national parties and they did not support either Democrats or Republicans in any great numbers, which is not to imply a lack of affection for the Democrats among this large unmobilized electorate. Their Democratic proclivities, however, had never been realized as Democratic votes. But the candidacy of Al Smith, the Depression, and the activist stance of the FDR presidency mobilized a large fraction of these nonvoters directly into the Democratic party. Just as the Civil War provided the event which carried one immigrant wave into the political system and gave the group a distinctive partisanship, the Depression and the presidential candidacy of a Catholic arrived at the time that a large portion of the second immigrant wave was susceptible to party mobilization. The data in figure 4.3 illustrate this process. The data plotted in the bottom line of figure 4.3 are the number of Republican voters (in thousands) in the ten counties with cities of heavy immigrant populations. Not all cities are represented, but the counties chosen are those with an immigrant population large enough in the 1920s and 1930s to provide an account of how the immigrants behaved.[22]

In 1920, a record Republican year, these ten counties delivered almost 2.3 million Republican votes, 65 percent of the total vote cast. In 1940, they contributed over 3 million votes for Willkie, but in that year 3 million votes amounted to less than 40 percent of the total vote cast. Over the entire twenty-year period the Republican presidential candidate averaged over 2.4 million votes. There is considerable stability about this average with the only substantial decline coming in 1936, when FDR won reelection with a substantial 60 percent of the national vote, and the only increase coming in 1940, when FDR won reelection with a smaller fraction of the vote than he gained in 1932. It is the second line in figure 4.3 that gives significance to the first line. The second line plots, in thousands, the total number of votes cast in these ten counties between 1920 and 1940. Unlike the stability of the Republican vote, the total number of votes cast increased markedly. The total vote increased 124 percent, while the Republican vote increased barely 34 percent (if 1940 is treated as a stable increase). The Republican party simply did not get its share of the increase in the size of the voting population, and this failure to attract the new voters resulted in a 30 percentage point decline in the Republican share of the vote. In the 1930s, in other words, the Democratic party benefitted from the arrival of new voters who had not voted until then, just as the Republicans benefitted by the arrival of new voters in the 1850s. Unless one is willing to believe that all or a substantial number of the 1920 Republican voters subsequently defected to the Democratic party and that the stability in Republican votes is contributed by some fraction of new voters replacing the defectors (a proposition that could not be comfortably supported by the results of recent research in voting behavior), it is an inescapable conclusion that the Democratic victories in the cities and the countryside after 1928 are less a consequence of changed behavior on the part of old voters than it is the result of the choices of new voters.[23]

To be sure, there was some defection to FDR, but that defection

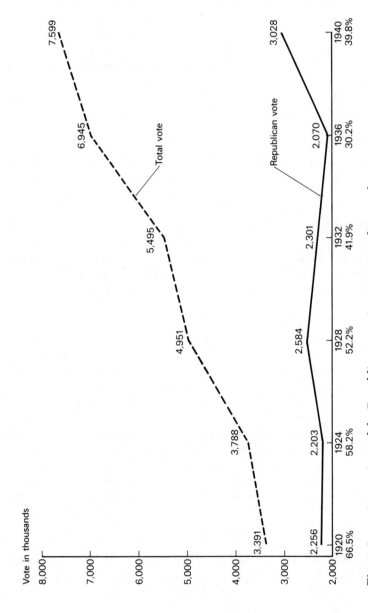

Fig. 4.3   Comparison of the Republican vote in ten metropolitan and industrial areas with the total vote, 1920–40

alone would not have provided the pluralities of the 1930s, just as the
defection from the Democrats would not have given Lincoln the
winning margin after 1860. There is some reason to believe that
many hundreds of thousands of Roosevelt voters in 1932 and
1936, who had previously voted for Republicans, returned to the
Republican fold in 1940 and 1944. The Republicans were at least
partly correct in asserting that "Roosevelt the man" was their
problem. When Roosevelt proved to lack a solution to all the nation's ills and when he broke the third-term tradition, many previously Republican states and counties returned to the fold. A
Republican resurgence in New England and the Middle West
is especially noticeable. Nevertheless, the new Democratic
majorities in cities and counties with large numbers of "ethnics"
remained firm. Defection may have elected Roosevelt in 1932 and
even in 1936, but by 1940 Republican defectors were returning.
The Roosevelt vote after 1936 was a Democratic vote.

The Coalitions

The realignments of the 1850s, 1890s, and 1928–36 all rested
upon the same new-voter phenomenon. The difference among
them is in the party that benefitted and the event that caused the
mobilization. In one instance it was the Civil War and in the latter
instances it was an economic depression. Al Smith, the Depression, and FDR were less important in changing the party preference of Republicans than they were in creating a preference and,
more important still, increasing severalfold the turnout rates of
citizens who had not participated before.

The "who" of party support arises out of the history that has
been sketched here. Some mix of religious, regional, ethnic, social
status, and occupational characteristics should delimit the groups
which make up the supporters of the parties. For example, virtually all Southerners should be Democratic. But Northerners will
be Democratic if they are of late immigrant stock and therefore
Catholic, and they will be Republican if they are of early immigrant stock and Protestant. The experience of the Depression of
1929 for the lower class and pro-union bias of the Democratic
party would lead one to expect to find Democrats among union
members irrespective of nationality or religious characteristics.
The reform and welfare bias of the Democratic party should typically lead us to expect to find fewer Democrats among the well-
to-do. The political recognition Roosevelt accorded blacks and the
welfare orientation of the national Democratic party clearly realigned the black population.[24] The next chapter documents the
presence of these coalition groups in the contemporary parties.

5 The Party Coalitions

An Empirical Derivation

The Party Coalitions: Historical Insight and Statistical Technique

Religion, nationality, race, region, economic status, occupation, and labor union membership are the social and demographic variables that the narrative in chapter 4 identified as the social cleavages that define the Democratic and Republican coalitions. But the party bias of these cleavages cannot be analyzed through a seriatum, bivariate comparison of each with party identification or the vote.[1] The social characteristics that predict partisanship are not sufficiently independent to permit such a strategy.[2] Some of the variables seem to account for the same variance in party preference. Since there is considerable overlap among the social characteristics that are related to partisanship, the American party system cannot be described in terms of a single dominant cleavage.[3] Previous realignments have built parties which are mosaics of social groups, defined by a permutation of several social traits.

The obvious task, then, is to specify the combination of social and demographic differences which yield groups with markedly different party preferences. There are several methods which might be used to identify the groups. The method used here combines an apriori selection of sociological differences with a statistical ability to predict party preference accurately. Chapter 4 offered historical reasons for believing that the traits listed in table 5.1 capture much of the variance in partisanship. By using statistical criteria to combine the variables in table 5.1, one can produce a number of groups which, because of their relatively unique partisanship, can be used to define the social basis of the contemporary party system.

The reason for adopting the statistical procedure outlined in Appendix A is that some independent test is needed to justify the permutations of social characteristics that define party coalition groups.[4] Many permutations are reasonable, but some will be useless, for they identify population segments lacking a distinctive partisanship. And, of course, it is equally possible that unaided intuition will fail to create a politically important (and historically interpretable) grouping. The statistical criteria for eliminating, retaining, and combining the social differences in table 5.1 becomes, therefore, very important.

The Social Correlates of Partisanship: An Empirical Derivation

Ethnoreligious differences account for party identification more effectively than any of the other characteristics in table 5.1.[5] Protestants are more likely to support the Republican party than are Catholics, and both are less likely to support the Democrats than minorites such as blacks and Jews. The grouping reported in table 5.2 provides no new insight into the social base of the parties; but some of the variation is a bit anomalous. The Republican preference of German-Americans has a conventional explanation.[6] Some of the intra-Catholic differences, however, are less explicable.

Polish and Irish Catholics are substantially more Democratic

Table 5.1   Percentage of Variance in Party Identification Correlated with Various Social, Economic, and Demographic Variables

Variables	Percentage
Ethnicity[a]	6.2
Region of residence	3.6
Index of social status	3.0
education	2.4
occupation	2.3
Union membership	2.0
Size of place of residence	1.1

[a]The specific categories of these variables are fully described in Appendix A.

Table 5.2   Party Preference of Eight Major Ethnoreligious Categories of the Electorate

Ethnoreligious Groups	Mean Party Bias[a]
German and Scandinavian Protestants	−.04
Protestants of other nationalities	.11
Other and no religion	.12
Polish and Irish Catholics	.46
All other Catholics	.32
Jews	.50
Blacks	.52
Spanish	.64
National average	.19

[a]Negative numbers indicate a Republican bias and positive numbers measure a Democratic bias. The numbers are the difference between the percent identifying with the Democratic party minus the percent identifying as Republicans. Unless otherwise indicated, the party bias measure is the way partisanship is assessed in the following tables and figures.

than other Catholics. On the average, they seem to be 60 percent Democratic, while other Catholics are less than 50 percent Democratic. The long history of Irish support for a Democratic party, extending back at least to the 1840s, might serve as a way of accounting for the difference. Why the Polish should be so Democratic is less clear. Cultural explanations are difficult to credit, since other Eastern Europeans are less supportive of the Democratic party than the Poles. While the Poles are 60 percent Democratic and only 13 percent Republican, other Eastern European Slavs are only 51 percent Democratic and 22 percent Republican.[7]

Alternative Explanations of Ethnoreligious Differences in Party Preference

These ethnoreligious groupings capture significant differences in party support; but the fact that some of the differences are difficult to explain lends credence to the proposition that they may be spurious and that they represent masks for unexamined variables. Are the ethnoreligious differences in party identification, for example, a catchall of regional social status, or rural-urban differences? The answer is that generally some of the ethnoreligious differences in party identification are a product of other characteristics, the most important of which is region.

Regional differences, however, are more varied than a South vs. non-South dichotomy. Table 5.3 examines the partisanship of seven different regions. It also compares the party identification of those who claim to be natives of each region with those who were raised elsewhere. The largest differences are obviously those between the South and the rest of the country. The South is at least 25 percentage points more Democratic than the nation as a whole. The states that border on the eleven states of the old Confederacy, while more Democratic than the rest of the nation, are considerably less Democratic than the Deep South.

A second interesting feature of these regional differences is the extent to which immigrants differ from natives. There are two areas where this produces important differences; in the South and in the Northeast and North Central regions. The southern differences are obviously a consequence of the heavy migration into the South that has taken place since the end of the Second World War. The migration has put into the region a population less Democratically inclined than the native population. The distinction between the native Southerner and the immigrant is important because expectations about the South depend upon native

Table 5.3.   Regional Differences in Party Bias

Regions[a]	All Residents	Among Natives	Among Immigrants	Difference[b]
New England	.12	.14	.05	−.09
Middle Atlantic	.03	−.01	.20	.21
East North Central	.08	.03	.23	.20
West North Central	.12	.13	.05	−.08
Deep South	.45	.50	.06	−.44
Border South	.30	.33	.19	−.14
Mountain and Pacific West	.21	.19	.23	.04

[a]The regions are the standard set used by the Survey Research Center.

[b]This is the arithmetic difference between the party bias of the native residents of the regions and the party bias of those who report being raised in some region other than the one in which they live. A negative number indicates that the immigrants to the region are more Republican in their party bias than the natives; while a positive number indicates that the immigrants are more Democratic than the natives of the region.

Note: In this and all similar tables the grouping of the characteristics is indicated by the lines which are drawn around the table entries.

Southerners. The immigrants are not Southerners whose party preference is colored by the same factors which determine the partisanship of the average native white Southerner.

The remaining regional differences between migrants and natives are, interestingly, a consequence of migration from the South to the North. Most of the immigrants to the industrial North have been Southerners, black and white. Although the Deep South and the Border South contain less than 30 percent of the population, they account for 59 percent of the migration into the industrial North.[8] These migrants out of the South are political mirror images of the migration into the South by Northerners. Migrants to the South are more Republican, while migrants from the South are more Democratic than the native population of the regions in which they settled. However, while migrants to the South are singled out as a group for the purpose of identifying the social characteristics of party supporters, migrants out of the South are not. There are three reasons for this discrimination. First, migrants to the South are singled out because removing them provides a more "crisp" group in which the study is interested, the native white Southerners. Second, many migrants out of the South are blacks. Blacks are, for obvious reasons, a priority group in the study of partisanship. Knowing that an individual is black is a more important piece of information for the specification of party identification than anything else about that person (as later data show). Finally, with the removal of blacks, there are only a few respondents representing migrants out of the South. The small number of cases, coupled with the fact that there are no compelling reasons for attempting an analysis of the residual, white migrants, argues against specifying migrants from the South as a group.

This analysis of partisanship in terms of region of residence and the region in which the respondents were raised leaves five regional groupings: native Southerners, immigrants to the South, border Southerners, residents of the Mountain and Pacific western states, and finally the residents of the Northeast and the Central and Plains states.[9] These five groups provide the best distinction of the regional basis of party identification. They also account for some of the ethnoreligious differences in party identification.

Table 5.4 indicates that intra-Protestant and nonminority white differences in party identification are almost completely a result of their regional distribution.[10]

Table 5.4.   Regional Basis of Ethnoreligious Differences in Party Bias

Ethnoreligious Groups	Native South	Immigrant South	Border South	Central and East	West
German and Scandinavian	.35	−.09	.16	−.10	.03
Protestants	(235)	(106)	(181)	(2492)	(649)
Other Protestant	.52	.00	.26	−.17	.08
nationalities	(2845)	(436)	(1046)	(4007)	(1349)
Other nonminority	.25	.09	.39	−.01	.20
whites	(693)	(328)	(340)	(2158)	(841)
Polish and Irish	.62	.66	.39	.46	.43
Catholics	(24)	(41)	(38)	(1068)	(122)
Other Catholics	.50	.56	.48	.28	.43
	(70)	(78)	(115)	(1859)	(339)
Jews	.48	.09	.19	.52	.57
	(14)	(19)	(34)	(648)	(67)
Blacks	.50	.50	.42	.53	.59
	(928)	(51)	(182)	(884)	(203)
Spanish	.66	.20	—	.55	.73
	(28)	(14)	(1)	(118)	(169)

There are only small differences in the partisanship of Protestants that are independent of their regional distribution. Consider the differences between native Southerners and those who live in the Central and Eastern states. Protestant nationalities hardly differ at all within the Northern and Eastern states; and among native Southerners, too, there are only small differences in partisanship that are associated with nationality. By contrast, for any given nationality group, there are large interregional differences in party preference.

Table 5.5   Controlled Comparison between Regions and Denominations

A: Absolute mean deviations within nationalities caused by regional
differences for:

German and Scandinavian Protestants	.15
Other Protestant nationalities	.20
Other nonminority whites	.28
Average	.21

B: Absolute mean deviations within regions caused by
nationality differences for:

Native Southerners	.14
Immigrant Southerners	.08
Border Southerners	.09
Central and Eastern	.16
West	.10
Average	.11

Table 5.5 presents a comparison of the party bias of the Protestant nationality groups controlling for the party bias of the regions and a comparison of the party bias of the regions controlling for the party bias of the nationality groups within the regions. The numbers in the table are simply the absolute mean deviations associated with region or ethnicity when the other is held constant. Consider the example of the native Southerner. The South (for the whole twenty-year period) is 50 percentage points more Democratic than Republican (table 5.4). German and Scandinavian Protestants in the South are only 35 points more Democratic than Republican, other Protestant nationalities are about 52 points more Democratic than Republican in their identification, and other non-Catholic and nonminority whites are about 25 points pro-Democratic. The average absolute deviations of these percentages from the party bias of all native Southerners is 14 points (table 5.5). This figure of 14 percentage points can be thought of as the difference between the party bias of the South and the nation contributed by the different party bias of the Protestant nationality groups within the South. The other numbers in the table are derived similarly. The party bias differences among the various Protestant nationalities would be 72 percent smaller if they were equally distributed across all regions. In contrast, if the Protestant denominations were distributed in the North in the same proportions that they are in the South, the party bias differences between the regions would be reduced by less than 11 percent.[11]

There are, to be sure, some nationality differences within the regions, but they are based on a small number of cases and it is difficult to credit them with much significance. In any case, the ethnic-caused differences are only pallid reflections of the regional variation in party preference among white Protestants. But regional factors do not explain the party bias of non-Protestant nationalities, nor do they add much to the Democratic bias of blacks.

At a minimum, then, the party coalitions are based on regional differences and membership in minority religions and racial groups.

Social Status Differences between Democrats and Republicans

The social-demographic groups with distinct party preferences in table 5.4 are regionally, racially, and religiously defined. These groups lack any characterization by social and economic status, something which has been an important discriminator of party preference for forty years. The New Deal injected some measure of class politics into the American party system, so social and economic status should help to identify further the social divisions that separate Democrats from Republicans. In particular, one might wonder if the intense Democratic preference among Catholics and blacks is not a reflection of the socio-economic characteristics of the two groups. The bulk of the white Catholic population arrived at about the turn of the century, lacking the technical skills which would guarantee success in the industrial society into which they moved. Coming from ethnic stocks with languages and a religion different from the dominant population, the turn-of-the-century immigrant Catholics drifted into the lowest rungs of the Northern social order. It is possible, therefore, that the pro-Democratic bias of Catholics is a reflection not of a cultural heritage of Democratic support, but in the underdog orientation of the national Democratic party and the underdog status of Catholics.[12]

Unfortunately, however attractive status hypotheses may be, they do not explain the party differences between Protestants and Catholics. At similar levels of socioeconomic status Catholics are always less Republican than Protestants. Consider table 5.6, which presents the mean party bias of each of the groups from table 5.4 by each level of social status (Appendix B describes the construction of the status index). There is a bit less support for the Democrats among the very highest status Irish and Poles but these differences, which rest on small Ns, pale in comparison with the differences between Catholics and Protestants of a similar social status, The partisanship difference between Polish and Irish Catholics and other Catholics is largely impervious to status differences. However, status differences do predict differences in

Table 5.6   Party Bias by Ethnic and Regional Grouping and Status

Ethnic and Grouping	Very High Status	II	III	IV	Very Low Status	Farmers
		Index of Socioeconomic Status				
White Protestants:						
Central and	−.42	−.35	−.24	−.01	.03	−.10
Eastern states	(1214)	(1242)	(1054)	(1544)	(2461)	(851)
Western states	−.27	−.08	.01	.23	.29	.19
	(441)	(447)	(445)	(486)	(800)	(102)
Border South	.14	.15	.34	.42	.31	−.06
	(161)	(198)	(173)	(297)	(605)	(113)
Deep South,	.56	.47	.48	.57	.51	.56
natives	(436)	(540)	(528)	(501)	(1238)	(509)
Deep South,	−.04	−.08	−.03	.17	.02	−.03
immigrants	(221)	(185)	(158)	(133)	(136)	(15)
Polish and Irish	.24	.42	.37	.62	.53	.71
Catholics	(162)	(264)	(180)	(285)	(381)	(19)
All other Catholics	−.02	.14	.31	.42	.44	.37
	(431)	(658)	(644)	(897)	(1344)	(135)
Jews	.36	.38	.57	.72	.70	
	(208)	(188)	(177)	(97)	(111)	(1)
Blacks	.52	.60	.62	.57	.57	.49
	(125)	(132)	(218)	(420)	(1256)	(92)
Spanish	.38	.61	.71	.58	.71	.69
	(16)	(27)	(44)	(51)	(183)	(6)

party identification for Catholics who are neither Irish nor Polish. Those in the two highest status categories are likely to be less Democratic than the population as a whole, while Catholics below the second category are more Democratic (the population mean is .19).

Overall, while it is possible to improve one's prediction of party identification by knowing something about the social status of an individual, one cannot explain the Democratic sympathies of the Catholic population in terms of their lower socioeconomic position.[13] While a better education or occupation is correlated with higher levels of Republican support among Catholics, the difference in the party identification of Catholics in the highest status category compared with those in the lowest category is never equal to the difference between Protestants and Catholics in similar status categories.

The Status Basis of Democrat Sympathies among Catholics: A Digression

This analysis does not take account of the distinction between the current social status of Catholics and the social status of Catholics when they entered the electorate. Consider the following amendment to the theory: The Catholic population developed a Democratic party preference because of their relatively disadvantaged position in the United States in the decades after their entry, because of their ties to urban Democratic political machines, because the Democratic party offered Catholics recognition with the nomination of Al Smith, and because the Democracy of the New Deal met the welfare needs of Catholics, a relatively deprived group. It is entirely possible that the Democratic preference of Catholics, learned during the years of Catholic deprivation, was passed on through parental and general subcultural socialization.[14] In short, the Catholic population might be Democratic today because the social mobility of Catholics did not prevent each generation from transmitting the Democratic preferences developed when their socioeconomic status was important.

Table 5.7 presents the relevant data. The problem with the preceding amendment is that the socioeconomic status of Protestants who entered the electorate before 1928 is not different from that of the Catholics who entered before 1928. Their party identification, however, is much more Republican. This similar social and economic status, with complete dissimilarity in party preference, clearly refutes the amended status explanation. The low status of their ancestors compared with white Protestants did not make Catholics Democrats today. There were no economic status differences of any consequence 50 years ago, and there are none now.

The differential appeal of the parties for Catholics and Protestants rests upon historical events interacting with cultural differences. Catholic and Protestant differences in party identification are not simply a reflection of social class.

Social Status and Republicanism

For other groups in the North, however, there is a clear tendency for status and party preference to be associated (see table 5.6). It has little impact on either blacks or Jews, but for most other groups there is a positive relationship.

Farmers are a particularly interesting group in this regard. Farmers tend to have the lowest socioeconomic status of any occupational group in the population. For every level of education, a farmer will have a lower score on the index of socioeconomic status than any other occupation because his is both low prestige work and not very remunerative. Given such a low socioeconomic status and the extent to which the Democratic party has been the champion of policies designed to aid the farmers, one might ex-

Table 5.7   Comparison of Social Status and Party Bias of Catholics and Protestants among Three Electoral Cohorts

| | Time of Entering the Electorate | | |
	Before 1928	In 1928–51	After 1951
Catholics:			
mean social status	−.46[a]	.17	.15
mean party bias	.35	.41	.35
Protestants:[b]			
mean social status	−.44	.23	.23
mean party bias	−.23	−.05	.00

[a]Negative numbers on the index of social status indicate a score below the average for the population, while a positive score indicates one above the population average. The party bias measure is, of course, negative when the group is more Republican than Democrat and positive when the group is more Democrat than Republican.

[b]Only Northern white Protestants are included in this group. The North here includes any state not in the Deep or Border South.

pect them to give strong support to the Democrats. But, as table 5.6 indicates, this is not the case. Outside of the South, farmers are a markedly Republican group.[15]

The weak association between party and social status among Southerners in table 5.6 covers some significant longitudinal differences. The extent to which the partisanship of upper-status compared with lower-status white Southerners has changed in recent years is apparent from table 5.8: No differences in party preference by social status for the 1950s became large differences by the 1970s. The upper- and lower-status groups in the South have changed their party preference at different rates. Their dissimilar partisanship in the later years argues for segmenting border and native Southerners by social status even though no differences appear in table 5.6.

Table 5.9 presents a final regrouping of the population which is sensitive to the strong ties between the Democratic party and organized labor. In literally every case, a respondent in a household with a union member could be expected to be more Democratic than members of a group not connected with a union member. But because some groups seemed important to keep intact, not all union members were placed into a union membership category. The point to the asymmetry of this regrouping was to remove union members but not disrupt the central party identification of a group that was of particular interest. Blacks, Jews, and border and native Southerners were, therefore, not put into a union group even if they were characterized by union

Table 5.8   Development of Status Differences in Party Preference in the South

	1950s	1970s	Change[a]
Border South			
very high status	.16	.20	.04
high status	.58	.02	−.56
middle status	.47	.19	−.28
low status	.32	.37	.05
very low status	.16	.31	.15
Native Deep South			
very high status	.73	.36	−.37
high status	.60	.24	−.36
middle status	.66	.24	−.42
low status	.66	.53	−.13
very low status	.48	.41	−.07

[a]This number is the percentage point change in the party bias of the group. A negative number is change toward the Republican party and a positive number represents change toward the Democratic party.

membership. These groups were judged far too interesting as political groups to have their characteristics dispersed by a less interesting political influence (union membership).

The Social Composition of the Parties

The fifteen groups that maximally discriminate party identification are presented below.[16] They provide the best prediction of party identification that can be obtained by social characteristics. Table 5.10 summarizes the groupings that have been developed in this chapter. In the left column the proportion of the groups in the population is shown. The next column presents the mean score of the groups on the index of party identification. The last set of columns present the distribution of Democrats, Independents, and Republicans in the groups, and their party bias. This table is based, as was most of the analysis which derived the groups, on the pooled interviews of the nine election studies for the years 1952 through 1972.[17]

1. The very high-status Northern white Protestants: Table 5.9 differentiates between members of this group located in the Central and Eastern states and those located in the Western states. This little recognized sectional division is interesting. Almost any explanation one might care to offer as an account of the differences (the silver orientation of the Bryan Democrats, the success of the Populists, etc.) has more than a few defects. Simply because it is a difference that does not have an available explana-

Table 5.9   Influence of Union Membership on Party Bias

Ethnic, Regional, and Status Grouping	Non-union	Union
Very high-status Protestants		
Central and Eastern states	−.43	−.27
Western states	−.27	−.12
Middle- and high-status Protestants		
Central and Eastern states	−.34	−.02
Western states	−.11	.19
Lower-status Protestants		
Central and Eastern states	−.09	−.16
Western states	.17	.41
Border Southern whites		
middle and upper status	.21	.16
lower status	.28	.43
Deep South		
immigrant	−.05	.34
middle- and upper-status natives	.49	.64
lower-status natives	.52	.62
Catholics		
Polish and Irish	.45	.51
higher status–other nationalities	.08	.19
lower status–other nationalities	.35	.51
Jews	.42	.76
Blacks	.56	.61
Northern Farmers	−.07	−.05
National Average	.14	.37

tion, the very high status Northern Protestants, regardless of where they come from in the North, are treated as a group. Basically this grouping includes anyone who is neither Catholic nor Jewish, who is not a union member or a farmer, and who lives outside of the South or the Border South. This group includes only those in the first category of the status measure (those with education beyond high school and a professional or managerial occupation). On a separate index of social-economic status this group is about 1.5 standard deviations above the social status of the population (see Appendix B). They are the top 20 percent of the northern white Protestant population by social status, and represent the "silk-stocking" component with which the Republican party has been identified. Any changes in the partisanship of this easily recognized segment of the electorate would be interesting both theoretically and politically.

2. Middle- and high-status Northern white Protestants: What is written about the very high-status group largely applies here, except that their social status is lower. This group averages about 0.6 standard deviations above the population in socioeconomic

Table 5.10   The Sociodemographic Basis of Party Preference

Coalition Groups	Proportion of Population	Mean Party Identification	Percent Democrat	Percent Independent	Percent Republican	Party Bias
Very high-status Protestants	6%	4.1	17	27	56	−39
Middle- and high-status Protestants	10	3.7	13	27	51	−28
Lower-status Protestants	12	3.0	34	29	37	−03
Border Southerners						
middle and upper status	2	2.7	48	25	27	20
lower status	4	2.2	58	19	23	35
Deep South						
immigrants	3	3.1	35	31	35	0
middle- and upper-status natives	6	1.8	61	28	11	50
lower-status natives	9	1.6	67	20	13	55
Catholics						
Polish and Irish	3	1.8	58	29	13	45
other nationalities—higher status	4	2.7	36	36	28	8
other nationalities—middle and lower status	7	2.1	53	230	18	35
Jews	3	1.5	58	34	8	50
Blacks	9	1.4	69	20	11	58
Northern farmers	4	3.2	37	20	44	−07
Union members	19	2.2	51	29	20	31

status. It represents about 35 percent of the Northern white population and is the respectable middle class which has a traditional affinity for the Republican party.

3. Lower-status Northern white Protestants: Again, only social status differentiates this group from the preceding two. These respondents tend to have a mix of education and occupations which put them beneath the middle level of the society (status categories four and five): On an extended index of social and economic status, they average about 0.7 standard deviations below the population average and constitute the lower 45 percent of the Northern white Protestant population in social status.

4. Middle- and upper-status white Protestants in the Border South: Culturally, this group represents a transition between the Republicanism of Northern white Protestants and the Democratic sympathies of Southern whites. The upper third of the status distribution of the region is represented in this group: Their SES score is about 0.8 standard deviations above the national norm.

5. Lower-status white Protestants in the Border South: This group is similar to the proceeding group except in social status and, of course, party preference. Two-thirds of the white population of the Border South is represented here. The group is about 0.8 standard deviations below the national norm in social status.

6. Immigrants to the Deep South: This group includes white Protestants residing in the South who were raised outside the South. The group is much more inclined to be Republican than the typical native Southerner. The rationale for this group is negative. It is valuable only because, if it were not distinguished, the Southerners would not be adequately specified.

7. Middle- and upper-status native Southerners: Again, this group is Protestant in religious preference. It includes individuals raised in and currently living in the eleven states of the old Confederacy. The group represents about 40 percent of the white Southern electorate and the relative social status of the group is about 0.7 standard deviations above the norm.

8. Lower-status native Southerners: About 60 percent of the white Southern electorate is represented in this category. The group is about 0.8 standard deviations below the population in social status. Overall, they are not markedly different from the preceeding group in party preference. There are, however, sharp differences over time in their party preference.

9. Polish and Irish Catholics: This group has a near-normal socioeconomic status reflecting the fact that the Irish are well off and the Poles rather less well off. The groups are equal in size and seem similar (if students of ethnicity are to be believed) only in

their preference for the Democratic party.[18] If the "silk-stocking" WASPs of the first category are the essence of Republicanism, the Polish and Irish Catholics are the essential Democrats. It is perhaps no accident that Poles and Irish (and particularly the latter) are represented beyond their numbers in the leadership of the Democratic party.[19]

10. Higher-status Catholics: This group excludes Polish and Irish Catholics. Ethnically, it is composed of Catholics of many nationalities who seem to share only a rather high status and as a consequence, it would seem, less of the modal Catholic preference for the Democratic party. The group is defined by the two highest categories of status, and it has a socioeconomic status about 1.1 standard deviations above the population. They are about 25 percent of all Catholics.

11. Middle- and lower-status Catholics: Similar to the previous group except in status, this group is defined by social status categories three and below. The group is about 0.4 standard deviations below the population in social status. About 50 percent of all Catholics are represented here. The Democratic preference of this group is stronger than that of higher-status Catholics but less than that of the Polish and Irish Catholics.

12. Jews: All Jews are represented in this group. As an inspection of the preceding tables will indicate, the Democratic preference of Jews is largely unaffected by any other social characteristic. While union membership seems to imply greater support for the Democratic party (as it does among all population groups), Jews are considered a priority social group in this analysis, and Jews who are members of unions are still categorized as Jews.

13. Blacks: All blacks are represented in this group. The comment for Jews applies to blacks, too.

14. Northern farmers: Northern farmers were a negative group much as Southern immigrants were a negative group for Southerners. The point of separating out Northern farmers was not to examine changes in the partisanship of farmers over time so much as to remove from the preceding groups the confounding correlation of a farm occupation with a Republican party preference. As table 5.6 indicates, though, only Northern and Border South farmers are included here. Farmers were not deleted from the other groupings. The party preference of white Southerners, for example, was not better specified by knowing that the Southerner was a farmer, and so the characteristic of being a Southerner was treated as a priority trait.

15. Union member: As table 5.9 makes clear, union membership strongly affects whether an individual will consider himself a

Democrat. The strongest effect of union membership was found among Northern white Protestants.The Democratic sympathies of Catholics were also affected by union membership. In order to isolate its influence on partisanship, the union membership category is populated only by Northern white Protestants and white Catholics. In both cases the removal of union members from the grouping ensures that group differences in party preference and changes in the party identification of the groups does not represent the influence of organized labor.

Table 5.10 is summarized in figure 5.1. Throughout this chapter and in subsequent chapters the attitudes of the groups are ex-

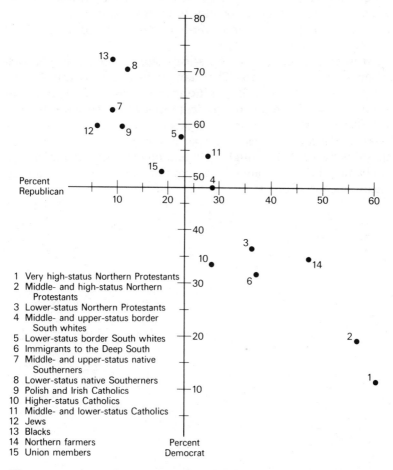

1   Very high-status Northern Protestants
2   Middle- and high-status Northern
      Protestants
3   Lower-status Northern Protestants
4   Middle- and upper-status border
      South whites
5   Lower-status border South whites
6   Immigrants to the Deep South
7   Middle- and upper-status native
      Southerners
8   Lower-status native Southerners
9   Polish and Irish Catholics
10 Higher-status Catholics
11 Middle- and lower-status Catholics
12 Jews
13 Blacks
14 Northern farmers
15 Union members

Fig. 5.1   Spatial representation of the relative party preferences of fifteen party coalition groups

pressed as "bias indices" (as percentage differences). To obtain some clear grasp of what these bias indices mean in a spatial sense, and to understand exactly how different the fifteen groups are in their party preference, the percentage Democrat and Republican in each group are summarized in the following figure. Figure 5.1 presents two axes which (vertically) plot the percent Democrat and (horizontally) the percent Republican. The intersection of these axes is the twenty-year average of the percent who are Democrat and Republican in the population. The higher the position of the group the more Democratic it is and the farther to the right the group is located the more Republican its party identification. A very Democratic group would be in the upper-left quarter. A group with a high or balanced proportion of Democrats and Republicans would tend toward the upper-right quarter; and a group in the lower-left quarter would have a high proportion of Independents.

An informed observer of American politics would not be surprised by any of the groups. They have an historical basis in American politics, and they yield an intuitively correct typology to describe the social and demographic groups which support the parties. Because the groups are relatively constant, they can be interrogated at different times. Their party preference can be traced for the years from 1952 through 1976 and changes in this preference can be noted. If the change is substantial enough, there would be reason for describing it as a realignment.

Part 3

The Contemporary Realignment

New Coalitions

6 The Realignment of the Parties

The extravagance of recent elections, in terms of the candidates that have been presented, the issues that have been raised, and the lopsidedness of the results of the vote, is coincidental with important changes in the groups from which the parties typically draw their support.[1] Old bastions of the parties are no longer secure. The Democratic vote has declined in the South and increased in New England and in the Central and Plains states. These are not purely changes in "presidential Republicanism" in the South; and changes outside the South are greatest in traditionally Republican states without major urban areas. Democratic officeholders are common at the state and national level in New England and the Midwest. The number of Republican officeholders is increasing throughout the South.

Beyond elections there are indications of stress within the party coalitions. This is particularly true of the Democratic party. The clash between "hardhats" and "radicals," for example, has been seen as a slipping of the Democratic moorings of ethnics and blue-collar workers. Confrontations between blacks and these same white groups betray the social conservatism of a considerable number of Democratic identifiers.[2] Growing liberalism among groups usually regarded as Republican portend a similar weakening of the Republican party.

The response of social scientists and journalists to this scenario is varied. Some have argued that a realignment is either underway or imminent. Burnham and Phillips provide contrasting interpretations of this realignment. Burnham perceives a "heads-and-tails" realignment: A liberal but well-off segment of the electorate that therefore has supported the Republican party is moving to reinforce an ideologically liberal but economically disadvantaged segment of the population that already supports the Democrats. A great middle, characterized by a conservative preference for the status quo, is to become the basis of the Republican party.[3] Phillips sees a two-decade-long strain resulting in Republican dominance.[4] Others, in contrast, have regarded recent elections as responses to relatively short-term, election-specific issues which will leave the parties largely untouched, especially if neither party embraces one of the divisive issues.[5]

This chapter will demonstrate that the "ayes" have it, that there is a realignment underway, that several traditional sources of Democratic and Republican voting strength are shifting their allegiance, and that the groups which are changing the most were instrumental in building the winning pluralities in the 1964, 1968, 1972, and 1976 presidential elections.

Aggregate Stability, Dealignment, and Realignment

From one point of view figure 6.1 shows a great deal of stability in the electorate. While the Republicans have lost proportionately more of their support in recent years, the relative proportion of Democrats to Republicans (the party bias of the electorate) has been remarkably constant. Both parties have suffered (on average) a 5 percentage point decline in identifiers, with the result that Democrats continue to outnumber Republicans by about 19 percentage points. The party bias has fluctuated a bit, especially during the 1950s, but there is no discernible trend in the Democratic advantage.[6]

There is, however, irrefutable evidence of a decline in attachment to the parties. Independents have increased almost 60 percent from about 23 percent of the electorate in the 1950s to just under 40 percent by the middle 1970s. Clearly, some degree of electoral dealignment has occurred.

But nothing in figure 6.1 will help to answer whether a party-voter realignment has transpired. The increase in Independents does not address the question of realignment at all. An individual can change his party identification and become a Democrat when he was a Republican or he can abandon the parties by asserting that he is an Independent. But formally a realignment occurs only when the parties exchange supporters. At least up to the point where the number of Independents becomes so numerous that one might question whether there is significant support for any party, a simple increase in the proportion of Independents in the electorate does not indicate a realignment (see chapter 2). The evidence for a realignment, therefore, must come from an analysis of the social groupings which typically differ in their support for the parties.

The particular way in which groups of varying sizes have changed their partisanship, coupled with the direction of that change, has left the parties with the same relative strength; but

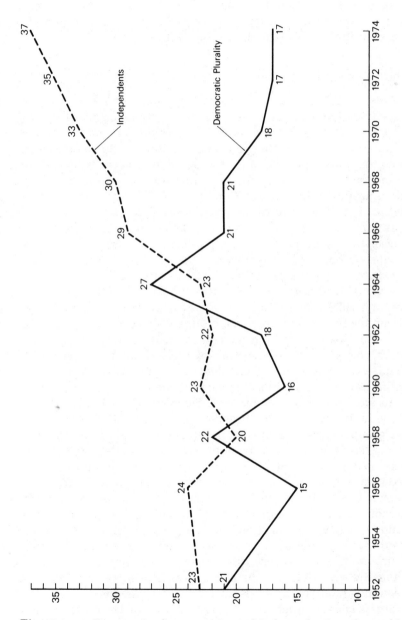

Fig. 6.1   Increase in the proportion of Independents and a stable Democratic plurality

Republican and Democratic identifiers are not distinguished by the same social and demographic characteristics by which they were marked in the past, at least not to the same degree. The social basis of the party coalitions has changed; it is in these changes that a realignment can be demonstrated. Electoral dealignment has contributed substantially to the shift.

The Source of Realignment

Most of the 15 demographically defined party coalition groups have undergone a change in their party preference over the past 20 years. Only 4 groups, containing about 34 percent of the population, have not changed their partisanship to some extent. Six groups with 48 percent of the population have become more Democratic either through an actual increase in Democratic identification or by a loss of Republican identification to independence. The 18 percent of the population distributed over the remaining 5 groups has become less Democratic, either by an increase in the proportion of Republicans or through loss to a greater number of Independents.

Figure 6.2 compares the party identification of each group for the years 1952 through 1960 (the 1950s) with the years 1968 through 1976 (the 1970s). There is a considerable difference between the two periods for some groups. Table 6.1 summarizes the changes. The first column presents a measure of the percentage point change in the proportion of each group which consider themselves Democrat, Independent, or Republican. The next two columns break down this change: the numbers in the second column are simply the change in the percentage of Independents, those in the third column measure the change in the party bias of the group.[7] A positive change in the party bias indicates that the group has become relatively more Democratic in the 1970s than it was in the early 1950s, while a negative index number would indicate a greater proportion of Republicans relative to Democrats. The fourth column of Table 6.1 presents an asymmetric Somer's δ, which is based upon predicting the distribution of the index of party identification with the year of the study for each group. This "longitudinal correlation" takes on a value different from zero when the distribution of party preference in the group is changing over time. As the correlation is positive, the group is becoming relatively more Democratic; and when it is negative, the group is becoming relatively more Republican. The correlation is a convenient device for indicating the degree to which the change indexed in the preceding columns summarizes a trend over time

Table 6.1   Summary Indexes of Change in the Distribution of Party Identification for the Fifteen "Coalition Groups"

Coalition Groups	Change in Party Identification	Change in Independents	Change in Party Bias	Correlation
Northern Protestants				
very high status	14	13	16	10
middle and high status	11	10	12	5
lower status	10	5	15	6
White Southerners				
middle and upper				
status border	25	10	−40	−14
lower status border	17	17	− 4	1
immigrants to the				
Deep South	11	11	− 8	− 5
middle and upper				
status, Deep South	38	31	−46	−24
lower status,				
Deep South	18	17	−20	−13
Catholics				
Polish and Irish	5	5	− 4	− 3
other Catholics of				
higher status	14	14	− 4	− 3
other Catholics of				
middle and lower				
status	9	5	13	3
Jews	9	9	− 6	− 3
Blacks	18	− 4	32	8
Northern farmers	7	− 4	9	3
Union members	9	9	− 4	− 2

Note: Change in party identification is the total percentage point change that has taken place between the two time periods in the distribution of Democrats, Republicans, and Independents. Note 7 more fully describes how this percentage is calculated.

Change in Independents is the simple arithmetic difference between the proportion calling themselves Independent in the 1972 and 1976 studies and the proportion Independent in the 1952 and 1956 studies. A positive number indicates more Independents in the later period.

Change in party bias is the arithmetic difference between the party bias of the group in the seventies and the party bias of the group in the early fifties. A positive number indicates relatively more Democrats, a negative number more Republicans. To determine the percentage, rather than the percentage point change, simply divide the number by two.

The correlation is a Somer's δ predicting party preference with the year of the study.

(rather than just oscillation). All of these numbers demonstrate considerable change in the partisanship of the coalition groups.[8]

Most of the change in the distribution of partisanship is contributed by the ten groups which are changing at a rate above the

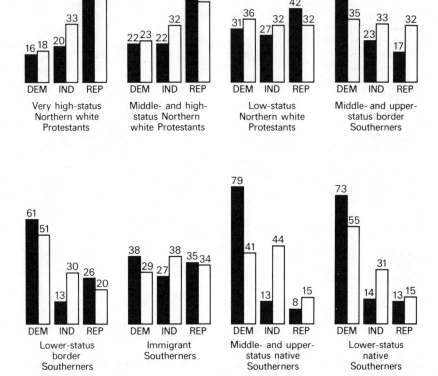

Fig. 6.2   Changes in the partisanship of the coalition groups since the 1950s

average for the groups. Not surprisingly, these ten groups are interesting for what they have contributed to political debate and analysis in the last decade. These groups will be looked at in some detail below.

The Southern Democracy

The courtship of white Southerners by the Republican party beginning in the middle 1950s and intensifying in the early 1960s has had an effect.[9] Southern whites are leaving the Democratic party. Grass-roots organizational work by the Republican party

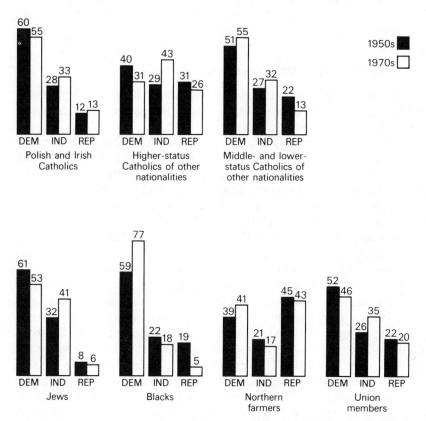

and the ever clearer political (and especially racial) liberalism of the Democratic party is eliminating the discrepancy between the party predisposition of Southerners and the rest of the nation. The change is so substantial that Southerners, who represent only about 20 percent of the electorate, contribute almost 39 percent of the change in partisanship that is found in the entire electorate. It is difficult to chart the year at which this change was initiated. An average figure for all Southerners indicates that 1952 is the high watermark of Democratic strength. The 60-plus percent of white Southerners who identified with the Democratic party over the Republican party in 1952 is never approached again. The perturbations of the line probably reflect only the election-specific forces which influence the party preference of some voters.[10] The "soft-

ness" of Democratic identification in the South after 1952 became a precipitous fall after 1964. The data seem to lend themselves to a periodization which finds the years 1952 through 1960
as one era of party preference, the years 1962 through perhaps
1966 as another, and the years after 1966 as a third period in
which the level of Democratic identification over Republican
identification is about equal to that of the nation as a whole.

The Status Cleavage in Southern Partisanship

Probably the most interesting feature of figure 6.2 is the difference between upper- and lower-status Southerners in the appeal of the Democratic party.

By 1936, the sorting of Democrats and Republicans in terms of
social status was marked, even if the two were not perfectly correlated.[11] In the South, in contrast, the status differential in party
preference did not exist. The economic cleavages of Southern
political life were handled by intraparty factions, or they were
ignored. The Populist elements in the Southern Democratic party,
represented by the Huey Longs, spoke for, at least insisted they
spoke for, the poor and disadvantaged within the party. The respectable elements and business tended to organize as an opposing faction.[12] The intensity of this cleavage varied from state to
state, and it was more intense in some periods than in others. But
it was usually present, and it was a functional equivalent for a
competitive party system which encapsulated status difference.
The "arrival" of the Republican party introduced party as an
alternative to faction. As late as 1952 there was virtually no difference in party preference associated with status. But from the
high watermark of 1952, partisanship begins to differ by socioeconomic status. The better-off Southern whites in both the Deep
South and the Border states have changed the most. Lower-status
Deep South whites have also become less Democratic, but at a
slower rate than the higher-status individuals. Only the lower-
status whites in the Border South have failed to change.

Of course, the higher-status whites in these areas of the South
are not as Republican as their non-Southern counterparts. But, as
these data and the summaries of table 6.1 indicate, there has been
a substantial change from the unanimous Democratic sympathy
characteristics of the South in the past.

The role of the age cohort factor in these changes will be
analyzed in chapter 7, for now, and it should be pointed out that it
is a factor in the changes. Younger Southerners, those who came

of age after 1960, seem to pace about 4 to 6 years ahead of older cohorts. The distribution of party preference in the whole population in 1972 can be found among young Southerners in 1966. The young have also been very important in the total amount of change that has occurred. Although they constitute less than a quarter of the Southern white population, they contributed 48 percent of the total increase in the proportion of Independents and 35 percent of the decline in the level of Democrat identification.

There is very little evidence of a rural-urban source for these changes. It is true that the partisanship change has been the largest in the more urban areas of the South (where 50,000 defines the larger urban area), but urbanization does not seem to constitute the causal phenomenon. The extent to which both higher-status and younger voters are concentrated in the larger cities is likely to be the primary explanation for the observable differences between urban and rural areas in shifts in party identification.

The Effect of Migration

The place of the immigrant to the South in these changes merits attention. The South has grown considerably in the past 20 years. Part of this growth is natural population increase but much of it is a direct consequence of migration from other areas of the country. Since the South was peculiar in the strength of its ties to the Democratic party, migration should have diluted the Democratic bias of the region. Indeed, some have argued that virtually all of the change in the South is a consequence of migration.[13] A close look at the data indicates otherwise.[14]

Most of the decline in Democratic support has come from changes in the party identification of individuals who were raised in the South. If there had been no migration to the South prior to the 1952 and 1956 elections, the South would have been 76 percent Democratic and most of the remaining 24 percent would have described themselves as Independent. The effect of migration prior to those years was to reduce the Democratic majority to 73 percent. By 1972 and 1976 the Democratic portion of the native white Southern population declined to 51 percent, and adding in the immigrant portion of the population reduced the Democratic plurality only seven more points, to 44 percent. Had there been no migration to the South, the proportion of Democrats would still have declined 26 points. Only 20 of the 29-point decline in Democratic identifiers has been contributed by nonnative Southerners. Table 6.2 summarizes all of these changes.

Table 6.2   The Effect of Immigration on Southern Partisanship

Status Groups	Percent Democratic	
	1952–56	1972–76
Native Southerners		
middle and upper status	78	45
lower status	75	55
Immigrant Southerners	49	23
Total	73	44
Sources of Decline	Percentage Points	Percent
Change in Partisanship of Native Southerners	23	80
Differences in the party preference of immigrants and natives	3	10
Increase in the proportion of immigrants	3	10
Total decline	29	100

A Final Note on the Uniqueness of the South

The extent to which white Southerners have abandoned the Democratic party is even clearer if one compares Southern and Northern shifts in party identification. The dominant feature of contemporary changes in the party system has been its erosion, manifested by the growth of Independents. On the average, almost 78 percent of the changed partisanship of the coalition groups results from the dealignment of the electorate, its general loss of partisanship. But while dealignment is an important process in the realignment of the New Deal party system in general, it plays a much smaller role among white Southerners. Within the South, the decline in the Democrats has registered increases for the Republicans.

The noteworthy feature of the data in table 6.3 is that the decline of the Southern Democrats has actually improved the party bias in a Republican direction. Figure 6.1 showed that, despite a surfeit of concern about the health of the Republican party, their relative distance behind the Democrats has been constant since the early 1950s. Although the Republicans have proportionally suffered a greater loss to independence than the Democrats, the absolute decline in their numbers has been no greater than the Democrats, resulting in a constant 19 point Democratic bias in the electorate. But that steady bias has been sustained by patterns of partisan change among white southerners that differs from the rest of the country. The numbers in table 6.3 are not changes within regions, rather, they are estimates of the regional contributions to the total national change that occurred between the

Table 6.3   Changes in Partisanship of Northern and Southern whites from the 1950s to 1976

	Democrats	Independents	Republicans
All but Southern whites	−2.4	+10.2	−7.9
Southern whites	−5.4	+ 3.4	+2.0
Total	−7.8	+13.6	−5.9

decade of the 1950s and 1976. Among all other regions and groups the Democratic bias has increased more than 5 points between the 1950s and 1976. Adding the South into the calculation shifts the pattern of erosion in a way that disadvantages the Democrats. Both parties have lost support, but Republican losses have been reduced by the waxing affection of the South for the GOP.

Change Outside the South: Fewer Republicans

The importance of the South to the Democratic party is considerable. If one were, for example, to remove the South from the electorate, the electoral and congressional majorities of the Democratic party would virtually disappear; and, with the exception of Johnson's election in 1964, there would not have been a Democratic president after 1936. The loss of the South would seem to assure Republican dominance. That this has not happened (and that there is no indication that it is about to happen) indicates the existence of pro-Democratic trends in segments of the Republican coalition or an intensification of Democratic support in normally Democratic groups.

About 64 percent of the "silk-stocking" Protestant population identified as Republicans in the fifties. By the late sixties and early seventies the proportion of Republicans in this group had declined to 50 percent. The changes in the other Northern Protestant groups are only slightly smaller. In the fifties the middle-status Protestant group was 34 points more Republican than Democrat, but in the seventies the advantage had declined to 22 points. In the fifties lower-status Protestants were 11 points more Republican, and by the seventies this had converted to a 4 point Democratic advantage.

While the changes here are not nearly so large as those in the South, they are considerable, and they mark a decline in Republican identification among a segment of the population that has long been identified as intensely Republican. Unlike the South, these changes are disproportionately concentrated among the young. So concentrated, in fact, that the majority of the change would not have taken place were it not for the difference in the partisanship of the young and the old among Northern Protestants.

The ubiquitous farm vote that has been a pivotal influence on social policy because of the structure of congressional representation is also less Republican over time. In spite of the New Deal and a proliferation of farmer-oriented policies and programs designed by the Democratic party, farmers outside of the South have displayed a preference for the Republican party over the Democratic party, especially in comparison with the national distribution of party identification. The Republican bias of northern farmers is declining more slowly than it is among other groups (see table 6.1), but because of the farmer's place in our political history it is interesting to note the change they are undergoing. However, the slowness of the change combined with the fact that farmers are a rapidly declining portion of the population reduces the practical significance of this transformation.

Other Changes: More Democrats among Blacks and Jews

Paralleling the decline of Republican support in traditionally Republican segments of the population is an increase in the Democratic bias of normally Democratic groups. Blacks are a significant portion of the Democratic coalition because of the level of support they give Democratic candidates and for their strategic geographical concentration.[15] The conversion of blacks to the Democratic party dates from the middle 1930s and is clearly a consequence of the welfare programs of the Roosevelt administration and the political recognition that his first administration accorded blacks.[16] With Roosevelt, the pictures of Abraham Lincoln were "turned to the wall" and the wholesale conversion of black voters to the Democratic party took place.[17]

The change in black partisanship was less complete in the South. Southern blacks exhibited a substantially higher level of Republican identification well into the 1960s. While Republican identification averaged about 14 percent among Northern blacks in the 1950s and 1960s, it averaged about 24 percent for Southern blacks. Abraham Lincoln's picture, it would seem, was harder to turn away from in Dixie, where the local Democratic party was not the party of racial moderation and progress that it was in the North. In the South, it was the Republican party which was the party of racial moderation and the Republican party which was available as an opposition to the segregationist white population.[18] To be sure, a considerable fraction of this Civil War Republicanism had evaporated by the middle of this century, and if the remaining portion was unimportant to the relative electoral strength of the parties by the 1950s, it remains significant that Southern blacks were distinctively more Republican than their Northern counterparts and that several blacks who had long been active in Southern Republican affairs were able to produce Republican votes where blacks were registered to vote.[19] Throughout the 1950s, for example, analyses of Southern politics were able to estimate some types of voting trends by discounting and adjusting vote totals for the nearly unanimous Republicanism of black voters. However, the events of the early sixties pushed more black Southern Republicans into the Democratic party.[20] The percent of black Republicans in the South in the sixties was half what it was in the fifties; and after 1964 there is virtually no difference in the proportion of blacks in the South who were Republican compared with the proportion in the North who are Republican (about 6 percent). Considering sample variability, after 1964 something less than 10 percent of blacks are Republican, a bit more than 20 percent are Independent, and the remaining 70 percent are Democrat.

Jews represent another minority with a distinct political party preference. The data here indicate that Jews are becoming less Democratic over time and for some offices they are tending to vote less for Democrats; but they have not become more Republican. The decline in Democratic identification has increased the proportion of Independents among Jews. Virtually all of this change in partisanship seems to be concentrated among the young. The 9 point increase in Independents is completely a function of the high rate of Independents among Jews who entered the electorate after 1960.

The Ethnics and the "Hardhats"

Although a contrary impression has been fostered in recent years, the Democratic party is still the political home of Catholics and the working class represented in labor unions. While there are differences in the degree to which Catholics identify as Democrats (Irish and Polish Catholics are staunch Democrats compared with other Catholics), there are no significant changes over time in these differences. On the whole, the ethnics and the "hardhats" are less likely to be Independent now than in the past and, compared with the national figures, slightly more Democratic.[21]

The Democratic party bias of Polish and Irish Catholics, higher-status Catholics of other nationalities, lower-status Catholics of other nationalities, and union members has changed slightly. Polish and Irish Catholics have become even more Democratic in these two decades, as both the proportion of Republican identifiers and Independents has declined. Over time there may be slightly more Democrats among lower-status Catholics, and there seem to be slightly fewer Democrats among the higher-status Catholics. More than compensating for any Democratic losses in these groups is the decline in Republicans. Between the 1950s and the 1970s there is a 6 point decline in Republican identifiers among the Irish and Poles, among high-status Catholics of other nationalities the decline is 4 points, and among the lower-status the decline is 7 points. In each group, as a result, the Democratic plurality is stable or larger, never smaller.

The pattern is similar for that other bulwark of Democratic support, union members. They are becoming relatively more, not less, Democratic. The more mixed voting behavior of these groups has led several observers to perceive a decline in Democratic support among ethnics and unionized workers. But only among higher-status Catholics is there a Republican trend in voting. Whether it is a harbinger of a large change in their party bias is an interesting possibility that cannot be examined with these data. However, applying the eminently reasonable principle that we learn to believe in and value what we do, there is reason to expect that a larger change in the party identification of higher-status Catholics is likely.[22]

Change in the Party Coalitions

Up to this point, the analysis of shifts in party identification has concentrated on the party preferences of classes or categories of voters. The analysis of a realignment, however, also requires an examination of the group profile of the parties.

Table 6.4 displays the social-group characteristics of Democratic and Republican identifiers in the 1950s and the early 1970s. The percentages in the table are the proportion the different groups represent of the parties. It is clear, for example, that in the early fifties, white Southerners were overrepresented in the Democratic party and underrepresented among Independents and Republicans. Although constituting only 22 percent of the population, the five types of white Southerners constituted 31 percent of Democrats, 13 percent of Independents, and less than 11 percent of Republicans. By the early seventies, in contrast, white Southerners were about 25 percent of the population but they are now only 25 percent of all Democrats, 25 percent of Independents, and 23 percent of Republicans. A little arithmetic indicates con-

Table 6.4   Changes in the Social Group Characteristics of Republican and Democratic Identifiers since the early 1950s

Coalition Groups	Democrats 1950s	Democrats 1970s	Republicans 1950s	Republicans 1970s
White Northern Protestants				
very high status	1.4%	3.2%	9.0%	13.9%
middle and high status	5.1	5.0	19.1	17.8
lower status	7.4	8.9	18.7	14.7
Border Southerners				
middle and upper status	1.7	2.3	.6	3.9
lower status	2.9	4.6	3.1	3.2
Southerners				
immigrants	2.2	2.2	2.2	5.4
middle and higher status natives	9.0	5.6	1.4	5.0
lower status natives	15.5	10.7	3.6	5.1
Catholics				
Polish and Irish	3.2	3.4	1.9	1.2
others—higher status	2.1	4.0	2.4	5.3
others—middle and lower status	8.0	8.7	5.5	3.9
Jews	4.5	3.2	.8	.7
Blacks	10.1	16.2	4.9	2.4
Union members	22.0	19.4	18.0	13.2
Northern farmers	4.9	2.6	8.8	4.3
	100.0%	100.0%	100.0%	100.0%

siderable proportionate change. Blacks are another group through which the shift in party supporters can be demonstrated. In the early fifties, blacks were overrepresented in the Democratic party by 72 percent in the early seventies.

Although the very high-status "silk-stocking" white Northern Protestants are still woefully underrepresented among Democratic identifiers, they have more than doubled their representation in the past two decades. Proportionally, (though not absolutely) they have enlarged their fraction in the Democratic party faster than any other group. These two groups, plus the five white Southern groups, are responsible for more than half of the total 14.5 percent change in the social group profile of the Democratic party.[23] The Republican party, in contrast, is more Southern, less black, and less Catholic now than it was two decades ago.

Of course, some fraction of this transformation of the party coalitions reflects the changing size of the groups in the population. There are, for example, more blacks and college-educated professionals now compared with twenty years ago. But these changes reflect more than just demographic shifts.

Table 6.5 presents the expected size of the group, the observed size of the group, and the discrepancy between the two percentages. A positive number in the deviation columns indicates that

Table 6.5   Comparison of the Expected and Observed Size of the Groups among Party Identifiers

Coalition Groups	Change in Group Size	Democrats Expected 1970s[a]	Democrats Deviation (Observed − Predicted)	Republicans Expected 1970s	Republicans Deviation (Observed − Predicted)
White Northern Protestants					
very high status	71%	2.4%	.8%	15.4%	− 1.5%
middle and high status	− 2	5.0	0.0	18.7	− .9
low status	−10	6.7	2.2	16.9	− 2.2
Border Southerners					
middle and upper status	105	3.5	− 1.2	1.2	2.7
lower status	41	4.1	.5	4.4	− 1.2
Southerners					
immigrants	13	2.5	− .3	2.5	2.9
middle and upper-status					
natives	19	10.7	− 5.1	1.7	3.3
lower-status natives	−11	13.7	− 3.0	3.2	1.9
Catholics					
Polish and Irish	−17	2.7	.7	1.2	0.0
others—higher status	114	4.5	− .5	5.1	.2
others—lower status	− 3	7.8	.9	5.4	− 1.5
Jews	−22	3.5	− .3	.5	.2
Blacks	6	10.7	5.5	5.2	− 2.8
Union members	−13	19.2	.2	15.7	− 2.5
Northern farmers	−57	2.1	.5	3.8	.5
Percentage change			10.9		12.2

[a]These numbers can be compared with those in table 6.4. The deviation results from a comparison of the 1970s data in table 6.4 with the expected 1970s data in this table.

the group is a larger fraction of Democratic or Republican identifiers than population shift alone would predict. A negative number indicates the group is proportionally less numerous than expected. Had there not been a realignment during this twenty-year period, the Democratic and Republican parties should, controlling for demographic shifts, exhibit a constant group profile over these two decades. This has not happened. Independent of demography, the social-group profile of Democratic and Republican identifiers has altered since the fifties.

For example, between 1952–56 and 1970–74 the "silk-stocking" group (college-educated professionals who are white Northern Protestants) increased from about 4.1 percent to 7 percent of the population, a 71 percent increase. If demography alone were the explanation, one would expect the group to contribute 2.4 percent of the Democratic identifiers and 15.4 percent of all Republicans. As table 6.5 indicates, their actual contribution to the parties is different.

Across all groups, the difference between the expected size of the groups among party identifiers and their observed proportion is the index of the realignment of the parties.[24]

Table 6.6 summarizes the contribution of the groups to the realignment. After adjusting the change in the group profiles of the parties for the contribution demographic factors alone have made to the change, there is about an 11 percent alteration in the group profile of the Democratic party and about a 12 percent change in the group profile of Republican identifiers.[25] The increasing proportion of blacks and Northern Protestants in the Democratic party accounts for a bit less than 40 percent of the change in the Democratic party, and the declining proportion of Southerners is responsible for 47 percent of the change. The remaining change is attributable to Catholics, union members, Jews, and the farmers. White Southerners are also responsible for much of the change in the Republican party. Almost half of the 12 percent change in the social basis of Republican identification is contributed by white Southerners. White Northerners contribute almost a fifth of the change, the declining share of blacks in the Republican party

Table 6.6.   Contribution of the Coalition Groups to the Realignment of the Parties

Groups	Democrats (10.9%)	Republicans (12.2%)
Northern white Protestants	14%	19%
Southern whites	47	49
Catholics and union members	11	17
Blacks	26	12
All others	3	3

contributes another 12 percent to the change, and about 20 percent is contributed by Catholics, union members, and farmers.

It is difficult to determine how much of a realignment is represented by these changes. An interpretation is labored because of the growth in the number of Independents. Intuitively, this change should be counted in any estimate of the change in the social-group profiles of the party; but exactly how it should be counted is not clear. Even if the Independents are ignored on the grounds that we are interested only in party supporters, there is still no clear way to estimate the amount of change. The net 11 and 12 percent shifts in the social-group profile of the parties (see the bottom row of table 6.5) must be related to a theoretical maximum to have any interpretation. The problem, of course, is that there are several denominators that might be considered, and no clear reason for selecting one over another. If, on the one hand, the maximum change is represented by a situation where the parties become coterminous with a single social group, then the change here is not large. If, on the other hand, the maximum change that can be expected is a complete exchange of the social base of the parties, resulting in a Republican party in the seventies with a social base like that of the Democratic party in the fifties (with adjustments for changes in group size in the population) and vice versa, the parties have changed a great deal. Alternatively, if the maximum change that could be expected is for party supporters to be virtually undifferentiated by social characteristics, then the change has been even greater. Simply in the interest of providing a referent, assume that the last definition of maximum—party supporters are not differentiated by social characteristics—is the best.[26] Under this assumption the maximum change that could be found among Democratic identifiers is a bit less than 16 percent. Using 16 percent as the theoretical maximum, the Democratic party has changed 69 percent of the maximum. If the same assumption is used for the Republican party, the theoretical maximum is over 23 percent. Comparing the theoretical maximum with the observed change for Republicans indicates that the social-group profile of the Republican party has changed about 52 percent of the maximum possible.

The New Deal Coalitions and the 1976 Election

The Ford and Carter coalitions reflected this realignment.

Many observers saw a resurrection of the New Deal party system in the candidacy of Jimmy Carter. He appeared uniquely qualified to reassemble the warring elements of the old coalition. Among Southerners he was expected to soften the anti-Southern image acquired by "the" Democrats, and in doing so, encourage the white South to cast a heavy Democratic vote once again.[27] His strong record in support of black aspirations ensured that the South could be enticed without damage among blacks and their supporters in the North. Indeed, it was Carter's support among Georgia blacks that made it possible for him to receive a hearing.[28] The locus of power in the Democratic party (Southern congressmen notwithstanding) has been in the North for forty years, and the maverick image of the white South would have precluded any serious attention being given to Carter's nomination campaign had he not enjoyed a strong reputation among Southern (Georgia) blacks. Although his moral fervor threatened to brand him as a modern-day William Jennings Bryan, and signs of restiveness could be seen among Northern Democrats before and during the autumn, most did not believe that Carter's religion, accent, or remoteness from big-city politics and organized labor constituted insurmountable handicaps.[29]

When Carter won the South and most of the big states and their cities with a campaign in which unemployment, taxation, and inflation were paramount issues, the old Democratic coalition did, indeed, seem in robust health. The prescient observers who had predicted the reknitting of the coalition seemed vindicated. The old issues were back, as were the traditional electoral college votes.

But to assume that the "reinstating" election of 1976 also represented a resurgence of the New Deal party would be a mistake.[30] To be sure, the Democrats won, something they had not done since 1964. But the coalition that elected Jimmy Carter displayed all the differences from the New Deal that the 1960s realignment would lead us to expect in a post-1970 election.[31]

The New Deal built a Democratic majority out of strong support in the white South, among Catholics (through big-city party organizations), blacks, Jews, and union members. While white Northern Protestants were not absent, especially if they were union-affiliated, the Democratic vote among Northern WASPs who were not union members was stingy. In the 1948 election, perhaps the last election of the New Deal era, almost 85 percent of Truman's vote was cast by Southern whites, Jews, blacks, Catholics, and union members.[32] Southern whites gave 78 percent of their ballots to Truman, Catholics cast a 64 percent Democratic vote, 70 percent of the votes of the union members went to Truman, and blacks and Jews were also strongly Democratic, 90 and 88 percent Democratic, respectively.

The Truman vote among Northern Protestants lacking the union affiliation averaged 31 percent, and it was lower among upper-status WASPs. Even the candidacies of Eisenhower and Kennedy did not disturb the coalitions substantially. Attracted by Eisenhower and repelled by Kennedy, Dixie still cast a majority of its votes for the Democratic ticket through 1960, and Jews, Catholics, and blacks, though buffeted by the tides of electoral fortune, were identifiably Democratic in 1952, 1956, and 1960.

The 1976 election represented a contest between two substantially different coalitions. Just over 43 percent of white Southerners supported Carter, a pale reflection of a history of over 70 percent support for Democratic candidates. Catholic support for the ticket was anemic. Only a bare majority—53 percent—voted for Carter. The Democrats did well among only 3 traditional members of the New Deal coalition: blacks (95 percent), Jews (73 percent), and union members (61 percent). Jimmy Carter won the election because turnout among blacks made their 95 percent support more significant, and because Northern WASPs are now more Democratic.[33]

Table 6.7, which contrasts the social-group coalitions that cast Democratic and Republican votes in 1948 and the 1950s, with 1976, illustrates that the changed party bias described above was not transitory. Jimmy Carter's winning coalition was not a traditional Democratic coalition. Compared with the 1950s the proportion of Northern WASPs in the Democratic camp increased by 40 percent, blacks by 117 percent, and Southern whites declined by a quarter. There were corresponding changes in Ford's support compared with Eisenhower's in the 1950s and Nixon's in 1960. So while the personalities of recent elections (and other short-term factors as well) were instrumental in shaping the 1964, 1968, and 1972 elections, there have also been enduring changes. Carter was not able to reassemble the old Democratic coalitions because the issues that have undermined it supercede any individual personality. The realignment was not reversed by Carter's candidacy, nor has it been affected by his presidency. Many of the issues that provided a rationale for Democratic or Republican sympathies in the 1920s, 1930s, or 1940s are either less important today or, where they are still significant matters of controversy, they have altered their meaning and begun to erode the traditional party bias of the groups.[34] And because these new issues fuel the partisan fires vigorously, a single candidate, however well connected he is to various party blocs, cannot be expected to undo the changes they have set in motion.

Table 6.7　　Change in the Social-Group Composition of the Democratic and Republican Voting Coalitions

Coalition Groups	Democratic Voters		Republican Voters	
	1948–60	1976	1948–60	1976
Northern Protestants	15%	21%	44%	38%
Southern whites	21	17	15	24
Catholics	17	19	12	15
Blacks	7	15	2	1
Jews	7	4	1	1
Union Members	27	22	17	15
All others	5	2	10	6

Summary: The Realignment of the Parties

The changes that have been uncovered in the social correlates of party identification clearly point to a realignment of the parties. Although this change in the clientele is interesting in itself, it is more important for what it portends for the policies and electoral strategies of the parties. The significance of these changes may be particularly pronounced on the race issue. Blacks are critical to Democratic dominance, and in some states they are the segment of the electorate which keeps the Democratic party competitive. No Democratic president and no individual who aspires to national leadership in the Democratic party could alienate blacks as a group; he would simply doom his political future at the outset. A Republican president, however, if partisan tactical advantage dictates, can ignore the demands of blacks and not endanger his support. Less than 3 percent of Republican support is provided by blacks. Blacks quite simply are not a necessary calculation in Republican electoral success to the degree that they are for Democrats. Reinforcing this trend is the loss of a large portion of the Southern electorate by the Democratic party. The general social conservatism and the very specific racial conservatism characteristic of the region has traditionally restrained the markedly less conservative and more pro-black Northern wing of the party. As the South becomes a less reliable segment of the Democratic party and a more familiar part of the Republican vote, the influences of the South on the Democratic party will decline.

The Effect of New Populations

The Post-1960 Cohort

Demography alone accounts for a considerable portion of the transformation of the party coalitions. Simply because of shifts in the size of groups (blacks and "silk-stocking" WASPs, for example), the party coalitions have undergone changes. Cohort replacement, however, has also been important. Consider just the figures from the survey data. More than a quarter of the 1952 electorate had been removed by death at the start of the 1970s (assuming an average life span of about 72 years); about 48 percent of the early 1970s electorate was not eligible to vote in 1952. In other words, only a bare majority of the electorate of the 1970s had been active before 1952.[1]

This would not be an important consideration if it were possible to rely upon intergenerational socialization to sustain the party system. But parental value preferences require some reinforcement to be retained throughout the life cycle, or, in this case, even to be adopted by the post-1960 cohort at the rate that characterized their parents. None of the voters who entered after 1960 have had any personal familiarity with the issues that realigned the parties in the 1920s and 1930s. Although the rhetoric and symbols of the New Deal period may still energize a few, their ability to attract the allegiance of the newer cohorts is slight. The issues that made sense of partisanship in the New Deal—the relationship of the government to the state of the economy and the welfare needs of the society—are largely resolved (Eisenhower's presidency and Goldwater's defeat established that). And since the middle of the 1960s issues around which the parties have not consummated a tacit agreement to disagree—race, crime and social disorder, a foreign war, lifestyle debates—have been the preeminent concerns of the society. As a result the new cohorts of only a few groups have been given obvious reasons for subscribing to a partisan banner. Blacks, in particular, have been strongly wedded to the Democratic party as a result of the Goldwater candidacy in 1964. But the party bias of most coalition groups was redirected by the failure of younger voters to identify with the parties. In each case new voters, albeit of different types, are responsible for the party transformation documented in chapter 6.[2]

The New Voters

If the post-1960 cohort had entered the electorate with the same partisanship as their elders, and only the aging of the electorate and the response of the voters to the way the parties addressed the new issues affected overall committments to the parties, the increase in Independents would have been smaller. Such a scenario can be simulated by making some statistical adjustments for the impact of these later voters.

Suppose that, in the 1960s and 1970s, one examined only the partisanship of voters who had been eligible to vote before 1961.[7] By definition, therefore, the post-1960 cohort could not have influenced the decline of partisanship. The loss of voters who were in the electorate in the fifties and the abandonment of partisanship—actual change in the loyalties of voters over time—would be the only possible explanation for the decline in Democratic and Republican identifiers. While the death of 1950s voters explains some of the change, it does not explain all of it, both because natural replacement has not been that high and because differences in the partisanship of voters who were in the electorate before 1950 and those who entered in the fifties were not that large. Most of this change has been caused by the post-1960 cohort. Over all, about 58 percent of the change in the distribution of party identification between the fifties and the seventies is a result of the difference between the young and old in their party preference.

The importance of the post-1960 cohort to the overall change in party preference is also reflected in their impact on their partisanship of each coalition group. Figure 7.1 is a two-dimensional graph which presents the proportion of Democrats on the vertical axis. For each social group, three sets of percentages are displayed. The starting point is a plot of the percentage of Democrats and Republicans in the group in the early fifties. A group with a large proportion of Democrats and a small proportion of Republicans would be located in the upper-left quarter of the graph. When the Republican percentage is much larger than the Democratic percentage, the group is located in the lower right. As the proportion of Independents increases, the group tends to move toward the lower-left quarter. The upper-right quarter of the graph would never have any cases because gains by one party limit the maximum percentage of the other, since the total can never exceed 100 percent. A second set of percentages locates the

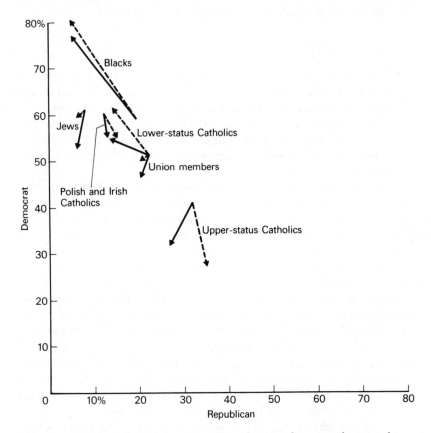

Fig. 7.1   The effect of the post-1960 cohort in changing the party bias of the coalition groups

proportion of Democrats and Republicans in the group for the years 1968 through 1976. These two coordinates are connected with a solid line. The longer the line, the greater the change in the party bias of the group.

The contribution of the young to these changes is indicated by the dotted line connecting the Democrat and the Republican percentages in the fifties to the Democrat and the Republican percentages, for the pre-1961 cohort, in the seventies. That is, the dotted line indicates how the group would have changed if the young had not had a party bias different from the older members of their group. In almost every case, the young cause the solid line to be longer—indicating greater change in the party bias of the group—than the dotted line (where the post-1960 cohort is deleted). This effect of the post-1960 cohort is fairly uniform. Except for white Southerners and blacks, the addition of the young

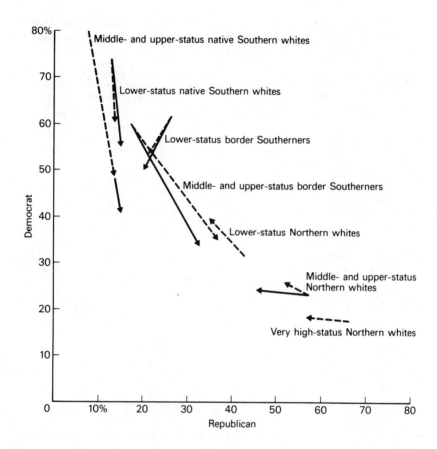

changes the party bias of each group more than it would change if the young were not considered. Table 7.1 summarizes these effects.

The effect of the young on the social-group profile of the parties is more muted. The eleven percent change in the group characteristics of Democratic identifiers and the 12 percent in the social basis of the Republican party would be 10 and 9 percent, respectively, without the young. Their contribution to the transformation of the party coalitions is smaller than their contribution to the aggregate change in partisanship because, with a couple of exceptions, the rate of independence among the post-1960 generation does not significantly differ by social group. Their potential for further changing the party coalitions is considerable. But to this point they have contributed more to dealigning than to realigning the party system.

The Young and the South

The most prominent groups in this realignment of the Democrats and the Republicans have been the young, the Southerners, and blacks. The latter two groups have been sorted into

Table 7.1   Summary of the Percentage Point Change in the Party Preference of the Coalition Groups and the Portion Contributed by the post-1960 Cohort

Coalition Groups	Percentage Point Change in the Party Preference of the Group	Percentage Point Change Contributed by Post-1960 Cohort
Northern White Protestants		
very high status	14	7
middle status	11	6
lower status	10	5
Border South		
middle and upper status	25	5
lower status	17	4
Deep South Whites		
immigrants	11	4
natives		
middle and upper status	38	8
lower status	18	5
Catholics		
Polish and Irish	5	3
all other nationalities		
upper status	14	8
middle and lower status	9	8
Jews	9	8
Blacks	18	4
Union members	9	5
Northern farmers	7	2

exclusive categories, with the result that it is possible to identify how much of the total change has been contributed by each of them. While the preceding table also permits some judgments about how important the young have been in the alteration of the party bias of each coalition group, this mapping of the cohort dynamics of the realignment requires some attention to regional differences in the impact of the new and old voters on the parties.

Table 7.2, which compares the partisanship of Northerners and Southerners for the period from 1952 through 1960 with their partisanship in 1976, presents the data in full.[4]

The differences between the regions are substantial in two ways. First, in the South, unlike the North, the change in the partisan balance does not simply reflect a decline in partisanship. As chapter 6 indicated, only Independents increased in the North.

Table 7.2   Percentage Point Changes in Partisanship by Cohort and Region, 1952–60 Average to 1976

	Democrat	Independent	Republican
North[a]			
pre-1960 cohort	−0.2	+3.9	−3.7
post-1960 cohort	−2.2	+6.3	−4.2
White South			
pre-1960 cohort	−4.2	+2.6	+1.6
post-1960 cohort	−1.2	+0.8	+0.4

[a]Includes all those who are not in one of the five Southern white categories.

In the South, by contrast, a healthy proportion of the decline in the Democrats, about 37 percent of it, bolstered the number of Republicans in the electorate.[5] The second major difference between the regions is found in the contribution of the post-1960 cohort to the changes. In the North, this new cohort, contributed over 60 percent of the measured change in partisanship, while in the South it contributed less than a quarter. Because the North (at least as it is defined here) constitutes almost 80 percent of the population, the Northern young largely determine the overall importance of the post-1960 cohort. But just because they are so large a group, they mask more subtle changes that occur regionally. Disaggregated into cohorts within regions, the nature of partisan change appears more complex. The young, Northern cohort represents about 42 percent of the Northern population but over 62 percent of the partisan shift. In the South, by contrast, the young are underrepresented. The young, Southern post-1960 cohort constitutes about 41 percent of the Southern white population, but it added only 23 percent of the decline in the Democrats. Table 7.3 presents a summary of the cohort contributions by region and, just

Table 7.3   Contribution of Regional Cohorts to the Gross Change in Partisanship

	Share in Gross Change in Partisanship	Size of Group in 1976
North		
pre-1960 cohort	25%	45%
post-1960 cohort	40	33
South		
pre-1960 cohort	27	13
post-1960 cohort	8	9
	100%	100%

to provide a referent with which to judge these values, the proportion of the total population the regional cohorts contribute in 1976.

The forces responsible for this realignment are working more strongly upon white Southerners than they are upon most groups in the society. As a consequence the older cohort is violating the general tendency for new voters to provide the cutting edge of changes in party systems. There may well be a general proposition to be drawn from this serendipitous result. Its meaning will be returned to after a similar change in another coalition segment, blacks, another group which is on the cutting edge of the forces pushing the transformation, is examined.

Blacks: An Instance of Voter Mobilization

The importance of blacks transcends their surge toward the Democrats. Theoretically, they are interesting because they appear to be a contemporary instance of the mobilization of a group which was much more apolitical and uninvolved with the party system than the rest of the population. Their movement into the ranks of the Democratic party reflects the influence of the entering post-1960 cohort, some actual changes over time in partisanship conversion, and the mobilization of previously apathetic and unaligned blacks.

An examination of the discrepancy between the voting choices and partisanship of blacks offers an entry point for analyzing this phenomenon.[6]

If nonvoting blacks had participated in the Eisenhower elections, the Democratic vote among blacks would have fallen from 72 percent to 66 percent. By the late 1960s, however, the discrepancy between the preferences of voting and nonvoting blacks had disappeared. In the 1968, 1972, and 1976 elections, the 95 percent Democratic vote among blacks would not have declined as much as 2 percentage points with the participation of the nonvoters. This convergence of the preferences of voting and nonvoting blacks reflects a mobilization of the kind analyzed in chapters 3 and 4.

The Goldwater candidacy in 1964 and its associated Southern strategy, the increasing influence of white racial militants among Southern Republicans, and the prominence of the national Democratic party in the civil rights activity of the period gave blacks considerable incentive to support the Democrats.[7] It is doubtful that Goldwater was as racially prejudiced as the white Southerner to whom he appealed. But there is no doubt that his 1964 campaign in the South meant to leave, and did leave, the impression that a Goldwater administration would be minimally involved in legislating private conduct toward blacks. Blacks and Southern whites saw in his candidacy a solicitous concern for the white Southern way of doing racial business. The white Southern response to this behavior was an acceleration of their departure from the Democratic party; the black response was a virtual abandonment of the Republican party.

But the abandonment of the Republicans by blacks took place in different ways in the North and the South. In the North the change seems to have been a fairly straightforward shift to a Democratic identification. The process in the South is more interesting, and it bears similarities to the electoral mobilization that characterized prior realignments.

The number of blacks voting in the 1950s was less than the number who did not vote. About 45 percent of all age-eligible blacks voted in the Eisenhower elections, while over two-thirds of whites reported voting in those years. Between the early fifties and the early seventies the black voting rate grew 43 percent. Virtually all of it reflected an increase in black turnout in the South. Eighty-three percent of the growth in black voting is a result of turnout among Southern Blacks rising from 14 percent to 51 percent. The turnout rate of Northern Blacks increased only five percentage points to 67 percent.[8] Paralleling the growth of turnout among Southern Blacks was a decline in apathy and disinterest toward party politics. Prior to 1964, more than 20 percent of Southern blacks did not respond to the questions that assess party identification. After 1964 the rate of nonresponse and apolitical responses to the party identification questions declined to the national average.

These changes are not independent. The convergence of the presidential choices of voting and nonvoting blacks reflects not only a conversion of blacks from the Republicans but a mobilization from apathy to a Democratic identification among a large and politically inactive black population. The politicization of blacks by voting-rights groups and the pro-black position of the Democratic party mobilized nonvoting blacks at exactly the moment that political events were imprinting them with a preference for the Democratic party.[9] The nonvoting blacks who had preferred Eisenhower and Nixon (but especially the former) betrayed their lack of a partisan anchor by their responsiveness to short-term forces. But the strong forces of the years around 1964 gave blacks a substantial committment to the Democrats and considerable immunization to the short-term forces of later elections.

This explanation for the shift in the partisanship of blacks can be tested. It is not possible to test it directly, but it is possible to examine some data patterns that are deducible from this thesis. If

virtually all of the previously apolitical blacks entered the electorate with a Democratic preference, it is reasonable to regard all of
the apolitical and apathetic blacks found in the surveys in the
1950s as latent Democrats. Treating these apoliticals as latent
Democrats revises upward the Democratic bias of blacks in the
1950s. But its effect in the South is substantially different from its
effect in the North. In the 1950s the party bias of Northern blacks
was 40 points more Democratic than Republican, excluding the
apoliticals from the estimation; it was 42 points Democratic with
their inclusion.

By 1970, when the party bias of Northern blacks increased to 67
percentage points, 25 of this 27 percentage point increase represented the conversion of Republicans or Independents. The remaining 2 percentage point increase in their Democratic bias reflects a decline in apathy and indifference toward the parties, that
is, the mobilization of latent Democrats.

In the South, by contrast, the decline in black apoliticals contributed much more to the intensification of a Democratic bias.
Between the fifties and seventies the party bias of Southern blacks
surged from 39 points Democratic to about 70 points Democratic.
Treating apathetic and apolitical Southern blacks as latent Democrats boosts their "actual" party bias in the 1950s to 56 points
Democratic, and the original 31 point shift to the Democrats is
reduced to only about 14 points. In other words, over half of the
change in the partisanship of Southern blacks is a consequence of
the mobilization of blacks who had found party politics to marginal to their concerns prior to the 1960s that they were unable to
relate to the question which assessed their party preference.[10]
Figure 7.2 presents the data.

Over all, as much as a third of the increase in the Democratic
bias of blacks is a result of the politicization of Southern blacks.
The relatively greater instability of their partisanship may reflect
this, in that a comparatively large number of blacks hold a partisanship and a sense of electoral involvement that can be traced
back only a decade.

Blacks and the White South

There is a satisfying neatness about the fact that blacks and
Southern whites should be the two groups whose realignment
represents more than the entrance of a "malsocialized" post-1960
cohort. Both can trace this difference to the importance of race in

the shifting party coalitions. For the South, on the one hand, race has intruded forcefully enough upon the older generation of whites for them to shake the inertia of partisanship more effectively than their contemporaries in the North. For blacks, on the other hand, the intrusion of race has given the party system a

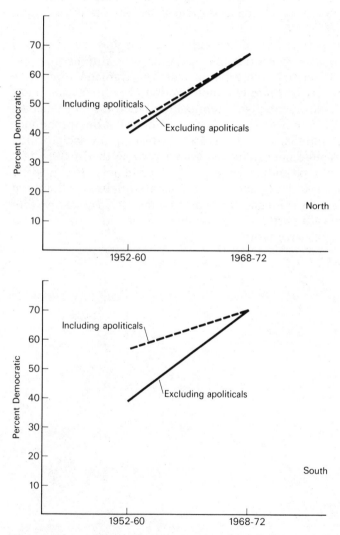

Fig. 7.2   Distinguishing conversion from mobilization among Northern and Southern blacks

salience it previously lacked. This salience (plus the dismantling of institutional barriers and the organizational work of civil rights groups) has had the greatest effect where there is the most room for an expansion of the black electorate, in the South. It is not surprising that Southern blacks responded as they did. It is, after all, a pattern that is predictable from what characterized the mobilization of other groups only slightly involved with the parties until some event made parties a salient feature of their world.[11]

From the perspective of needing to account for "who" caused this most recent transformation of the party coalitions, the preceding data illustrate the ways in which realignments might be forged. For blacks, there is a mobilization of political marginals (even if it is an incomplete mobilization when turnout rates are considered); for most whites, there is evidence of the importance of new generations, a fact Beck used to develop his socialization theory of realignment (with the added proviso that realignment events can also be antiparty forces which yield not a new majority but an erosion of party support in general); finally, for Southern whites, there is evidence that conversion is a response within groups who are particularly offended by the side "their" party adopts on a divisive issue.

Part 4

The Contemporary Realignment

Its Attitudinal Base

8 The Dynamics of Realignment II

The Role of Issues

There is nothing new about using issues to explain party-system transformation. The missteps of party strategists and the tides of social change which leave one or both parties unrepresentative of the concerns of their constituency have long been held responsible for shifts in party fortunes. But the conceptualization of some of these changes as electoral realignments has spurred attempts to systematize the relationship between party-system change and the issue positions of the parties. At least three kinds of issue changes have been pressed into service.

Major systemic changes that completely alter the public agenda and, in consequence, disrupt the settled pattern of party competition is the first of these issue changes.[1] The social and economic changes that fuel the conflicts around which the parties are organized have changed several times. The unfortunate feature of these transformations for the parties is the difficulty of traversing the distance between the old and the new agendas. The resolution of the more fundamental problems of the old agenda and the rise of new and more pressing concerns undercuts the stability of the existing party alignment. Unless the new agenda spawns issues that coincide with the concerns of the prevailing issue alignment, cleavages are created *within* the parties. Disagreements over new issues threaten unity forged around older issues, and since these older issues (or at least many of them) have lost much of their salience as the majority party's policy has mutated from outrageous to acceptable and, finally, to normal, the party system begins to lose its programmatic underpinnings.

Everett C. Ladd, the principal architect of the agenda approach, has identified at least three distinct sociopolitical periods and their associated agendas.[2] In his analysis the problems of nation-building, industrialization, and the urban-industrial state have given birth to political conflicts that created five distinct party systems. And in a more recent study, he and Charles Hadley argue that the contemporary dealignment of the parties results from economic and social changes which cut across the issues that currently sort voters into Democratic and Republican ranks.[3] This potential sixth party system (which they believe might emerge as a nonparty system) is a response to a lessening of concern with the constellation of cleavages and agreements around which the New Deal party system was constructed, and increased attentiveness to social and cultural issues which are poorly aligned with the welfare issues that are the bedrock of the New Deal Democrats.

A second issue explanation for party-system change emphasizes cataclysmic events which rebound against one of the parties.[4] Wars and depressions for which one of the parties is held responsible are the hallmark of this issue interpretation of realignments. Simply because there has been such a coincidence of realignments with social disasters, the two have become inextricably linked. The apparent failure of the public leaders of one of the parties (the governing one) to stave off, or solve, or mitigate the consequences of such events has been used to explain dramatic and long-lasting shifts in party fortunes. Massive defections from the party encumbered by the disaster explained its precipitous decline in the original version of this theory. The newer theory of realignment emphasizes the biased mobilization of voters who hold one of the parties responsible for the troubles of the period of their maturity.[5] But both are in agreement about the role of issues in the transformation.

The third issue explanation requires neither major social transformations which alter the concerns of the society nor cataclysms such as depressions and wars to disrupt the prevailing party system. Virtually any issue which divides the parties internally is a potential precipitant of electoral realignments. The preceding issue explanations of realignment represented major political, social, or economic events; but the significant feature of each is that it alienated segments of the party coalitions. Admittedly, it is difficult to imagine an issue provocative enough to disrupt a stable party coalition that is not at least a part of a larger set of concerns; but such issues are possible. Race relations represent an example. In the past decade, concern with the treatment and status of blacks has become bundled with social and cultural issues, but from the late 1940s until the late 1960s race matters were independent of most other public policy questions, and they were certainly threatening for the Democratic coalition. Two historical examples of the existence of a single divisive issue might include the alienation of German-Americans from the Democratic party during and following World War I, and the attractiveness of the Republican party among evangelical Protestants because of the association of Republicans with morality and temperance legislation throughout the last half of the nineteenth century.[6]

The major distinction among these three types of issue explanations of party realignment is the level at which the disruption
occurs. The agenda thesis is describing a major historical transformation which disrupts party coalitions because the constellation of concerns which tied groups into a single party have
changed in content and salience, leaving previous allies in opposition. The cataclysm explanation of realignments does not explicitly require a significant resorting of the groups which comprise the party coalitions. Although such a shuffling of support is
likely since the impact of some events, a depression, for example,
is unevenly felt, the focus of the cataclysm explanation of realignments is on the attribution of responsibility for some problem and the resulting abandonment of that party by a portion of
the electorate. The idiosyncratic issue explanation differs from the
preceding one in that the issue that cuts across the prevailing
party-issue alignment cannot, a priori, be described as a social
cataclysm. It is simply an issue about which part of the electorate
feels strongly, and, because the parties are unable to embrace all
positions on the matter simultaneously, the parties lose or swap
some of their support. If the issue seriously divides both parties,
the voters most affected by the issue will cross the partisan divide;
that is, the parties will swap some of their support. But if only one
of the parties (the Democrats, for example) is seriously divided by
an issue (race), the movement will be unbalanced and in a single
direction. In either case whether actual conversion occurs or
whether groups of voters simply abandon their prior affiliation,
the size of the party shift will depend upon the salience of the new
issue compared with those that structure the existing alignment. If
the old issues continue to attract voters, the most likely outcome
of a new, controversial issue is dealignment. Groups will abandon
their party but, because they cannot abide the alternative party,
they simply forswear allegiance to either.

Each of these explanations expects an issue to stretch to the
breaking point the capacity of one or both of the parties to continue to aggregate into a single party image (or something like it)
the pressing concerns of their traditional supporters. The explanations differ in the kind of issue that provokes a new alignment,
but they agree on the importance of its cutting across the existing
issue-party alignment. Ladd's agenda thesis emphasizes major social transformations, the cataclysm points to major dislocations as
the precipitate of realignment, and the single-issue explanation
focuses upon more proximate concerns (of whatever origin and
reflecting many social processes) that simply divide current coalition partners.

Social Groups, Party Support, and Crosscutting Issues

When queried for a reason for their party preference, individual voters respond on several levels of sophistication and abstraction. Some explain their partisanship by reference to the fact that they are liberal or conservative, that they are black, that they are workingmen or businessmen, that they support or oppose a national medical care system, or that they do (or do not) believe that government should address welfare legislation to defined classes of people.[7] Having said that, these same voters are likely to follow up with the assertion that they are Democrats (or Republicans) because the Democrats (or Republicans) take a preferred position on the important issues. That is, a voter is a Democrat because the Democratic party is the liberal party, or Republican because the Republican party opposes a national medical-care system administered by the national government, and so on. The central feature of this issue basis of party support is not the particular political opinion of the voter, but the extent to which the voter is able to attach that opinion to the parties. In short, voters are Democratic or Republican because they feel that the party they prefer represents their position on the issues. Whether this perception is objectively correct is substantially irrelevant. Since voters behave on the basis of what they believe to be true, it is the perceived issue position of the parties and not their objective position that determines the support given to them by voters.

The congruence between partisanship and the perceived position of the parties on most issues is quite high. Occasionally, and for some issues, a large portion of the electorate confesses confusion about the issue position of the parties, but, among those who perceive a difference between the parties, identifiers will invariably nominate their party as the one that represents them on the issues. Figure 8.1 graphs some of these data. In this figure Democrats, Independents, and Republicans are compared in terms of the proportion who identify either the Republican or Democratic party as more representative of their opinions on foreign policy, race, economic, and social issues. The horizontal axis is the proportion who nominate the Democratic party as better on the issue, and the vertical axis plots the proportion nominating the Republicans. An excess of Republican over Democratic nominations would put the point high and to the left in the graph, while a surplus of Democratic nominations would put the point low and to the right. The points cluster low and to the left if there is a high proportion of judgments of similarity in the party's positions. The points in figure 8.1 indicate that Republican identifiers believe that the Republican party supports their issues preferences; Democratic identifiers find their champion in the Democratic party; and the Independents nominate both parties more or less equally, with a large fraction perceiving no substantial differences between the parties.

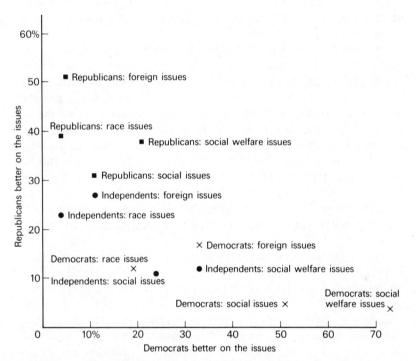

Fig. 8.1   Comparison of the perceived issue positions of the parties among Democrats, Independents, and Republicans

Whether the issue judgment preceded the partisanship is beside the point. The traditional interpretation of party identification argues that it does not, while some recent research indicates that a latent partisanship is developed or at least reinforced by cumulative election experiences.[8] But whichever interpretation of partisanship one favors, there is no doubt about the extent to which preference is associated with a perception of the parties' positions on issues. In the 1976 presidential election almost 60 percent of those who identified themselves as Democrats also identified the Democratic party as more representative of their feelings on one or more self-selected important issues. Only about 4 percent found the Republicans preferable on these matters. The pattern is repeated for the Republicans. A plurality displayed an "issue partisanship" that was clearly Republican, while about 13 percent seemed to find the Democrats more congenial on these important issues. Independents split more equally, with 27 and 11 percent, respectively, viewing the Democrats and Republicans as the party holding the "better" position on the issues. Only a small portion of the 1976 electorate held a perception of the policy orientation of the parties which conflicts with their self-identification as Democrats and Republicans

This explanation for the party preference of individual voters also serves as an explanation for the party preference of defined classes of voters. Southerners, for example, tend to support the Democratic party because they perceive the Democratic party to be closer than the Republican party to their preferences on the issues. The same can be said of the white, Catholic-ethnic population, which prefers the Democratic party because, as a group, they tend to believe that the Democratic party, and not the Republican party, is closer to them on the issues. Very high-status Northern whites support the Republican party because it is more favorably perceived on the issues than the Democratic party. Figure 8.2 plots these differences for several major population groups.

The tie between the different groups and the parties, therefore, depends upon the political-opinion profile of the group and the perception of the parties in terms of these opinions. Catholics are heavily Democratic because they have a set of opinions which are, they believe, better supported by the Democratic than the Republican party. Furthermore, the parties realize this. When a candidate takes a series of positions in a campaign and "talks to the issues," he is appealing to a constituency that shares these preferences. Because the parties know something about the opinion profiles of "their" voters, they also know what positions will be popular with their constituency, which positions they should avoid, and which positions will neither attract nor repel voters. The relationship becomes nonrecursive over time, but at some point the explanation for why some groups are likely to be Democratic and others Republican lies in the political-opinion profile of the group and the way the members of the group perceive the parties on the relevant issues.

Figure 8.3 graphs this model for the party-coalition groups. Line A graphs the observed differences between the groups in their party preference. This relationship is observed because of

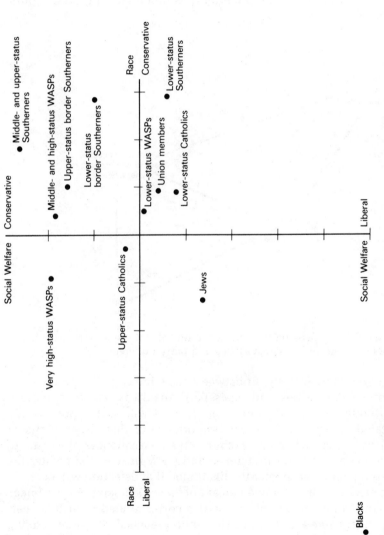

Fig. 8.2   Position of various party coalition groups on racial and welfare issues

group differences in issue preference (line B). The voters who are members of these groups should, more or less explicitly, compare the public position of the parties on the issues which they regard as important (line C). As a result there should be significant variation between the groups in the identification of which party best represents the issues preferences of the group (line D). Line E, linking party preference and connectedness, represents the dependence of the party bias of the group on the perception that one of the parties holds the preferred position on one or more significant issues.

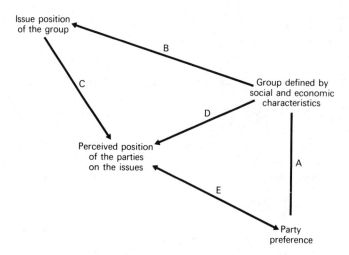

Fig. 8.3   Schematic representation of the relationship between sociodemographic characteristics and party preference

Often, however, the fit between one's image of the policy position of the parties and one's partisanship is less than perfect. Although it is fairly congruent for most voters, it is poorly integrated for some others. The importance of this "issue partisanship" is clear when one examines the consequences of a discrepancy between party preference and party images: the greater the discrepancy, the greater the likelihood that defection will occur in an election. Only about 4 percent of those Democrats whose image of the policy stands of the parties corresponded with their partisanship voted for Ford in 1976, but it reached 87 percent among those who felt that the Republican party was a better representative of their positions on the important issues. Among Republican identifiers, the voter for Ford dropped from almost 99 percent for those with a strongly Republican issue connectedness, to around 48 percent for those whose issue connectedness pointed them in a Democratic direction.

Of course only a small portion of the electorate was located in these most discrepant off-diagonal cells, about 5 percent in 1976 (it reaches almost 19 percent if independents who perceive a party difference are counted). But the proportion of issue-inconsistent partisans is less important than the way they behave. That such individuals overcome their party preference and cast a vote for the opposition testifies to the importance of reinforcing partisanship with issue preferences and perceptions of the parties (what is here called "issue connectedness"). Since issue opinions and issue perceptions of the Democrats and Republicans rationalize voters' ties to the parties, one would expect that changes in these perceptions should, at some point, affect their party identification. One might also expect the party bias of different groups to reflect their perceptions of the stance of the parties on the important questions of the day.

As figure 8.3 indicates, voters might change their perception of where the parties stand on the issues (or some issues), or the party leadership may undergo a change that alters the stance of the party toward some set of questions. But in either case, it is a shift in issue connectedness which alters the party-issue alignment.

Figures 8.4 and 8.5 illustrate this by graphing factor loadings from a matrix of correlations among party preference, issue preference, and the perceived position of the parties on these issues.[9] The graphs present the issue positions of Southern whites and their perception of the positions of the parties on these issues in the 1950s (fig. 8.4) and the 1970s (fig. 8.5). The changes that have taken place in the perceived position of the parties is the biggest difference between the parts of the graph. Opinions among white Southerners were as orthogonal to their partisanship in the 1950s as they are in the 1970s, albeit in slightly different ways. The larger change is in the relationship of these positions to the stance of the parties, where white Southerners once believed the Democratic party championed them, they are no longer so certain.

Clearly the role of issues in maintaining or disrupting the party alignment is more subtle than a focus upon the rise of new issues presumes. Figures 8.4 and 8.5 illustrates the need to consider images of the position of the parties as much as the relationship between party preference and issue preference. In each case, a

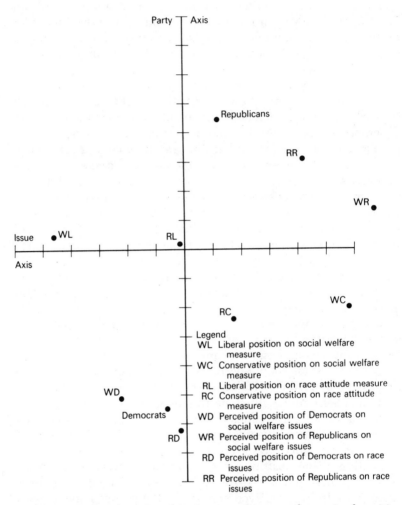

Fig. 8.4   Plot of partisanship, issue positions, and perceived position of the parties among white Southerners in the 1950s

crosscutting of the issue-party alignment by either new issues or new perceptions of the position of the parties on old issues threatens the existing alignment. Exactly how this process alters the party coalitions remains to be seen. From the preceding chapter there is every reason to believe that crosscutting issues do not (at least immediately) cause abrupt shifts in the party identification of individual voters. Most of the change should result from the failure of the party system to mobilize entering cohorts along traditional lines. But older cohorts cannot be completely insensitive to new issues and different party images. Disruptive issues should have some effect on them as well.

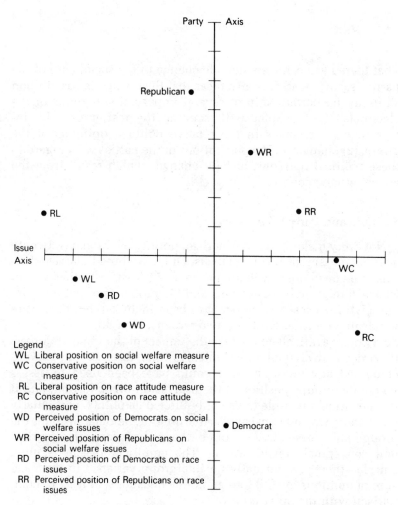

Fig. 8.5   Plot of partisanship, issue positions, and perceived issue position of the parties among white Southerners in the 1970s

9 The Attitudinal Basis
of the Realignment

That there has been considerable change in the social base of the parties seems clear. It is also clear that the change is based upon shifts in the partisanship of several important subgroups of the electorate. This chapter will examine the realignment by integrating: (1) changes in the relative political opinions of the group, (2) changes in the perceptions of the parties with regard to these political opinions, and (3) changes which result from the arrival of new cohorts.

Attitude and Party Change

Not every major issue in American politics over the past twenty years is measured in this analysis. Only two broad classes of issues are considered, welfare and race. At least two other sets of issues, foreign policy questions and the problems of public order and civil liberties, might also have been included, but they were not dealt with extensively for two reasons. First, there are too few data points available to analyze the impact of the issue of domestic order and civil liberties reliably. Only three of the surveys contained any questions that could have been used to assess where the groups positioned themselves on this question, and it did not seem advisable to use only three data points, particularly since there was no consistent patterning of the data. Second, the foreign policy issue was left out of the analysis for both empirical and conceptual considerations. The empirical reason is quite simple—there was virtually no intergroup variance in the measure of opinions toward foreign policy questions, at least in comparison with the other issues.

The conceptual reason for ignoring foreign policy issues is that they did not in the past, and do not today, divide the American public along the same lines as racial and welfare issues.[1] The criteria which distinguish individuals as "liberal" and "conservative" on foreign policy are largely, although not entirely, orthogonal to the cleavages which divide the electorate into Democrats and Republicans. The correlational link between changes

in party preference and changes in a group's modal opinion toward foreign policy issues is very weak.[2] Thus, although foreign
policy issues may be responsible for some change in party preference, its effect is different from the other issues that affect the
party bias of the groups.

Figure 9.1 is a two-dimensional plot of indexes which measure
a group's attitudes on racial and welfare questions.[3] The center of
these axes (the zero point) is the average for the entire population.
A group which is not different from the population in its feelings
on racial and welfare questions would score at the intersection on
the graph. A group which was markedly more liberal than the
population on racial and economic welfare questions would be in
the upper-right quarter of the graph, while a markedly conservative group would be located in the lower-left quarter of the graph.
Of course a group which was liberal on one issue but conservative
on the other would be either in the upper-left or lower-right quarter, depending upon the issue on which it was more conservative
or liberal than the population. A group which was relatively liberal on welfare questions but conservative on racial matters would
be located somewhere in the lower-right quarter. A group with the
opposite profile would be in the upper-left quarter.

The lines in figure 9.1 connect each group's score in the fifties
with the group's score in the seventies. The arrow points to the
score of the group in the 1970s. One would expect that groups
becoming more Republican would become more conservative on
the issues, and groups becoming more Democratic to become
more liberal on the issues.[4] Consider the very high-status Northern white Protestants: The proportion of Republicans to Democrats in this group has declined considerably since the early
1950s. Corresponding to this change in the party bias is a large
change in the proportion giving conservative replies on racial and
welfare questions. These high-status WASPs could not be fairly
characterized as conservative on racial issues, since their feelings
on this question were no more unfavorable to blacks than any
other group in the population. However, their position on the
welfare issue, coupled with the very small conservative plurality
on the racial issue, clearly marked them as a conservative portion
of the population. Their relatively strong preference for the Republican part over the Democratic part is, therefore, not surprising. If the transformation of a group's partisanship follows
changes in their modal (or mean) attitudes, we would expect, in
this instance, to find "silk-stocking" WASPs more liberal in the
1970s than they were in the 1950s. As figure 9.1 indicates they
have become more liberal.

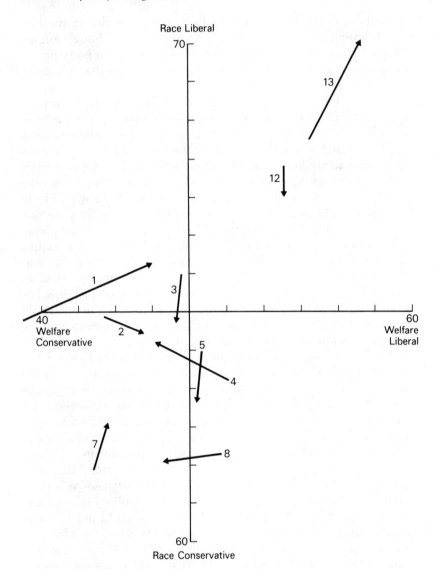

Fig. 9.1   Changes in the race and welfare attitudes of the coalition groups

If the adequacy of the attitude explanation of the party change could be assessed by the fit of the data for the "silk-stocking" group alone, the case could be rested. Unfortunately, there are few groups who are consistent in the direction in which their attitudes have changed, and fewer still whose change in attitudes have completely paralleled changes in party bias. Consider the attitude data in figure 9.1 more fully. Most groups have changed in a con-

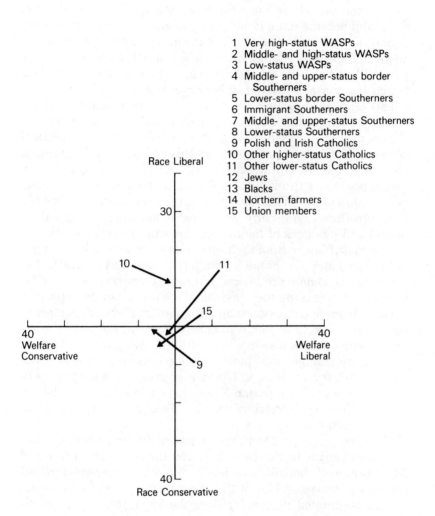

tradictory fashion, becoming more liberal on one issue and more conservative on another. By virtue of this inconsistency alone, there is a poor chance that changes in the party preference of the groups can be traced to changes in group attitudes on political issues. One expects groups becoming more liberal to become more Democratic, and groups becoming more conservative to become more Republican. But what is the expectation if the attitudes change in opposite directions?

One could consider the possibility of specific attitudes accounting for such changes. For example, one might ignore the slighly greater conservatism of the middle-status WASPs on the race issue in the seventies compared with the fifties and simply assume the priority of the attitude explanation by insisting that the group became more Democratic because it had become more liberal on welfare issues. A similar kind of argument would be made for high-status Catholics, while for Polish and Irish Catholics we could attribute the small decline in Democratic support to their increasing conservatism on welfare questions.

This strategy, however, has some problems. In the first place, even such an optimistic approach leaves unaccounted for as many changes as it successfully explains. Some of the unexplained cases are glaringly at variance with this ad hoc hypothesizing. If changes in specific attitudes were responsible for changes in party preference, the attitudes that are responsible should bear some relationship to the character of the groups. For example, since the Southern Democratic party was constructed upon the racial attitudes and practices of the region, one would expect to find the Southern drift away from the Democrats associated with changes in the racial attitudes of the South. But as figure 9.1 indicates, the South has become more liberal, not more conservative, on racial issues, which is quite the opposite of what one would expect.

There is more confusion than enlightenment about changes in party preference to be found in considering individual attitudes. There is no obvious way in which attitude change can be used to explain the changes that have (or have not) taken place in the party bias of several groups. The lack of change in a group's party bias is particularly important, since several groups have barely changed their party preference in the face of considerable change in their attitudes.

The data in figure 9.2 indicate the size of discrepancy that exists between changes in the party bias and the political attitudes of some groups. If changes in racial or welfare opinions precipitated changes in the party bias of the groups, the arrows in figure 9.2 should be pointed diagonally from the lower-left to the upper-right quadrant, or from the upper-right to the lower-left segment. For several groups just the opposite pattern is observed.[5] Attitudes can account for changes in the party bias of only five groups. The changing party bias of "silk-stocking" WASPs, lower-status border Southerners, lower-status native white Southerners, blacks, and union members is positively correlated with a liberal-conservative change in their attitudes.[6] For almost all of the other coalition groups change in at least one and occasionally both attitudes contradict the shift in their party bias.

Political Generations and Issue Change

This overview of the relationship between changes in attitudes and the party bias of the groups ignores the data presented in chapter 7. Most of the gross change in party identification has come from that segment of the electorate which entered since 1960. Not considering this generation factor explicitly reduces the significance of the data in figure 9.2. The attitude explanation should account for group changes in party bias that are contributed by the older cohort. By including the younger cohort in the analysis, the wrong data are compared to the theory. It seems possible that the attitudes of the young are also disproportionately responsible for altering the attitudinal profile of the groups. If both of these changes are occuring because of the post-1960 cohort, the young, who are 29 percent of the electorate in the 1970s, might be confounding a strong association between the changes.[7] For example, since the young in the South are more liberal on racial and welfare issues than their elders (though they are still more conservative than Northern young), they alone might be the reason for the negative correlation between changes in the party bias and changes in the welfare and race attitudes of Southerners as a group.

To examine the extent to which opinions are responsible for changes in partisanship, it is necessary to examine these attitudes only for the fraction of the group that has been in the electorate for the entire period, and, therefore, able to change their attitudes from the first period of time to the second.

Figure 9.3 presents a comparison of the relationship between changes in the party bias and changes in the issue preference for the pre-1960 cohort. The vertical axis represents the party bias and the horizontal axis plots a summary measure of opinions on the race and welfare issues.[8]

Obviously, no systematic improvement follows from removing the younger cohort from each group and remeasuring the change. The basically inconsistent relationship between party bias and attitude change remains. None of the uncorrelated change in the group's partisanship is explained. The reason for the similarity of the relationships in figures 9.2 and 9.3 is that the young cohorts in each group have almost the same relative attitude on race and welfare issues as the older cohorts. The effect of the young is almost exclusively on the party bias of the groups. The young are less identified with a party, and removing them only dampens the change in the group's party preference.

Considering the relationship between attitude change and party

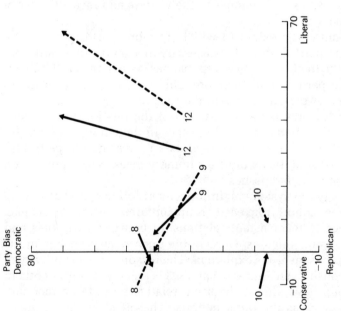

1 Very high-status Northern WASPs
2 Middle- and high-status Northern WASPs
3 Low-status WASPs
4 Upper-status border Southerners
5 Lower-status border Southerners
6 Lower-status Southerners
7 Upper-status Southerners
8 Polish and Irish Catholics
9 Other Catholics of lower-status
10 Other Catholics of higher-status
11 Jews
12 Blacks
13 Union members

The hatched line plots the relationship between changes in racial attitudes and changes in party bias while the solid line plots the relationship between changes in the party bias and changes in the economic welfare attitudes of the group.

Fig. 9.2   Comparison of changes in group positions on racial and economic welfare issues with changes in the party bias of the groups

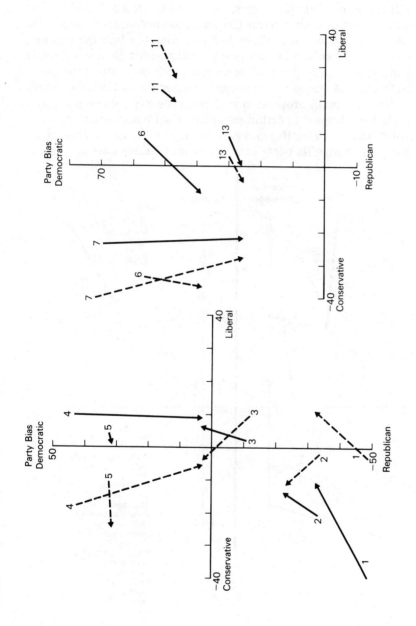

change generally, the young cohort actually helps each group convert attitude change into party identification change (compare figs. 9.2 and 9.3). The groups most affected by the young are higher-status Catholics, Jews, and middle-status WASPs. The older cohort of higher-status Catholics has become (perhaps) a bit more liberal since the fifties, but considerably less Democratic. The younger cohort of this group neither adds to, nor subtracts from, this slightly greater liberalism, but it does affect the party preference of the group. Younger, higher-status Catholics enter with only a small proportion preferring the Republican party and a relatively large proportion preferring the Democratic party. As a result, in the late sixties and early seventies the group as a whole does not change its party bias to any measurable extent.

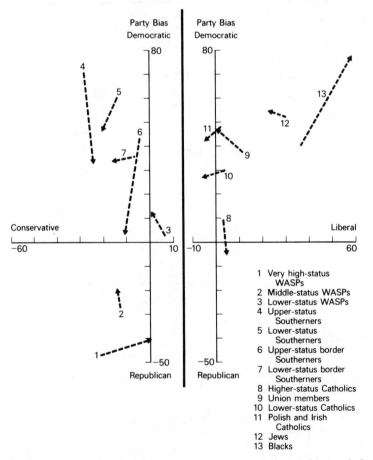

Fig. 9.3   Relationship between changes in the party bias and changes in the issue preferences of the older cohort for each of the coalition groups

The effect of the younger cohort of Jews is similar to the effect of the young cohort of higher-status Catholics. The issue preferences of the young Jewish cohort are not markedly different from those of the older cohort. Their party preference, however, is different. The older cohort has become slightly more Democratic since the fifties, but because the post-1960 cohort of Jews is much more Independent, the net change is a reduction of the Democratic bias of Jews as a group.

Lastly, middle-status WASPs have become both more liberal and less Republican almost completely because of the younger cohort. The older cohort of middle-status WASPs has lost some of its Republican bias; the young cohort only adds to the trend. But while the net attitude change of the group as a whole is toward a more liberal stance—which seems to explain the change in the group's party preference—there is virtually no change in the political attitudes of the older cohorts, or, at best, even a slight movement to the conservative pole. In the case of the middle-status WASPs, then, the young explain all the attitude change, and, compared with the Jews and the upper-status Catholics, comparatively less of the party preference change.

Generally, concentrating on the older cohort does not reduce much of the discrepancy between the expected and observed relationship between attitude change and party change found in figure 9.2. An examination of the older cohort leaves us with less of an explanation for the partisan change than can be had with the younger cohort included in each group. When the attitude data from figure 9.2 are averaged together, changes in the party preference and attitudes of four groups are inconsistent. If the young are removed from the groups, and only the older, pre-1960 cohort is considered, the party preference changes of six groups cannot be accounted for by the direction or magnitude of changes in group opinions on racial and economic welfare matters.

The multiple correlation between changes in racial and economic welfare attitudes and the changes in party preference accounts for less than 22 percent of the variance in the change in party preference across the groups. This is high by some standards, but if you consider that it is computed on grouped data, the 22 percent is singularly unimpressive. The attitudes alone account for only a little more than 2 of the 13 point change in the party bias of the groups between the fifties and the seventies.[9]

Figure 9.4 illustrates the inability of attitude change to account for the changes in the party bias of the groups. Only the pre-1960 cohort is included in the figure, which is comparing the observed change in the party bias of the group with the change predicted by

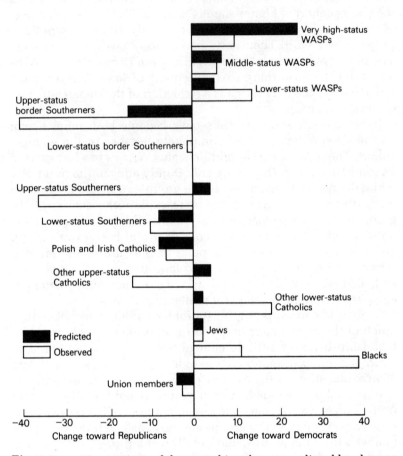

Fig. 9.4   Comparison of the party-bias change predicted by changes in the attitude of the party-coalition groups with the observed change

shifts in the racial and welfare attitudes of the group. The difference between the predicted and observed party bias measures the inability of shifts in opinion to explain the realignment of the groups. Five groups are predicted very well. Middle-status WASPs, lower-status border Southerners and lower-status Southerners, Polish and Irish Catholics, Jews, and union members have realigned (or not) both in the direction and at (approximately) the rate predicted by their attitude change. The party bias of the "silk-stocking" group has changed much less than expected, blacks much more, and the party preference of most Southerners has also changed much more than a change in attitudes would predict. The change in the party bias of upper-status Southerners is opposite to the direction predicted by their increasing liberalism.

The attitude model of party change is not completely wrong. It works for several groups; but only for a few groups does it work particularly well. The explanation for changes in partisanship must lie in other attitudinal factors, if it is going to be found among attitude variables at all.

Party Images and Partisan Change

The idea of party images is the central feature of the concept of connectedness. The model outline in chapter 8 assumed that political attitudes correlate with party preference because individuals are able to distinguish the parties in terms of their issue preferences. The images that citizens have about the issue stance of the parties permits them to use their political attitudes to explain why they support one party rather than the other. These images locate the parties as more or less close to the opinion of the individual voter, who can then characterize himself as closer to the Democratic party, closer to the Republican party, equally distant from both, or unable to decide the party to which he is closer. In either of the last two possibilities, the voter is unable to use his position on that issue to justify his support of a party.

That individuals can correctly identify the position of the parties is not at issue. Subjective reality is what the individual voter uses to make sense of his behavior. So to the extent that the individual believes that the parties differ on an issue, that belief can be used to justify the individual's preference for one of the parties. Moreover, there are several issues on which the parties may not have agreed positions. It is neither unreasonable nor surprising that voters may come to different conclusions about where the parties stand on a question.[10]

Parties do not always adopt clear positions on the issues. Occasionally the position of a party is blurred by party elites because there is no agreement on the issue among their supporters, and more might be lost than gained by embracing it. At other times (or for other issues) the party leadership is immobilized by internal dispute or conflicting interpretations of the preferences of supporters. Foreign policy issues have had this character for both parties in recent decades. Only with rare exceptions has there been a party line clear enough to permit voters to predict their support for a party on foreign policy questions. Until the 1960s, race has also been this kind of issue for the Democratic party.

The individual level logic can also be applied to explain

changes in the partisanship of groups. If the members of a group nominate the Democratic party as closer to them on the issues than the Republican party, one expects that group to prefer the Democrats over the Republicans. If, however, the group nominates the Republican party as a better representative of its opinions on the issues, then one expects the group to prefer the Republicans over the Democrats.

For this reason, images of the issue stance of the parties should accurately predict the party bias of the groups. The simple attitude explanation for changes in the party bias assumes that issue-party connectedness changes in the same direction. For some groups (as for some individuals) changes in issue preferences do produce changes in the connectedness of an issue with that party. But for others, connectedness and issue preference vary independently. A group (or the electorate's) perception of the stance of the parties on a question may shift because the parties have moved or because previous misperceptions of the position of the parties have been corrected. For these reasons, and variations on them, it is not surprising to find myriad configurations of beliefs about the position of the parties on public questions. The variety enhances the likelihood that attitudes will fail to account for changes in partisanship.

Figures 9.5 through 9.7 indicates the importance of the discrepancy between attitudes and the placement of the parties in explaining the realignment. The party bias index is plotted on the vertical axis and the horizontal axis represents issues. The points in the figures are the factor loadings obtained from a principal component analysis which forced a two-factor solution. If the American party system were a bifunctional party system concerned as much with public policy as with seeking office, the points should cluster.[11] The conservative positions of welfare, race, and foreign policy issues should be highly correlated with each other; they should also be correlated with Republican identification. The patterning of the Democratic points should be just the opposite. The points should be high and low, respectively, on the party dimension while the issue preferences and perceptions of the parties in terms of the issues should locate the factor loadings high in the upper-right quarter and low in the left quarter of each graph.

If, however, the supporters of the parties held a variety of different issue preferences the conservative and liberal points would be rather distant from the partisan points. The weak correlation between issue preferences and partisanship would yield factor loadings which are high on the issue dimension and low on the

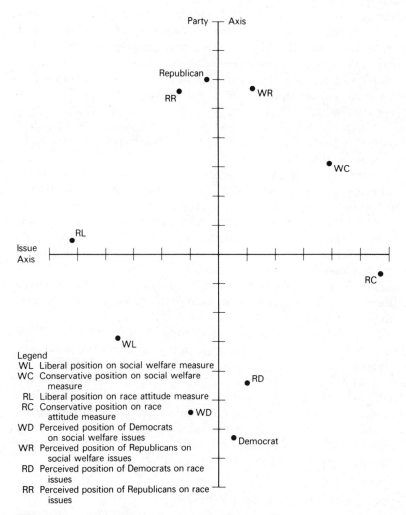

Fig. 9.5   Plot of factor loadings for partisanship, issue positions, and perceived party positions for the 1950s

party dimension, yielding a graphic representation which shows issues cutting across partisanship. The issue perception of the parties could load on the partisanship dimension, the issue dimension, or somewhere in between.

Figures 9.5, 9.6, and 9.7 offer some understanding for the failure of attitude changes to account for the party bias of the coalition groups. Figure 9.5 presents a dimensional representation of the relationship between partisanship, issues preferences, and perceptions of the issue stance of the parties for the years 1952 through 1960. Only welfare issues load on the issue and party dimensions in a manner which indicates the importance of economic welfare questions to the partisanship of Democrats and Republicans. Foreign policy issues are uncorrelated with either partisanship or economic welfare preferences, resulting in small factor loadings on both dimensions; and race opinions are weakly related to welfare opinions and uncorrelated with partisanship. Over all, the relationship of issues to party preference is weak and contradictory, and the principal issue cleavage that distinguishes Democrats from Republicans is, not surprisingly, the economic welfare question.

However, the perceptions of the parties' positions on the issues is strongly correlated with partisanship, more strongly than they are correlated with the issue preferences of the electorate.

Clearly, the American party system during the 1950s was organized around the economic welfare cleavage. The basic independence of other issues and partisanship was ignored and the parties were perceived by most to represent their position on the issues even though the data in figure 9.5 indicate there were as many "liberals" as "conservatives" in each party on the race and foreign policy questions.

Figures 9.6 and 9.7 show the changes that help explain why attitude change is not the principal factor in either the growth of Independents or the changes in the party bias of the various groups. Racial attitudes continue to cut across partisanship; by the 1970s welfare attitudes were less correlated with partisanship; foreign policy issues had become more articulated with other issues (they were loading on the issue dimension); but the most dramatic difference is the decline in the relationship between party preference and the perceived position of the parties.

Transformations in the Party's Images

Issue connectedness, therefore, rather than changed issue preferences in the groups might underlie shifts in their party bias. The data in figure 9.8 permit this analysis of the impact of changes in connectedness. Figure 9.8 presents changes in the connectedness of race and economic welfare issues for thirteen groups.

The vertical axis measures the connectedness of the race issue. The higher the group is positioned on the axis the more often the members of the group perceive the Democratic party taking the preferred position on race questions. As the group is located lower, on the negative side of the axis, the members of the group tend to perceive the Republican party as a better representative of

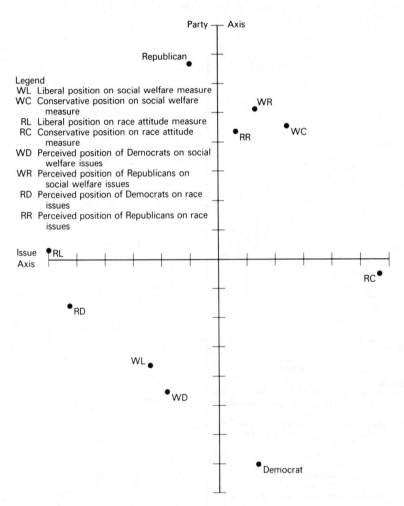

Fig. 9.6   Plot of factor loadings for partisanship, issue positions, and perceived party positions in the mid-1960s

their feelings on the question. The horizontal axis measures the perception of the parties on a series of economic welfare questions. Positive values indicate a belief that the Democratic party is the better representative of the individual's position on these matters, and a negative value indicates a belief that the Republican party is the better representative. The intersection on the graph is a point at which the parties are not distinguished by the group on either of the attitudes. Like figure 9.1, figure 9.8 locates the groups in the fifties and the seventies, and connects the two points with a line. As before, the arrow points to the 1970s score.

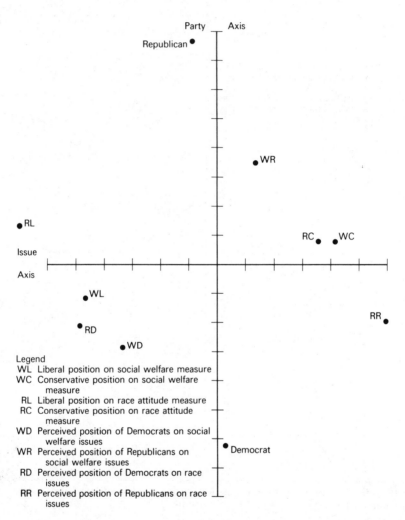

Fig. 9.7   Plot of factor loadings for partisanship, issue position, and perceived party positions for the 1970s

The contrast of figure 9.8 with figure 9.1 is striking. Figure 9.8 has relatively few inconsistencies. Groups which changed their perceptions of the parties changed them in a consistent direction for both issues. Where the change is not consistent—where a group is more favorable toward the Republicans on one issue and more favorable toward the Democrats on another—overall connectedness shifts are very small. By and large, the lines are running up from left to right, or down from right to left, as they should if perceptions of the parties change in a consistent manner. The three Northern WASP groups have come to regard the Republicans as less representative of their feelings on race and welfare questions than they believed them to be in the fifties. The four Southern groups have also changed since the fifties, and for them the direction of change is away from the Democratic party. Southerners find the perceived issue position of the Democratic party less acceptable in the seventies than they did in the fifties. Also interesting—and in contrast with the changes in attitudes in these groups—is the extent to which the slopes of change for the two variables are similar.

Most Northern white Protestants have changed their perception of the parties on racial and welfare issues at almost equal rates. Only the native Southerners appear to have changed their perceptions of the parties at an unequal rate, with perceptions on the racial issue changing at a slightly higher rate than their perceptions of the parties on welfare matter (not unexpected). The only white Protestant segment of the population that deviates much from what is almost a one-to-one change in perceptions of the party's positions on race and economic welfare issues are the higher-status border Southerners who have changed a dozen points in their perceptions of the parties on economic welfare issues but not at all on race matters.

Blacks have dramatically changed their perceptions of where the parties stand on racial and welfare issues. In the fifties blacks were moderately pro-Democratic on both of these matters. By the seventies they were dramatically more pro-Democratic on both questions, having increased their Democratic perceptions 25 points on race matters and 23 points on the welfare issue.

Overall, the groups have consistently changed their perceptions of the parties on racial and economic welfare matters. The only discrepancies in changes in party perceptions occurs among Catholics and Jews. For neither of these segments does the change in connectedness for one issue parallel changes in the other. Yet the size of these conflicting changes is very small.

The Relationship between Changes in Issue Connectedness and Changes in Party Bias

The data in figure 9.9 allow a close examination of correlation between these changes. The horizontal axis measures issue connectedness. Large negative numbers indicate a larger proportion

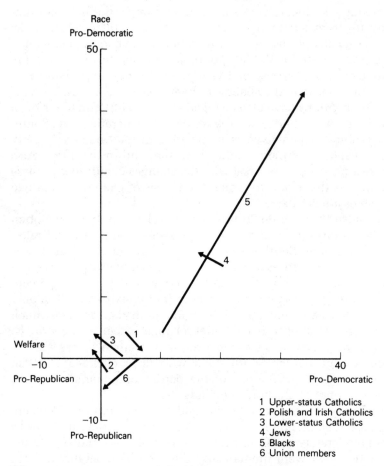

Fig. 9.8   Comparison of changes in issue-party connectedness for race and economic welfare issues for party coalition groups

believe themselves closer to the Republican party than the Democratic party on the issues. Large positive numbers indicate a larger proportion identifying themselves as closer to the Democratic party. Overall it is clear that change in the party bias of the groups is much more highly correlated with change in connectedness than change in attitudes. Only among higher-status Catholics are partisanship and connectedness changing in opposite directions. And even then, the discrepancy is very small. Among Jews, Polish and Irish Catholics, and lower-status Catholics of other nationalities there is party change but no observable change in issue connectedness. For each of these groups, the reason for the null correlation between the changes is that percep-

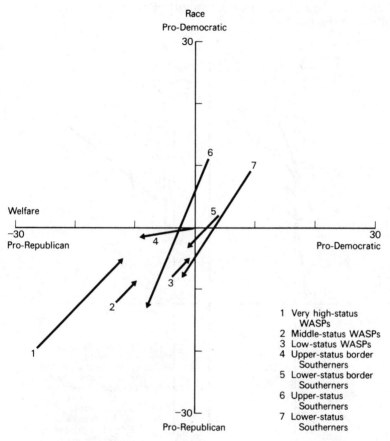

tions of the parties on race and welfare issues are changing in opposite directions (see figure 9.8).

Among native Southerners, where attitude change and party change are moving in opposite directions, connectedness explains the changes in partisanship. While many Southerners have become more liberal since the fifties on at least one and perhaps both race and economic welfare issues, they are not in any sense a liberal segment of the population. The connectedness concept accounts for this discrepancy because it measures the degree to which Southerners are aligning their attitudes and their party preference, and "correcting" a previous "discrepancy" between party preference and issue preference.

By the most conservative judgment there are only four groups changing their party bias without a corresponding change in issue connectedness. Moreover the instances where connectedness does not account for party change have more to do with the confounding effect of the younger cohort of each group than with a failure of the theory.

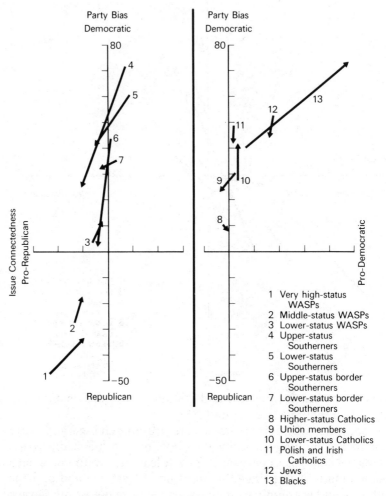

Fig. 9.9   Comparison of changes in the party bias of the groups with changes in the perceived issue position of the parties

As before, the young distort the relationship by having an overly large effect on the party bias of the groups. So here, too, it is necessary to remove the new cohort in order to distinguish between changes that are a result of generational replacement and those that result from a transformation over time in the attitudes and perceptions of members of the electorate. When this is done, it is clear that issue connectedness accounts particularly well for changes in the party bias of the groups (fig. 9.10). Shifts in the party bias are uncorrelated with the change in issue connectedness only for middle-status Northern WASPs and lower-status Catholics. In both groups there is a change in party bias with no measurable change in issue connectedness. However, for no group is partisanship and connectedness changing in opposite

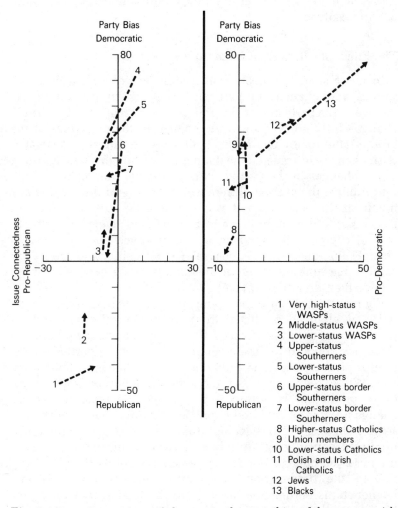

Fig. 9.10   Comparison of changes in the party bias of the groups with changes in the perceived issue position of the parties among the pre-1960 cohort

directions. The slopes between the variables differ but the direction of change is consistent with the theory. Excepting middle-status Northern WASPs and lower-class Catholics, groups that have become more pro-Democratic in their perception of the issue stance of the parties are now more Democratic in their party bias. Similarly, groups more Republican in their perception of the issue stance of the parties are more Republican in their party bias. By excluding the younger cohort, which affects the values of all the groups in the late sixties and early seventies but does not actually represent a change in over time, the conflicting patterns in figure 9.7 are resolved.

The Effect of Changes in Issue Connectedness

In contrast to the weak relationship between changes in attitudes and changes in partisanship—only 18 percent of the change in the party bias of the groups was correlated with attitude change—fully 46 percent of the change in the party bias of the groups (after removing the effect of the young cohort) is correlated with changes in issue connectedness.[12] Although the magnitude of the changes in the party bias is accurately predicted for only four groups, the average difference of the size of the residuals is much smaller here than it was considering attitudes alone in figure 9.4. And in no instance is the predicted change of the party bias of a group the opposite of the observed change. Overall, changes in the connectedness of issue positions accounts for about three times as much of the change in the party bias of the groups than do attitudes taken alone.

Figure 9.11 compares the change in the party bias of the groups with the changed predicted from issue connectedness and attitudes, removing the effect of the young. Considering both the issue position and the issue connectedness of the parties for the groups gives a very good prediction of the change in their party bias. With the exception of the higher-status border Southerners, every prediction is within 6 percentage points of the actual change and ten of the predictions are within 5 points of the observed change. On the average the change in party preference predicted considering attitude and issue connectedness misses the observed change by about 4 percentage points.[13]

Only the border Southern groups present any problems. Higher-status border Southerners are the least successfully predicted. While the group has changed its party bias 42 points, changes in opinion on racial and economic welfare issues and changes in the connectedness of these issues with the parties pre-

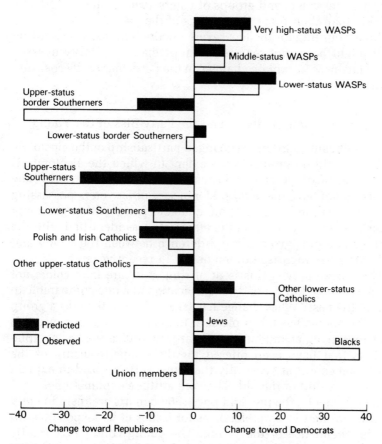

Fig. 9.11   Comparison of the observed change in partisanship with the change predicted by shifts in group attitudes and the perceived position of the parties on issues

dict only a 14 point shift away from the Democrats. Why the border South should deviate so far from the pattern for other groups has no obvious explanation.

For groups where change is overpredicted (e.g., Polish and Irish Catholics), the explanation is more at hand. Conveniently, it is reasonable to believe that the overprediction of change in party preference from changes in issue preference and issue connectedness indicates the extent to which a developed party preference is resistant to change. Party preference is not easily changeable and only very great pressure will precipitate an abandonment of that preference. Eventually the issue perceptions of the party should cause a change in party preference, but it should come as no surprise that voters and groups of voters abandon their party less quickly than their issue perceptions of the parties.

But accounting for the few severe mispredictions, as rewarding as it might be, is not required to appreciate the ability of issue connectedness to explain changes in the party bias of the coalition groups.

Issues, Issue Connectedness, and the Party Bias of the Young

A significant factor in the changed partisanship of the electorate and the coalition groups is the extent to which the electorate is composed of different people than the electorate of 1952. New voters do not have the party preference of older voters possessing similar social and demographic characteristics. Although young voters have always entered the electorate less identified with the parties than older voters, the difference between the young and old voters has increased dramatically in recent years.[14]

The puzzle is why this is occurring. Why are new voters not being socialized into a party identification at a rate comparable to that of the past? What change has taken place in them as a group or what change has taken place in the party system to cause this ever increasing abandonment of party identification? The explanations that have been offered for the nonpartisanship of the post-1960 cohort are basically the same as those used to explain the partisanship of the old. They are attitude explanations.

Unfortunately, the pre- and post-1960 cohorts are insufficiently distinct in their issue preferences for issues to be responsible for the independence of the young. The young cohort of virtually every coalition group is more liberal than the older cohort, but the differences end there; and simply being more liberal cannot account for their independence. An excess of liberals should (and does) yield a larger ratio of Democrats to Republicans (except in the South). To account for the sharply larger proportion of Independents, however, the young should be either (1) attentive to different issues than the older cohort, (2) unable to perceive differences between the parties in terms of these issues, or, (3) because the young are less burdened by party habits, more able to translate this inability to perceive party differences on the issues into independence. Again, even with such amendments, the issue explanation for the partisanship of the young fares poorly.

The importance that the young assign to welfare, racial, foreign policy, and cultural or life-style issues is virtually identical to that assigned by the pre-1960 cohort.[15] They are also virtually identical in their satisfaction with what they perceive government policy to be in each area. In short, the data (not shown) do not support the first explanation for the nonpartisanship of the young, that is, the young do not appear to be sensitive or especially exercised over issues in a way which distinguishes them from the pre-1960 cohort.

However, the young do see slightly greater differences between their issues preferences and what they perceive to be the position of the parties than do the older cohort. But as table 9.1 indicates, the differences in the connectedness scores of the two cohorts is quite small, and, in the case of racial issues, the opposite of what is expected. The overall pattern in table 9.1 is repeated for the coalition groups: For Northern Protestants, Southern whites, Catholics, Jews, and blacks there is a discernible tendency for the young, compared with the old, to view the parties as less representative of their issue preferences; but the differences are small. Only for the cultural or life-style issue are the differences large enough to warrant being described as a generation difference.

So although the young perceive smaller differences than the old do between the positions of the parties on welfare, race, foreign policy, and cultural issues, the differences are not large. At least they do not seem to be as large as the differences in the partisanship of the two cohorts would seem to require. The second explanation of the greater independence of the young can, therefore, also be laid aside. Although it is appealing to believe that the alienation of the young from the parties is caused by the tweedledum and tweedle-dee posturing of the Democrats and Republicans, the data do not support the idea, at least not very strongly.

The third attitude explanation for the independence of the

Table 9.1   Mean Connectedness Score for Pre- and Post-1960 Cohorts Across Four Issue Domains

Issue Domains	Pre-1960 Cohort		Post-1960 Cohort	
	All	Independents	All	Independents
Welfare	.98	1.07	1.07	1.24
Race	1.41	1.65	1.31	1.45
Foreign policy	.87	.99	1.00	1.13
Social issue	1.25	1.37	1.59	1.83

Note: Number is the mean difference between the position of the respondent on a seven point attitude index and his placement on the same index of the party. He perceives to be closer to him. The number, therefore, measures how well the nearer party represents the respondent's position. The scores range from zero (a perfect match) to six.

young does not require them to be sensitive to issues, nor must they perceive the issue positioning of the parties differently. In the third explanation, the young are less attached to the parties because they are more responsive to the increasingly tenuous ties between the parties and the dominant public issues. The older cohort of voters were grafted to the parties when the most salient issues were similar to the "New Deal issue" around which the party system is structured. For this group of voters one of the parties seems "right" in spite of the fact that it may be difficult to rationalize their commitment with the current stance of the Democrats and Republicans. In other words, the inertia of habit retards the erosion of partisanship that would inevitably follow an unbiased evaluation of party preference in light of the policy commitments of the parties, the importance they attach to these issues, and their satisfaction with the policies being pursued on these issues. The relative immunity of the older cohort to the new issues (or the manner in which old issues are articulated) prevents them from converting their dissatisfaction with the parties into independence at a rate characteristic of the post-1960 generation.

Although this retrieval of the attitude explanation is rhetorically convincing, the data in figure 9.12 do not lend it much credence. The regression of independence on the connectedness measures yields slopes for the old that are virtually identical to those of the young cohort. There are some small differences in favor of the hypothesis for the welfare and life-style connectedness measures, but they are as substantively trivial as they are statistically undifferentiated.

The erosion of the belief that the parties represent them on the principal issues seems to have altered the party bias of the pre-1960 generation, but their replacements have been inspired by other considerations. Perhaps we should consider the possibility that just as a pro-party event can mobilize a majority for a party among an entering cohort, a diffuse distaste for parties in general will encourage independence. Certainly something like a "culture of independence" appears to be responsible for the weaker attachment of the young to the parties since the late 1960s.[16]

The Agenda of the New Alignment

Race conflict is the major new element in the party-system agenda. Conflict over the "social" issue between advocates of social reform and social control has certainly played some role in the realignment, or the dealignment, of the parties. But the most visible difference between the party coalitions that entered the turbulent 1960s and those that exited in the middle 1970s is to be found in their new-found distinctiveness on race-related policy issues.

Figure 9.13 plots four different data points representing the positions of Democratic and Republican identifiers on race and social welfare issues in the 1950s and the 1970s. The direction of the change is indicated by the arrow which points to the average score of the party identifiers in the early and middle 1970s. The principal difference between party identifiers in the fifties was to be found in opinions about the need for government action to meet a variety of social welfare matters. Reflecting the New Deal agenda of "governmental nationalism," the Democrats tended to be supportive of government action in the area while Republicans opposed it.

Interparty differences on racial issues were usually much less distinct, with Republicans marginally more positive toward issues of concern to blacks. But as Goldwater and the Republican party began to "hunt where the ducks are" after the middle 1960s, the stance of the parties toward racial matters changed. Republican identifiers became less sympathetic toward blacks, Democratic identifiers adopted a distinctly pro-black posture compared with the 1950s, and the size of the interparty difference began to rival Democratic-Republican disagreement over social welfare matters. Some of this difference reflects attitude changes among voters and social groups whose partisanship is relatively unaltered. But a very large portion of the new difference between the parties on racial issues reflects the realignment of the social groups that formed the New Deal coalitions. The interparty difference on welfare issues would be about 12 percent smaller in the 1970s if the party coalitions looked now as they did in the 1956, 1958, and 1960 elections. Interparty racial differences would be almost 55 percent smaller. Table 9.2 presents the data on which these calculations are based. It also illustrates the reversal of the

Table 9.2	Issue Distance between Democrats and Republicans		
	Distance between Party Identifiers (Democrats mean score minus Republican)		
	1950s	1970s (actual)	1970s (adjusted)
Walfare	−29	−27	−23
Race	7	−20	−9

Note: Negative numbers indicate that the Democrats are more liberal; positive numbers indicate that Republican identifiers have a more liberal score. The adjusted score removes the effect of coalition changes.

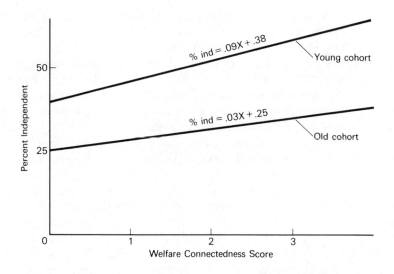

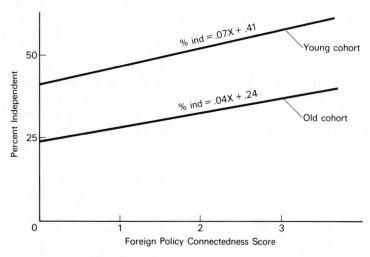

Fig. 9.12   Regression of connectedness scores on independence for young and old cohorts

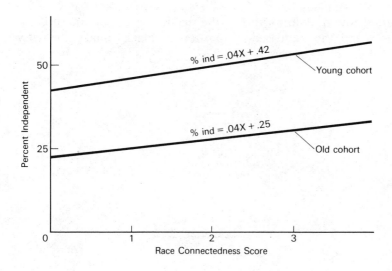

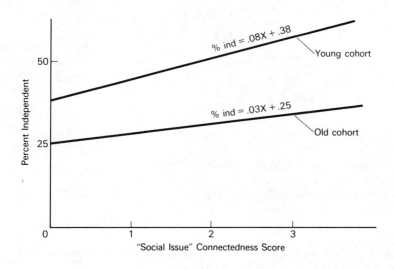

position of Democrats and Republicans on racial questions.
Throughout the 1950s the Republicans were 7 percentage points
more liberal than the Democrats. The pattern had reversed itself
by the elections of 1972 and 1976. In those years the Democrats
were 20 points more liberal, and while attitude change alone
would have made them a more liberal group in the 1970s (see the
second row of column three), the decline of the Southern Democrats and the increased proportion of blacks made the party
difference even larger.

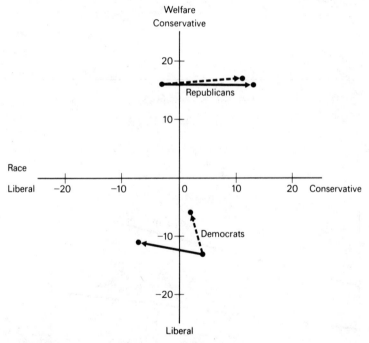

The broken line connects the attitudes of the party
identifiers in the 1950s with 1970s attitudes that
are adjusted for the changes in the party
coalitions.

Fig. 9.13   Changes in the race and welfare attitudes of Democratic and
Republican identifiers, 1950s to 1970s

There is a considerable amount of debate about the diagnosis of a more ideological electorate today compared with the 1950s. It would certainly be misleading to describe the parties as ideological coalitions, but there is no doubt that the policy agenda separating Democrats from Republicans has undergone a metamorphosis of substantial proportions. And since there is no reason to believe that race-related disputes will become any less important in the foreseeable future (and many reasons for believing the opposite), we should expect some stability in the reformulated coalitions described earlier. Racial differences, in particular, should become greater as the party leadership continues to respond to the altered social and ideological characteristics of their supporters.

Part 5

Conclusion

10 Party Systems and Party Coalitions

The Creation of a Peripheral Electorate

A principal feature of this realignment is its dependence on the growth of Independents. This reduced identification with the parties does not, of course, alter the fact of the transformation of the coalitions, but it does highlight some of its peculiarities. First, because the realignment does not constitute a critical realignment, the changes appear partial and incomplete, with long-term consequences that are difficult to predict. Virtually all of the realignments that have given the United States five different party systems have been made possible, if not precipitated, by an expansion of the electorate. The decline of the first party system and the rise of the Jacksonian Democrats saw the electorate grow from about 361,000 voters to almost 1,300,000 between the elections of 1824 and 1828. The transformation of the party system was so complete that the Federalists were moribund, even in New England, by 1832. The final formulation of the second party system with the birth of the Whigs was also a point of considerable electoral expansion. The number of voters increased from about 1.5 million in 1836 to about 2.5 million in 1840. The 50 percent growth of the electorate between 1852 and 1860 midwifed the third party system and the Republicans; the realignment of the 1890s was associated with an increase in the vote; and the triumph of the New Deal was made possible by a biased increase in the active electorate. In fact the only election in which the number of voters increased dramatically without a corresponding transformation in the party system was the contest of 1876. And even in that election one might make a very good case for the proposition that the election of 1876 was a watershed for the party system, since it was the election that facilitated the readmission of the South to the Union.

Of course, several different events explain the various increases in the electorate. The progressive extension of the franchise in the 1820s was clearly responsible for the electoral growth that took place throughout that decade and after, and the positions of competing elites on the question of the extension of the franchise played a major role in the direction in which new voters cast their ballots. The surge of voters in 1876 reflected the ability of the South to vote in presidential contests for the first time in a decade, and the expansion of the electorate in the 1920s reflected in part the enfranchisement of women. Yet not all of the growth of the 1850s resulted from changes in voting laws. Nor did all of the growth after 1920 (to say nothing of the decade before) result from female suffrage. Even if procedural changes were the principal explanation for the realignments, it would not change the fact that historical transformations of the party system appear to be a consequence of electoral growth.

It seems significant, therefore, that the current realignment is caused largely by a decline in support for both parties. It also seems significant that recent elections have been marked by a declining turnout rate. Both features distinguish the current transformation from more typical party changes in the United States. They also establish some affinities between the contemporary realignment and the development of the "system of '96."

Turnout declined after 1900 and turnout has declined almost without interruption since 1960. Some of this recent decline in the voting rate results from the growing independence of the electorate—their psychological demobilization from the party system—and some of it reflects behavioral changes among identifiers. In significant ways these recent changes parallel the turnout decline, roll-off, and split-ticket voting that characterized the "system of '96."

The comparison might overstretch the data, however. Party identification, not the vote, has been used to study the party coalitions here. While it is entirely possible that the changes of the last 15 years parallel those that spawned the "system of '96," it is impossible to be certain that we have witnessed the same phenomenon.

A very reasonable conclusion about this analysis is that, by using party identification to analyze coalition changes, this research has dealt with a leading indicator of critical realignments. All previous realignments could have been preceded by a similar biased contraction of the electorate. The sociological metamorphosis of the parties in the 1960s, therefore, may be a "pre-shock" and a harbinger of a critical realignment that is yet to come.[1]

Not all observers are persuaded that these data are as pregnant with meaning for the party system as the preceding comments imply. These skeptics see a persistence of partisanship in the intransitivity that characterizes the relationship between party identification and the vote, and they see coalitions that are more stable than the party identification measure indicates.

But the covert partisanship of the biased Independents can easily be overemphasized. In the first place, the apparent intransitivity in the index of party identification is specific to a limited number of variables. The "biased" Independents appear rather partisan only in their presidential choices. In other contests Independents are much less likely to support the candidate of the party toward which they lean than are the weak identifiers. They are also likely to evaluate candidates less positively than the weak identifiers. So although the leaning Independents share some of the characteristics of their more overtly partisan brethren, they do not, as some observers assume, display a stronger partisanship than the weak identifiers.[2]

The coalition changes have also been questioned with these data on "closet" Independents. Andrew Greeley has demonstrated that there are at least two kinds of Independents.[3] One is characterized by a "true" disregard for partisanship which can be seen in election-to-election variation in the vote choice. The second kind of Independent is marked by a functional attachment to the party of his social group. That is, if one compares Independents in terms of their social group, it is clear that those from social groups with Democratic leanings, for example, Catholics and Jews, are much more Democratic in their vote and liberal in their issue opinions than Independents from Republican social groups (Northern WASPs, for example). But these data are not persuasive evidence of the persistence of the old coalitions, because the Independents display a voting bias that is sensitive to the way the groups of which they are members have changed their partisanship.

For example, if white Southern Independents disguised a preference for the Democrats, their behavior and attitudes should display it. In fact, Southern Independents have some strongly Republican proclivities. Figure 10.1, which contrasts the predicted and observed Democratic vote of the groups in 1976, indicates this. The predicted Carter vote in figure 10.1 is obtained by weighting the party identification of the group by the *average* choices of all Democrats, Independents, and Republicans who voted in the 1976 election.[4] This technique offers a precise party-based prediction of the behavior of any population segment because it asks whether any group voted as did others with their particular identification.

For example, 76 percent of all leaning Democrats voted for Carter. If the leaning Democratic category accurately captured the

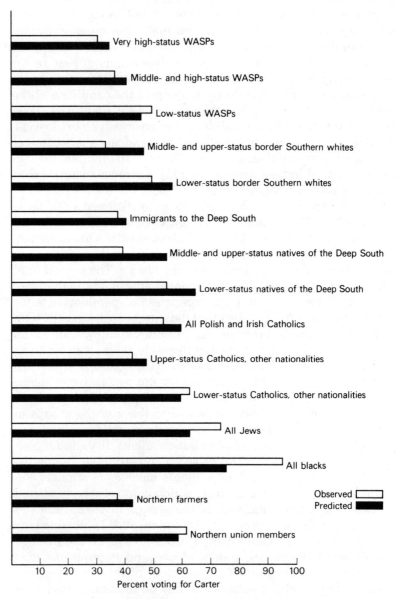

Fig. 10.1   Comparison of the observed and predicted vote for Carter by the coalition groups

behavior of all leaning Democrats, we would expect them all to vote 76 percent for Carter irrespective of whether the individual is black, Jewish, or Southern white. However, dramatic differences among such leaners indicate the pull of other variables. One of these other variables is the secular pull of partisan changes within the various coalition groups. As figure 10.1 indicates, the secular pull is visible.

The swing of the election mispredicts the behavior of the groups in interesting ways. Southerners voted almost 10 percentage points more for Ford than predicted, and Jews and blacks voted from 11 to 20 points more for Carter than expected. The direction of this misprediction follows the change in their party bias and in the size of the groups in the party coalitions. Independent Democrats among blacks and Southern whites are not the same kind of partisans and to assume that all these Independents can be relied upon to vote for Democratic candidates would be a mistake. Similar data for 1972 follow almost exactly the pattern of the data in figure 10.1.

In the short run the voting behavior of this peripheral electorate is more difficult to predict than the behavior of one more committed to the parties. With a larger fraction of the electorate expressing no attachment to the parties, not only is it difficult to predict how the electorate will vote but it is even difficult to know if they will vote. Partisans are concerned that their candidate win the election; nonpartisans care less who wins and they are less inclined to go to the trouble of voting. In the long run the consequence of the growth of Independents is hard to assess, and one very reasonable scenario is that it presages the emergence of a critical realignment electorate, which may be available to either of the parties in the future.

The Available Electorate

Some indication of the "availability" of the coalition groups is found in the proportion of each group who are unable to identify the party which holds a preferred position on the most important problem facing the country (according to the respondent), and the proportion who cannot identify either party as one which is best for people like themselves.[5] In 1974 the proportion of each of the coalition groups which could not find a champion for their most important problem was quite large (about 50 percent). In light of how their party bias has changed, it is interesting that this proportion was particularly large for upper-status Catholics (53 percent), Southerners (51 percent), and Northern Protestants (over 60 percent). Perhaps as important is the inability of the members of these coalition groups to identify one of the parties as "best for people like themselves" (over 40 percent). Given that the groups display a party bias exactly because they were able to make a summary assessment about the party that was "best for people like themselves," it seems important that only lower-status Catholics, blacks, and Jews are able to make that assessment in any numbers today. Virtually every other group is as likely not to see a choice in the parties as they are to find a choice.

The New Agenda of a Reformulated Coalition

What then becomes of a party system based on social group cleavages when the social groups do not find a rationale for their partisanship in the prevailing party agenda? The most available model would predict continued erosion of the party system among elite and mass. Candidates will be able to secure election without too much regard to the party symbol; as the symbol becomes less salient to voters, control of the party organization will be devalued. Over time all of these changes influence each other. The result would appear to be a party system with the qualities of a hibernating mammal; not quite dead, not even moribund, but not very lively either, neither exerting much influence on its immediate environment, nor being very affected by it.

This prospective insignificance will not (necessarily) undo the coalition changes in the last two decades. In fact the lack of vitality in the party system is important for the limit it places on the amount of conflict that normally attends a realignment. But that does not mean that this realignment is not a significant transformation in the party system. A realignment draws its significance from the likelihood that it is a symptom of a reformation of a part of the public-policy agenda. Groups have moved about because the policy preferences they have used to make sense of their party commitment have been disturbed. It is from this reformulated axis of cleavage between the parties that the realignment draws it importance.

A Sixth Party System?

The New Deal party system has been refurbished. With its new ideological rationalization it can probably persist for some time. But it is a weak system. This does not mean that one or both of the parties will cease to exist. It does imply an exhaustion of the force behind the realignment we have witnessed. Additional change is likely to be a secular process, a further realization of the changes put in motion during the 1960s. What is needed for a dramatic rebuilding of the parties is an agenda which will galvanize voters and office-seekers. It seems very unlikely that any of the issues of recent years have such potential.

But what issues do? As chapter 8 indicated, the issue portion of our model of realignment permits everything from a major transformation in the social structure to a specific and relatively "small" issue to disturb party coalitions. The key property of a realigning issue is that it can inject significant policy disagreement into the party, where "significant" is understood to refer to an issue about which otherwise allied groups have strongly felt and divergent opinions. It is easy to see race issues as embodying this property, and it is possible to identify other contemporary disputes as threatening the existing coalitions. But it is substantially more taxing to identify emerging or latent conflicts which might serve to build the parties.

To identify these issues we must be prescient enough to identify the social changes which might create a new political agenda by virtue of their impact on population segments with a specific stake in existing social and economic relationships. Our search for such critical realignment issues has been strikingly parochial. Permutations of existing quarrrels have constituted the outer limit of what most analysts have offered as the dominant cleavage of the next party system. But it seems unlikely that these issues—race, the "social issue," and the like—will ever draw enough attention to restructure the party system. The opposing sides on these matters are much too unbalanced numerically to allow party elites to seriously consider building an electoral coalition with them in the United States. Their potential seems to be disruptive, as this and other analyses have indicated.[6]

So what might be the forging issues for a new party system? There is no answer in this analysis beyond the injunction to look for issues that create communities of fate within the population, for they are the items which produce political conflict in the first instance and collective and coordinated political activity (parties) in the second. Disputes between those with a stake in a growing public sector and those who seem to bear the cost of it might provide a new alignment agenda. Alternatively we might look to the growing penetration of the national economy by the international economy as a source of critical disputes.[7] More a cliché than a fact until recently, domestic economies everywhere have become heavily influenced by economic activity that virtually lacks any national boundaries. Governments are hard pressed to regulate this activity as it becomes a larger portion of national economic activity. Moreover, since some sectors of the economy compete in international trade while others do much less well and still others are incapacitated by it, it creates political groups as the affected segments attempt to use the political system to protect their advantages and shore up their weaknesses. To be sure, neither of these particular questions seems capable of building major political oppositions at the moment. However, there are certainly visible instances of these conflicts. The diffuse dislike and distrust of government that animates Proposition 13s, balanced-budget amendments to the Constitution, negative votes on taxing proposals, and the low estate of public officials is some evidence of the reality (albeit possibly transient) of the first questions. The rumble attending multinational corporations, uncompetitive domestic industries like steel and textiles, and more robust sectors like agriculture might also be the harbinger of intense, widespread conflict capable of rebuilding the parties.

Unfortunately there is no way of determining if the uncommitted electorate can be mobilized by group conflicts over these or any other issues. It is possible, as some have argued, that we are entering the age of mass politics without parties. Certainly, it is true that the parties no longer have the virtual monopoly on the electorate they once enjoyed. Nevertheless, the nature of modern parties is that they are expressions of cleavages within mass publics. To the extent that styles of life, perspectives, and the costs and benefits of social activity are differently distributed among social classes, ethnic groups, or regions, it is hard to believe that a sense of collective threat will not encourage the formation of political coalitions. It is equally hard to believe that these coalitions will not receive some organizational expression as parties. The missing element in the contemporary electorate is a public agenda sufficiently compelling to overcome popular indifference to the parties.

Appendixes

Appendix A

Deriving the Coalition Groups

There were several criteria for deciding when a characteristic defined a group. The most important was the extent to which the creation of a new group improved the prediction of party identification. There would be little point in creating a classification with little discriminatory power, no matter how intrinsically interesting it seemed.

By itself, however, this was not a sufficient criterion for the creation of the group. Because a large number of cases were used in this analysis, it was easy to produce a reduction in statistical error that, by a conventional test, would be regarded as significant. There were, for example, over 3,000 cases grouped into the English Protestant category. With so many observations, it is difficult to imagine a subclassification of this group by any of the other variables which would not, by a conventional test of statistical significance, reduce the variance. Therefore, in addition to the criterion of improved prediction in the conventional statistical sense, a group was not created unless it was possible to demonstrate a difference between the party identification of the potential group and the party identification of the population from which the group was being drawn.

The second test required that before a group could be considered as a new group it was necessary that the absolute deviation of the mean party identification of the potential group be greater than the average absolute deviation of the means of every other potential group in the table. Consider the following example: the criterion population here is composed of respondents who are immigrant Southerners, that is, residents of the South who report being raised in some other part of the country. The issue is whether their social status is a useful predictor of their party preference. The following table presents the percentage point difference between the proportion considering themselves Democrats and the proportion considering themselves Republicans. The party bias differs enough by social status that a conventional analysis of variance indicates a statistically significant reduction in the error sum of squares. By this conventional test, status becomes a variable by which immigrant Southerners might be further distinguished. By the test of differences in the means, there are two groups which depart from the grand mean by more than the average .07 points. The fourth and fifth groups depart .20 and .13 points, respectively, from the grand mean. By the first and second tests, therefore, these two status groups are a potential regrouping of immigrant Southerners. Such a test could be done on a matrix of cells of virtually any size.

The immigrant Southerner example provides an illustration of several other tests of the "suitability" of a group. A third test required that the group be of a minimum size. If immigrant Southerners were to constitute a group whose change in party identification over time would be analyzed, it was important to keep the size of a potential group above some minimum number for each year. The minimum at which confidence in the results of an analysis could not be maintained is difficult to decide. In samples of the size and type used for this analysis, many kinds of subgroups do not produce reliable figures. Finally, 40 was decided upon as the minimum number necessary for the establishment of a group. Ultimately, this criterion was arbitrary. There is no reason to believe that group estimates based upon 35 or 40 cases are reliable, while those using 25 are not. Yet prudence and prior experience indicate that, except for certain types of samples, there is a good chance that estimates using 40 cases would be reasonably stable. The measurement fluctuation of groups based on 40 respondents did not seem any larger than the groups based on larger numbers of cases. Because the figures for these smaller groups did not seem particularly variable, groups based upon as few as 40 interviews in a particular year were created.

This minimum size rule was not followed in two instances. The first exception was in the case of the border Southern whites who were divided by social status in spite of the fact that the number of cases was below the minimum in the early samples. The reasons

Table A.1   Socioeconomic Status Differences among Immigrants to the South

	Mean Party Bias	Number of Cases
Very high status	−.02	224
High status	.01	189
Middle status	.04	159
Low status	.20	138
Very low status	.13	139
Farmers	.04	15

for creating this interesting group (see chaps. 5 and 6) superceded the problem of small numbers in the early years. The second instance of a group with too few cases is the category of immigrant Southerners. Immigrant Southerners were found to be responsible for some dilution of the party and attitude characteristics of white Southerners and this required that they be removed from the categories of upper- and lower-status white Southerners. Since immigrant Southerners did not provide a group with which the analysis was specifically concerned, the fact that there are so few of them in the early samples does not present a problem.

The fourth criterion for the definition of the group required that ordered variables be monotonically combined. This means that a characteristic which scales an order—more or less education, higher or lower socioeconomic status, etc.—could not be combined out of their order. The highest and lowest categories of ordered variables, for example, could not be combined against the middle categories of the measurement. In the Southern immigrant example, assuming that the number of cases in the categories had been larger, the groups could not have been defined because it would have required combining the lowest category of the measure of socioeconomic status (farmers) with higher categories and contrasting them with the middle status immigrants to the South.

It may be true that one can occasionally justify a combination or reduction of a measure which violates the order of the variable involved, but the general presumption against such a procedure seems justifiable. The social meaning of groups defined without the rule of monotonicity would be unclear and it would certainly introduce the possibility of some startling combinations. Ultimately such a rule turned out to be, if not unnecessary, at least without substantive significance since there were no instances where it had to be invoked.

The final criterion was dictated by the longitudinal design of the study. The full data set is ten surveys carried out over a period of twenty years. It was not practical to follow the procedure described above for each of the surveys. It was possible to pool the surveys because there was no reason to believe that there was not a great deal of similarity from survey to survey in the groups that would be found. Indeed, if there was not some stability in the groups, the entire notion of stable coalitions of voters associated with one or the other of the parties would be useless. Pooling the interviews from all of the years reduced the effort necessary to identify the groups at a manageable level. Yet it also had the effect of masking changes in the partisanship of some groups, at least it might have had this effect. A given set of characteristics might.

not, for example, distinguish party identification in the early fifties, but it might locate some very substantial differences in party identification in the late sixties and early seventies. Conversely, large differences in the early fifties might disappear by the seventies. This pattern of change over time would be very important, but unless it were of an unusually large magnitude, there is a chance that such a difference would not show up in a pooled data analysis. Native white Southerners, for instance, when examined by pooling the data for all years, do not show party preference differences by any other characteristics. If, however, they are examined a year at a time, it becomes clear that although there are no social-status differences separating native white Southerners in the early fifties, there is a markedly higher Republican bias among the better-off members of this group by the late sixties and early seventies. On the face of it, this would appear to be an interesting phenomenon since it indicates a differential rate of change. It would be important, therefore, to make the status distinction. With this consideration in mind, all of the clustering of social characteristics was done by pooling the data. But if there was any suggestion in (or apart from) the data that a further distinction of a grouping was indicated, the group was examined over time by the characteristic which was thought to provide a further difference in party identification.

The following marginals describe the variables which were used to identify the coalition groups. The data reported in table 5.1 of chapter 5 use the categories appearing below. The unweighted number of cases is 16,786. For discussion of educational and occupational status, see appendix B.

Table A.2   Initial Ethnoreligious Categorization

Anglo-Saxon Protestants	5%
Scandinavian Protestants	3
German Protestants	11
Other Protestants	45
Irish Catholics	3
German Catholics	3
Polish	2
Other Slavs	2
Italians	3
Other Catholics	8
Jews	3
Blacks	9
Spanish	1
All others	3

Table A.3   Regional Categorization

Eastern states	
New England	6%
Middle Atlantic	18
Central	30
Western states	
Pacific	12
Mountain	3
Border South	8
Southern states	24

Table A.4   Size and Place of Residence

Central city	12%
Central city suburb	15
Large city (above 50,000)	18
Small city and rural	55

Table A.5   Educational Attainment

Less than high school	44%
High school	32
Post high school	24

Table A.6   Occupation of the Head of Household

Professional, managerial, and higher-status white-collar occupations	29%
Lower-status white-collar occupations, e.g., clerical, sales, etc.	13
All blue-collar occupations	51
Farmers	8

Table A.7   Index of Educational and Occupational Status

Very high status	15%
High status	13
Middle status	15
Low status	20
Very low status	30
Farmers	8

Appendix B

Measuring Socioeconomic Status

There are several ways to index the social status of a household. The data reported in chapter 5 use two different, but not independent, methods. Neither possesses any particular advantage over alternative indices of social status which use more, fewer, or, perhaps, even different measures, except the ease with which they can be explained and interpreted.

The first index is an arithmetic combination of standardized measures of the respondent's education (coded as years of formal schooling), the income of the household (coded as dollars), and the occupation of the head of the household (recorded as a prestige ranking according to the Census SES scores). The standardized measures were summed and standardized a second time. The report values, therefore, are for a multiple-item index with a mean of zero and a standard deviation of one. This version of the social-status index is used for three different data presentations. It is used in table 5.7; it is used to describe the mean social status of the final groups derived in chapter 5; it is also used in the following table, which reports the algorithm used to create the index of social status which defined the groups.

The second index used only the education of the respondent and the occupation of the head of the household. The index ranges from those who have professional or managerial occupations and some post high school education (the "very high status") to those without a high school degree who have blue-collar occupations (the "very low status"). Farmers are separated into a category without regard to education. The roman numerals identify the way the cells were combined.

		Occupational Classes			
	Professional, managerial, higher white collar	Clerical, sales, lower white collar	All blue collar	Farmers	Education Distribution
Less than complete high school	III[a] .74%[b] 5.4%[c]	IV -.36 3.5%	V -1.92 29.8%	VI -3.15 4.8%	43.6%
Complete high school	II 2.29 8.8%	III 1.07 5.4%	IV -.12 16.4%	VI -1.06 1.8%	32.3%
At least some college	I 3.57 14.7%	II 2.09 4.0%	III .59 4.5%	VI -.21 .1%	24.1%
Occupational distributions	28.9%	12.9%	50.7%	7.5%	100%

[a]Description of the Status classifications:

   I   Very high status
   II High status
   III Middle status
   IV Low status
   V Very low status
   VI Farmers

[b]This is the mean score of those in the cell on the index of socioeconomic status described above.

[c]This is the proportion of the total population in the cell.

Appendix C

The Attitude Measures

The attitude measures used for the analysis in chapter 9 are based on multiple questions. The exact number of questions used in any one year varied considerably. Table C.1 lists the questions that were used by their variable reference number in the codebooks published by the Inter-University Consortium for Political and Social Research.

Table C.1	SRC/CPS Codebook Numbers for the Issue and Connectedness Measures			
Election year	Attitudes		Connectedness	
	Welfare	Race	Welfare	Race
1952	45	47	56	
1956	32, 38, 53, 59	44, 47	34, 40, 55, 61	46, 47
1958	21, 23, 27	31, 35	22, 24, 28	32, 38
1960	52, 54, 58, 66	62, 70	53, 55, 59, 68	63, 68
1964	66, 71, 74, 78, 344	97, 100, 105, 408	68, 77, 80	99, 103, 410
1966	21	25, 43	24	29
1968	60, 62, 64, 66, 456	73, 75, 78, 81, 83, 84, 88	61, 63, 65, 67	74, 77, 79
1970	41	77, 106	60, 108	94
1972[a]	172:613, 208	103, 104, 202, 629	176:617, 194:602	189:595, 218
1976	3241, 3225, 3271	3217, 3257, 3264	NOT USED	

[a]Variable numbers separated by a colon indicate questions that were split across the pre- and post-election samples, with half of the sample asked the question in the pre-election wave and half the sample asked the question in the post-election wave.

The variables presented in the preceding table have been summarized into four indices, attitude indices for economic welfare and racial attitudes, and two connectedness measures, one for the economic welfare attitude and another for the racial attitude. The indices are constructed to range from −1 to +1 for any individual. A respondent who consistently gave conservative answers to all of the issue questions or who consistently nominated the Republican party as closer to his position on the issues would have a score of −1; while another who gave consistently liberal answers or consistently nominated the Democratic party as closer to his position on the issues would have a score of +1. The potential range of the score for any group is from −1 to +1. Of course, the observed range of scores is always less than this.

The number is a percentage difference. What it indicates depends on whether the index is measuring attitudes or connectedness. When it is measuring issue preferences (attitudes), the number indicates the excess, in percentage point terms, of liberal over conservative answers, or conservative over liberal answers. When the number is negative, the conservative answers are more frequent than the liberal answers within the group, and when the number is positive, the liberal answers are more frequent than the conservative ones. The connectedness measures are scored similarly. A negative value indicates that the group perceives the Republican party closer to them on most of the issues and a positive one indicates that the group perceives the Democratic party to be a better representative of its issues preferences than the Republican party.

The population average for these measures varies from year to year. Since these yearly averages are more likely to reflect methodological than substantive variables, the mean score for each year has been removed. As a consequence, the population score for each year is zero. The score for each group measures the relative liberalness/conservativeness and Democratic/Republican connectedness for the group. The characterization of a group as liberal or conservative, or pro- or anti-Democratic in their issue preferences, therefore, is always relative to the population.

The analysis in chapter 9 is based on a comparison of the various scores of the groups between the 1950s and the late 1960s and early 1970s. The 1950s values are the averages of the scores for the years 1952 through 1960. The scores for the later period are the average values for the variables for the years 1968, 1970, and 1972. Figure 9.12 and table 9.1 are the only places which use 1976 data.

Notes

Chapter 1

1. William H. Flanigan and Nancy H. Zingale, "The Measurement of Electoral Change," *Political Methodology* 1 (Summer 1974): 49–82.

2. One can make a good case that the parties and political party elites are often slow to realize that the issues which still excite the leadership and activists have largely been resolved for the general public. But it does seem that after a point parties stop manipulating questions that no longer concern the public.

3. It should also be pointed out that issues are not constantly in a state of flux. Over a short period of time "long-term" issues may be fixed, and on occasion over a rather long period of time issues can be frozen for the population or some segment of it. In such an instance socialization alone can be relied upon to keep the descendants of partisans committed and there should be markedly less new issue content to the party divisions.

How representativeness occurs is not very clear. Research which sheds some light on the process may be found in Lewis A. Dexter, "What Do Congressmen Hear: The Mail," *Public Opinion Quarterly* 20 (Spring 1956): 16–27; Philip E. Converse, Aage Clausen, and Warren E. Miller, "Electoral Myth and Reality: The 1964 Election," *American Political Science Review* 59 (June 1965): 321–36; Donald E. Stokes and Warren E. Miller, "Party Government and the Saliency of Congress," *Public Opinion Quarterly* 26 (Winter 1962): Congress," *American Political Science Review* 57 (March 1963): 45–56; and Sidney Verba and Norman Nie, *Participation in America: Political Democracy and Social Equality* (New York: Harper & Row, 1972).

4. John R. Petrocik, "Changing Party Coalitions and the Attitudinal Basis of Realignment: 1952–1972" (Ph.D. diss., University of Chicago, 1976), pp. 2–3.

5. Some sense of this is in Richard M. Scammon and Ben Wattenberg, *The Real Majority* (New York: Coward, McCann, & Geoghegan, 1970); Samuel Lubell, *The Hidden Crisis in American Politics* (New York: W. W. Norton, 1970).

6. See Norman H. Nie, Sidney Verba, and John R. Petrocik, *The Changing American Voter* (Cambridge: Harvard University Press, 1976).

7. Walter Dean Burnham, "American Politics in the 1970s: Beyond Party," in *The Future of Political Parties* (Beverly Hills, Calif.: Sage Publications, 1976); Everett C. Ladd and Charles D. Hadley, *Transformations of the American Party System* (New York: W. W. Norton, 1975); Warren Miller and Teresa Levitan, *Leadership and Change: The New Politics and the American Electorate* (Cambridge: Winthrop Publishers, 1976); John Sundquist, *Dynamics of the Party System* (Washington, D.C.: Brookings Institution, 1973); Richard Rubin, *Party Dynamics* (New York: Oxford University Press, 1976); Nie, Verba, and Petrocik, *The Changing American Voter*.

8. "A Theory of Critical Elections," *Journal of Politics* 17 (February 1955): 13–18. Sundquist captures this theme well in the first chapter of *Dynamics of the Party System*.

9. It would be easier to list those who have not expected a shift in party

majorities. Duncan MacRae, Jr., and James A. Meldrum, in "Critical Elections in Illinois: 1888–1958," *American Political Science Review* 54 (September 1960): 669–83, emphasize shifting majorities less than most. Nie, Verba, and Petrocik, in *The Changing American Voter,* also do not use the "changing majority" definition. Historians who have interpreted American party history as a conflict of cultural groups have also emphasized the "party majority" aspect of realignment least. A noteworthy example of this is Paul M. Kleppner, *The Cross of Culture: A Social Analysis of Midwestern Politics, 1880–1900* (New York: Free Press, 1970).

10. The normal vote equation for the period 1964–72 is virtually identical to the equation Converse presents in "The Concept of the Normal Vote," in *Elections and the Political Order,* ed. Angus Campbell et al. (New York: John Wiley & Sons, 1966). According to Thad Brown, the values in the equation are different only after the third decimal place. Whether this stability is reassuring or not depends upon whether one believes that the equation should change in response to the increase in Independents and defection rates. The normal vote is sensitive principally to the relative proportion of Democrats to Republicans. If that proportion remains stable, and if the relative *differences* in the voting behavior of Republicans and Democrats are stable, there is no reason for the normal vote to change. Since the electorate has been about 19 points more Democratic than Republican for two decades and since the relative propensity of Democrats and Republicans to turn out to defect has not changed, it is reasonable to believe that the stability of the normal vote is not an error, at least not within the assumptions of the normal-vote concept.

11. The part that gerrymanders have played in the decrease in marginal districts is subject to debate. Incomplete research and discussions with politicians who should know have led me to believe that a considerable amount of gerrymandering took place between 1964 and 1967, but especially after 1964, when the Johnson landslide produced Democratic majorities in several state legislatures, just in time to enact Supreme Court mandated reapportionments. Edward Tufte has published two articles and a comment in which he argues the gerrymander explanation; see "The Relationship between Seats and Votes in Two-Party Systems," *American Political Science Review* 67 (June 1973): 540–54; "Communications," *American Political Science Review* 68 (March 1974): 212; "Determinants of the Outcome of Midterm Congressional Elections," *American Political Science Review* 69 (September 1975): 812–26. Other explanations assume changes in the behavior of either voters or congressmen; see Robert S. Erikson, "The Advantage of Incumbency in Congressional Elections," *Polity* 3 (Spring 1971): 395–405; Robert S. Erikson, "Malapportionment, Gerrymandering, and Party Fortunes in Congressional Elections," *American Political Science Review* 66 (December 1972): 1234–45; Warren Lee Kostroski, "Party and Incumbency in Postwar Senate Elections," *American Political Science Review* 67 (December 1973): 1213–34; David Mayhew, "Congressional Elections: The Case of the Vanishing Marginals," *Polity* 6 (Spring 1974): 295–317; John A. Ferejohn, "On the Decline of Competition in Congressional Elections," *American Political Science Review* 71 (March 1977): 166–76. The articles by Mayhew and Ferejohn offer the most persuasive data against the gerrymander explanation. Part of Ferejohn's research tested Mayhew's thesis that incumbency is greater after 1966 because congressmen have increased their visibility among their constituents. He was unable to find data to support the greater visibility thesis. A companion article to Ferejohn's, Morris P. Fiorina, "The Case of the Vanishing Marginals: The Bureaucracy Did It," *American Political Science Review* 71 (March 1977): 177–81, offers two case studies of the relationship between congressmen and their constituents which illustrate how Mayhew's effects do insulate congressmen from electoral tides. For data on the

advantage of incumbency in the South, see Richard G. Hutchinson, III, "The Central Effect of Incumbency and Two-party Politics: Elections to the House of Representatives from the South, 1952–1974," *American Political Science Review* 69 (December 1975): 1399–1401.

12. A list such as this can be found in almost any book or article dealing with the topic of realignment. The original source is, of course, V. O. Key, "A Theory of Critical Elections," *Journal of Politics* 17 (February 1955): 3–18. *American Politics* (New York: W. W. Norton, 1970), chap. 1; John Sundquist, *Dynamics of American Politics.*

13. This has been fully documented in Nie, Verba, and Petrocik, *The Changing American Voter*, chap. 4, 6, and 12 especially. Turner and Schneier report that insurgency has increased since 1960. It is especially noticeable among coastal Republicans and Southern Democrats, two prominent groups in the current realignment. The most insurgent within these groups are, interestingly, those whose districts tend to support the opposition party in presidential elections. On this see Julius Turner and Edward V. Schenier, Jr., *Party and Constituency: Pressures on Congress*, rev. ed. (Baltimore: Johns Hopkins Press, 1970).

14. See Herbert McCloskey, P. J. Hoffman, and R. O'Hara, "Issue Conflict and Consequence among Party Leaders and Followers," *American Political Science Review* 54 (June 1960): 406–29; Verba and Nie, *Participation in America*, chap. 16; David Nexon, "Asymmetry in the Political System: Occasional Activists in the Republican and Democratic Parties, 1956–1964," *American Political Science Review* 65 (September 1971): 716–30; Everett C. Ladd, *Patterns of Differentiation since the New Deal* (Beverly Hills, Calif.: Sage Publications, 1973).

15. Anne N. Costain, "An Analysis of Voting in American National Nominating Conventions, 1940–1976," *American Politics Quarterly* 6 (January 1978): 375–94.

16. His first work using this premise is "The Changing Shape of the American Political Universe," *American Political Science Review* 59 (March 1965): 7–28. Rates of split-ticket voting, turnout, fall-off from presidential elections, and roll-off from the top of the ticket all changed sharply after 1900. These changes as well as the solidification of the Republican majority amounted to a major change in the "shape of the political universe" and they indicated the arrival of the fourth party system. Burnham's analysis of the 1964 election also points to novelties in the *pattern* of voting behavior in that year, and his subsequent analyses of congressional elections draws a portrait of new patterns of party competition.

Burnham's interpretation of the source of these differences has been challenged by several people, notably Jerrold Rusk and Philip Converse. Their formulation of the meaning of these changes is persuasive. But since Burnham's thesis has not been so diminished that it is completely unconvincing, it is worth the effort to search for the major changes in political behavior that a party realignment should precipitate or respond to. See Jerrold G. Rusk, "The Effect of the Australian Ballot Reform on Split-Ticket Voting, 1876–1908," *American Political Science Review* 64 (December 1970): 1120–38; Philip E. Converse, "Change in the American Electorate," in *The Human Meaning of Social Change*, ed. Angus Campbell and Philip E. Converse (New York: Russell Sage Foundation, 1972), pp. 263–337. Burnham responds in *Critical Elections and the Mainsprings of American Politics*, chap. 4; "The Theory and Voting Research: Some Reflections on Converse's 'Change in the American Electorate,'" *American Political Science Review* 68 (September 1974): 1002–1010. Converse and Rusk respond in "Comment on Burnham's 'Theory and Voting Research,'" and "Comment: The American Electoral Universe: Speculation and Evidence," both in *American Political Science Review* 68 (September 1974): 1024–49.

17. The term "insularity" is from W. D. Burnham, "Insulation and Responsive-

ness in Congressional Elections," *Political Science Quarterly* 90 (Fall 1970): 411–36. See also note 11 above on the security of incumbency.

18. Nie, Verba, and Petrocik, *The Changing American Voter*, chap. 4.

19. Richard Funston, "The Supreme Court and Critical Elections," *American Political Science Review* 69 (September 1975): 795–811; Benjamin Ginsberg, "Critical Elections and the Substance of Party Conflict: 1844–1968," *Midwestern Journal of Political Science* 16 (November 1972): 603–25; Benjamin Ginsberg, "Elections and Public Policy," *American Political Science Review* 70 (March 1976): 41–49; Thomas P. Jahnige, "Critical Elections and Social Change: Towards a Dynamic Explanation of Party Competition in the United States," *Polity* 3 (Summer 1971): 465–500; Everett C. Ladd, *American Political Parties* (New York: W. W. Norton 1970); Everett C. Ladd and Charles D. Hadley, *Transformations of the American Party System* (New York: W. W. Norton, 1975). The "areas of agreement" and "axes of cleavage" phrases are from Jahnige. A recent study which examines agenda transformation from the perspective of roll call votes in Congress is Barbara Deckard Sinclair, "Party Realignment and the Transformation of the Political Agenda: The House of Representatives," *American Political Science Review* 71 (September 1977): 940–53. Turner and Schneier also discuss realignments and their effect on the congressional parties in examining party cohesion scores around the period of major electoral realignments (see *Party and Constituency*, p. 216). Apparently realignments yield more cohesive parties, at least in the short term.

20. Herbert F. Weisberg and Jerrold G. Rusk, "Dimensions of Candidate Evaluation," *American Political Science Review* 64 (December 1970): 1167–85; Jerrold G. Rusk and Herbert F. Weisberg, "Perceptions of Political Candidates: Implications for Electoral Change," *Midwest Journal of Political Science* 16 (August 1972): 388–410.

21. V. O. Key, "A Theory of Critical Elections," *Journal of Politics* 17:3–18.

22. The literature on the social basis of the parties is extensive. See Robert A. Kelly, *The Cultural Pattern in American Politics: The First Century* (New York: Alfred A Knopf, 1979); Samuel Lubell, *The Future of American Politics* (New York: Harper & Row, 1952); J. M. Allswang, *A House for All Peoples: Chicago's Ethnic Groups and Their Politics, 1890–1936* (Lexington: University Press of Kentucky, 1971); Ronald P. Formisano, *The Birth of Mass Political Parties: Michigan 1827–1961* (Princeton: Princeton University Press, 1971); Richard J. Jensen, *Winning the Midwest: Social and Political Conflict, 1888–96* (Chicago: University of Chicago Press, 1971); Paul Kleppner, *The Cross of Culture: A Social Analysis of Midwestern Politics, 1850–1900* (New York: Free Press, 1970); Raymond E. Wolfinger, "The Development and Persistence of Ethnic Voting," *American Political Science Review* 59 (December 1965): 896–908; Michael Parenti "Ethnic Politics and the Persistence of Ethnic Identification," *American Political Science Review* 61 (September 1967): 717–26; Raymond E. Wolfinger, "Some Consequences of Ethnic Politics," in *The Electoral Process*, ed. M. Kent Jennings and L. Harmon Zeigler (Englewood Cliffs: Prentice-Hall, 1966); Lawrence Fuchs, *The Political Behavior of American Jews* (Glencoe: Free Press, 1956); Nathan Glazer and Daniel P. Moynihan, *Beyond the Melting Pot* (Cambridge: MIT Press, 1963); Mark R. Levy and Michael S. Kramer, *The Ethnic Factor: How America's Minorities Decide Elections* (New York: Simon & Schuster, 1972); Eugene Burdick and Arthur J. Brodbeck, eds., *American Voting Behavior* (New York: Free Press, 1959), chap. 8, 15, 18; Angus Campbell et al., *The American Voter* (New York: John Wiley & Sons, 1960), Chaps. 12–17; Angus Campbell, Gerald Gurin, and Warren E. Miller, *The Voter Decides* (Evanston: Row-Peterson, 1954), chap. 5; Angus Campbell and Robert L. Kahn, *The People Elect a President*

(Ann Arbor: Institute for Social Research, 1952). The most eminent monograph dealing with the social and demographic correlates of party preference and the vote are Paul F. Lazarsfeld, Bernard Berelson, and Hazel Gaudet, *The People's Choice* (New York: Columbia University Press, 1948); and Bernard Berelson, Paul F. Lazarsfeld, and William N. McPhee, *Voting* (Chicago: University of Chicago Press, 1954). Good historical treatments of the social group characteristics of the American parties can be found in Wilfred Binkley, *American Political Parties: Their Natural History* (New York: Alfred A. Knopf, 1958); William Nesbit Chambers and Walter Dean Burnham, eds., *The American Party Systems: Stages of Development* (New York: Oxford University Press, 1967); David Burner, *The Politics of Provincialism: The Democratic Party in Transition, 1918–1932* (New York: Alfred A. Knopf, 1968).

23. See chap. 8 below and chap. 13 of Nie, Verba, and Petrocik, *The Changing American Voter.*

Chapter 2

1. James L. Sundquist, *Dynamics of the Party System: Alignment and Realignment of Political Parties in the United States* (Washington, D.C.: Brookings Institution, 1973).

2. Throughout this study the definition of party bias should be understood as the relative proportion of Democrats to Republicans. The party bias of a group does not depend solely upon the proportion of the group that is either Democrat or Republican. That a group has become 55 percent Democratic when it was 70 percent Democratic does not mark a change in the party bias of the group unless the proportion of Republicans in the group has changed by a different number of percentage points. For example, if the proportion of Republicans declined from 25 percent to 10 percent, there would be no change in the party bias of the group because the proportion of Democrats would still outnumber the proportion of Republicans by 45 points. If, however, there had been no change in the proportion of Republicans, then the party bias would have changed from 45 points Democrat (70 percent Democrat − 25 percent Republican = 45 points) to 30 points Democratic (55 percent Democrat − 25 percent Republican = 30 points). The change from 45 points to only 30 points Democratic constitutes a change in the party bias of the group. For the concept of "party bias," although not the definition used here, I am indebted to Sundquist, *Dynamics of the Party System.*

3. V. O. Key, "Secular Realignment and the Party System."

4. A good summary of this is in Sundquist, *Dynamics of the Party System,* chaps. 2 and 3. See also E. C. Ladd, *American Political Parties* (New York: W. W. Norton, 1971).

5. In *The Cross of Culture* (New York: Free Press, 1970), Kleppner provides a good account of this for the United States. Walter Dean Burnham's "The United States: The Politics of Heterogeneity," in Richard Rose, ed., *Electoral Behavior* (New York: Free Press, 1974), pp. 653–726, is also a good summary and bibliography for this theme.

6. See W. Phillips Shively, "A Reinterpretation of the New Deal Realignment," *Public Opinion Quarterly* 35 (Winter 1971/72): 621–24; Samuel Lubell, *The Future of American Politics* (Garden City, N.J.: Doubleday Anchor Books, 1955), chap. 3; and Daniel J. Elazar, "Megalopolis and the New Sectionalism," *Public Interest* 11 (September 1968): 67–85; Kleppner, *The Cross of Culture*; and David Burner, *The Politics of Provincialism: The Democratic Party in Transition, 1918–1932* (New York: Alfred A. Knopf, 1968).

7. The schemes used to study political parties are far too numerous to be chroni-

cled here. Textbooks usually begin by listing a few, and various literature reviews attempt some discussion of contending approaches. For the textbook approach, see Frank J. Sorauf, *Party Politics in America* (Boston: Little, Brown, 1972). The most comprehensive review of the literature, which also cites and reviews other reviews, is in Leon D. Epstein, "Political Parties," in *The Handbook of Political Science*, ed. Fred Greenstein and Nelson Polsby (Cambridge: Addison-Wesley, 1976), pp. 229–77.

8. Joseph A. Schlesinger, "Political Party Organization," in *The Handbook of Organization*, ed. James G. March (Chicago: Rand McNally, 1965), pp. 764–801; Sigmund Neuman, *Modern Political Parties* (Chicago: University of Chicago Press, 1956); Edward M. Sait, *American Parties and Elections*, rev. ed. (New York: D. Appleton-Century Co., 1939); E. E. Schattschneider, *Party Government* (New York: Holt, Rinehart, 1942); Leon D. Epstein, *Political Parties in Western Democracies* (New York: Praeger, 1967); Richard Rose, ed., *Electoral Behavior*, (New York: Free Press, 1974); Lee Benson, *The Concept of Jacksonian Democracy: New York as a Test Case* (Princeton: Princeton University Press, 1961); Richard Jensen, *Winning the Midwest* (Chicago: University of Chicago Press, 1970); Paul N. Kleppner, *The Cross of Culture* (New York: Free Press, 1970); Ronald Formisano, *The Birth of Mass Political Parties: Michigan, 1827–1861* (Princeton: Princeton University Press, 1971); "Toward a More Responsible Two-party System," Committee on Political Parties of the American Political Science Association (1950); James Q. Wilson, *The Amateur Democrat* (Chicago: University of Chicago Press, 1962); Herbert McCloskey, "Consensus and Ideology in American Politics," *American Political Science Review* 58 (June 1964): 361–82; see Ladd, *American Political Parties*; see also Everett C. Ladd and Charles D. Hadley, *Transformations of the American Party System* (New York: W. W. Norton, 1975) and *Political Parties and Political Issues: Patterns of Differentiation Since the New Deal* (Beverly Hills, Calif: Sage Publications, 1973).

9. Seymour M. Lipset and S. Rokkan, *Party Systems and Voter Alignments* (New York: Free Press, 1967).

10. *Electoral Behavior* (New York: Free Press, 1974).

11. Philip E. Converse, "Some Priority Variables in Comparative Research," in Rose, *Electoral Behavior*, p. 729.

12. Ibid.

13. Lipset and Rokkan, *Party Systems*, p. 5.

14. For a representative listing see note 23 above.

15. *Newsweek*, 12 October 1964, p. 35.

16. For several illustrations of this kind of ethnic antagonism see Len O'Connor, *Clout* (Chicago: Henry Regnery, 1974). See also Arend Lijphart, "Political Theories and the Explanation of Ethnic Conflict in the Western World: Falsified Predictions and Plausible Postdictions," in *Ethnic Conflict in the Western World*, ed. Milton J. Esman (Ithaca: Cornell University Press, 1977).

17. Wilfred Binkley, *American Political Parties: Their Natural History* (New York: Alfred A. Knopf, 1958); Samuel Hays, "Political Parties and the Community-Society Continuum," in *The American Party Systems: Stages of Political Development*, ed. William Nesbit Chambers and Walter Dean Burnham (New York: Oxford University Press, 1967); Hays, "The Social Analysis of American Political History, 1880–1920," *Political Science Quarterly* 80 (1965): 373–94; and Lee Benson, *The Concept of Jacksonian Democracy*.

18. James Wright, "The Ethno-cultural Model of Voting: A Behavorial and Historical Critique," *American Behavioral Scientist* 6 (May–June 1973): 653–74.

19. Kleppner, *The Cross of Culture*, p. 35. This theme is central to the analyses

presented by Formisano, *The Birth of Mass Political Parties*, and Jensen, *The Winning of the Midwest*.

20. Walter Dean Burnham's *Presidential Ballots: 1838–1892* (Baltimore: John Hopkins University Press, 1955) presents and analysis of this sociocultural cleavage in the first half of the book and the extent to which the Republican and Democratic parties represented the cultural and social biases of groups in the population is presented in a dynamic framework in Thomas P. Jahnige, "Critical Elections and Social Change: Towards a Dynamic Explanation of Party Competition in the United States," *Polity* 3 (Summer 1971): 465–500.

21. Samuel Lubell, *The Future of American Politics*. Two early examples of this approach are: Harold Gosnell and William Coleman, "Political Trends in Industrial America: Pennsylvania an Example," *Public Opinion Quarterly* 4 (September 1940): 473–86; and William F. Ogburn and Nell Snow Talbot, "A Measurement of the Factors in the Presidential Election of 1928," *Social Forces* 8 (December 1929): 175–83. Two early survey-based studies which viewed the parties through this kind of sociodemographic prism are Paul F. Lazarsfeld, Bernard Berelson, and Hazel Gaudet, *The People's Choice* (New York: Columbia University Press, 1948) and Bernard R. Berelson, Paul F. Lazarsfeld, and William N. McPhee, *Voting* (Chicago: University of Chicago Press, 1954).

22. Burnham, *Presidential Ballots: 1836–1892*.

23. In addition to Kleppner, see (for a recent study) Robert Axelrod, "Where the Votes Come from: An Analysis of Electoral Coalitions: 1952–1968," *American Political Science Review* 66 (March 1972): 11–21. Other notable works include Samuel Lubell, *The Future of American Politics*; J. M. Allswang, *A House for All Peoples: Chicago's Ethnic Groups and Their Politics, 1890–1936* (Lexington: University Press of Kentucky, 1971); Ronald P. Formisano, *The Birth of Mass Political Parties: Michigan 1827–1861* (Princeton: Princeton University Press, 1971); Richard J. Jensen, *Winning the Midwest: Social and Political Conflict, 1888–1896* (Chicago: University of Chicago Press, 1971); Paul Kleppner, *The Cross of Culture: A Social Analysis of Midwestern Politics, 1850–1900* (New York: Free Press, 1970); Raymond E. Wolfinger, "The Development and Persistence of Ethnic Voting," *American Political Science Review* 59 (December 1965): 896–908; Michael Parenti, "Ethnic Politics and the Persistence of Ethnic Identification," *American Political Science Review* 61 (September 1967): 717–26; Raymond E. Wolfinger, "Some Consequences of Ethnic Politics," in *The Electoral Process*, ed. M. Kent Jennings and L. Harmon Zeigler (Englewood Cliffs: Prentice-Hall, 1966); Lawrence Fuchs, *The Political Behavior of American Jews* (Glencoe: Free Press, 1956); Nathan Glazer and Daniel P. Moynihan, *Beyond the Melting Pot* (Cambridge: MIT Press, 1963); Mark R. Levy and Michael S. Kramer, *The Ethnic Factor: How America's Minorities Decide Elections* (New York: Simon & Schuster, 1972); Eugen Burdick and Arthur J. Brodbeck, eds., *American Voting Behavior* (New York: Free Press, 1959), chap. 8, 15, 18; Angus Campbell et al., *The American Voter* (New York: John Wiley & Sons, 1960), chaps. 12–17; Angus Campbell et al, *The Voter Decides* (Evanston: Row-Peterson 1954), chap. 5; Angus Campbell and Robert L. Kahn, *The People Elect a President* (Ann Arbor: Institute for Social Research, 1952). The most eminent monographs dealing with the social and demographic correlates of party preference and the vote are Paul F. Lazarsfeld, Bernard Berelson, and Hazel Gaudet, *The People's Choice* (New York: Columbia University Press, 1948); and Bernard Berelson, Paul F. Lazarsfeld, and William N. McPhee, *Voting* (Chicago: University of Chicago Press, 1954). Good historical treatments of the social-group characteristics of the American parties can be found in Wilfred Binkley, *American Political Parties: Their Natural History* (New York: Alfred A.

Knopf, 1958); William Nesbit Chambers and Walter Dean Burnham, eds., *The American Party Systems: Stages of Development* (New York: Oxford University Press, 1967). An exceptionally fine analysis of the formation of the New Deal coalitions in terms of the social groups that comprise the basis of Democratic support can be found in David Burner, *The Politics of Provincialism: The Democratic Party in Transition, 1918–1932* (New York: Alfred A. Knopf, 1968).

24. A useful and sophisticated analysis of the differences between simple electoral fluctuation and electoral realignment is in William M. Flanigan and Nancy H. Zingale, "The Measurement of Electoral Change," *Political Methodology* 1 (Summer 1974): 49–82.

25. W. D. Burnham, "The Changing Shape of the American Political Universe," *American Political Science Review* 59 (March 1965): 7–28.

26. Duncan MacRae, Jr., and James A. Meldrum, "Critical Elections in Illinois: 1881—1958," *American Political Science Review* 54 (September 1960): 669–83.

27. John L. Shover, "Was 1928 a Critical Election in California," *Pacific Northwest Quarterly* 58 (October 1967): 196–204.

28. Ibid., table 1 and fig. 1–4.

29. Gerald Pomper has popularized this technique in "Classification of Presidential Election," *Journal of Politics* 29 (August 1967): 535–66. MacRae and Meldrum were probably the first to suggest the technique, in "Critical Elections in Illinois."

30. The likely error of his substantive conclusions is made clearer in chap. 5.

31. See chap. 4 of this book and chap. 5 of Nie, Verba, and Petrocik *The Changing American Voter.*

32. This is possible because two factors affect the overall support enjoyed by a party in the electorate. The first factor is the relative size of the groups whose members consider themselves Democrats or Republicans. The second factor is the party bias of the groups. The party allegiance of a group or many groups may change (the party-bias factor) but if that change is cancelled out in the aggregate by perhaps smaller changes in the party bias of proportionally larger groups, the net change can result in no shift in the marginal support enjoyed by the parties at the polls. Yet the social-group profile of the parties may have changed considerably.

33. These symptoms of a realignment are cited in most studies of realignment but are found originally in Key, "Theory of Critical Elections," *Journal of Politics* 17 (February 1955): 3–18. It should be pointed out that these indicators are largely inferred or presumed and not easily demonstrated with data. Since most of the realignments that we are able to identify are historical, it is not possible to interview voters during these times to assess their level of interest in the election, and the like. The one indicator that does not depend upon personal interviews is the turnout rate, and there does not seem to be any reason to doubt that turnout increases during realignment periods.

34. Barbara Hinckley, C. Richard Hofstetter, and John H. Kessel, "Information and the Vote: A Comparative Election Study," *American Politics Quarterly* 2 (1974): 131–58.

35. Lazarsfeld, Berelson, and Gaudet, *The People's Choice,* indicate that the "normal vote" in 1940 was Republican in spite of the FDR successes (p. 23). This hope of the Republican party for 16 years was that the heavy Roosevelt vote was only a vote for the individual and not a vote for the Democratic party. They believed that defecting Republicans would return to the fold when FDR was no longer the Democratic candidate. In part they were correct, for large numbers of Republican defectors returned to the Republican column beginning with the election of 1940. Unfortunately for the Republican party, in the period a new Dem-

ocratic majority was constructed and all the returning defectors were insufficient to reestablish Republican dominance.

36. There is reason to believe that candidate personality is also a formidable factor at even the lowest levels of government. Candidates are frequently more easily recognized when their office is at a lower level and often touching the daily lives of voters in visible ways. The result of this greater visibility is that party may be a less important factor in the voter's calculations when he votes for many offices with narrow constituencies. The Stokes and Miller congressional study indicated how this works, and professional campaign organizations have built this factor up as the "candidate-recognition" variable; they have paid considerable attention to maximizing the proportion of the electorate able to recognize their candidate. See Donald E. Stokes and Warren Miller, "Party Government and the Saliency of Congress," in *Elections and Political Order*, ed. Angus Campbell et al. (New York: John Wiley & Sons, 1966).

37. Sidney Verba and Norman Nie, *Participation in America: Political Democracy and Social Equality* (New York: Harper & Row, 1972), chap. 15. The importance of this "mobilization of bias" for realignments is developed in chap. 4. For more on this see E. E. Schattschneider, *The Semi-Sovereign People* (New York: Holt, Rinehart, & Winston, 1960).

38. There are many studies of this matter, and they are not unanimous about the size and significance of the bias. One of the most recent studies, and methodologically a strong one, concludes that the bias exists. See David W. Moore and C. Richard Hofstetter, "The Representativeness of Primary Elections: Ohio, 1968," *Polity* 6 (Winter 1973): 197–222.

39. Stokes and Miller, "Party Government and the Saliency of Congress" in *Elections and the Political Order*, ed. Campbell et al., and Robert S. Erikson, "The Advantage of Incumbency in Congressional Elections," *Polity* 3 (Spring 1971): 395–405.

40. In a slightly different form this idea has been discussed as "presidential Republicanism." Several scholars, following Key, have discussed the phenomemon with regard to the South. In this instance, we are not discussing voting habits that have to do with discerning differences between a national and state party symbol, but with an incumbency effect that gives an advantage to candidates of the party which in days past enjoyed a majority that is now eroding. Something like this probably helped New England and Midwestern Republicans win House elections until recent years. As a recent paper shows, a similar advantage is benefiting Southern House Democrats. See Richard G. Hutchinson, "The Inertial Effect of Incumbency and Two-party Politics: Elections to the House of Representative from the South, 1952–1974," *American Political Science Review* 60 (December 1975): 1399–1401. Hutchinson shows that the decline in Democratic House seats in the South has not been as rapid as the decline in Democratic party identification among Southerners.

41. Paul N. Kleppner, *The Cross of Culture*.

Chapter 3

1. Burnham's contributions on this score are extensive and varied, but the gist of his arguments can be found in *Critical Elections and the Mainsprings of American Politics* (New York: W. W. Norton, 1976), and in "Revitalization and Decay: Looking toward the Third Century of American Electoral Politics," *Journal of Politics* 38 (August 1976): 146–72; see also Everett Carll Ladd, *American Political Parties* (New York: W. W. Norton, 1970); Thomas P. Jahnige, "Critical Elections and Social

Change: Towards a Dynamic Explanation of National Party Competition in the United States," *Polity* 3 (Summer 1971): 465–500; and David Butler and Donald Stokes, *Political Change in Britain* (New York: St. Martins Press, 1969), chaps. 3–6 and 11–14.

2. Philip E. Converse, *The Dynamics of Party Support* (Beverly Hills, Calif.: Sage Publications, 1975).

3. James L. Sundquist, *Dynamics of the Party System: Alignment and Realignment of Political Parties in the United States* (Washington, D.C.: Brookings Institution, 1973). This book summarizes better than any other the prevailing perspectives on electoral change.

4. See Sidney Verba and Norman Nie, *Participation in America* (New York: Harper & Row, 1972) and Lester Milbrath and M. L. Goel, *Political Participation* (Chicago: Rand McNally, 1977). For a full discussion and analysis of the relationship between involvement and shifting, see William N. McPhee and William A. Glaser, *Public Opinion and Congressional Elections* (New York: Free Press, 1962), chaps. 1, 6; Philip E. Converse, "The Concept of the Normal Vote" and "Information Flow and the Stability of Partisan Attitudes," in *Elections and the Political Order* ed. Angus Campbell et al. (New York: John Wiley & Sons, 1966); John R. Petrocik, "Voter Turnout and Electoral Oscillation," Paper presented at the Conference on Voter Turnout, San Diego, May 1979. As an aside, it is worth noting that Campbell's conclusions may be based on idiosyncratic data. Samuel Kernell has found that the effect reported by Campbell was larger (and maybe even present only) in 1958 than in any other recent election. See Samuel Kernell, "Presidential Popularity and Negative Voting: An Alternative Explanation of the Midterm Congressional Decline of the President's Party," *American Political Science Review* 71 (March 1977): 44–46.

5. A general analysis appears in Adam Przeworski, "Institutionalization of Voting Patterns, or Is Mobilization the Source of Decay," *American Political Science Review* 69 (March 1975): 49–67.

6. Kristi Andersen, *The Creation of a Democratic Majority: 1928–1936* (Chicago: University of Chicago Press, 1979).

7. Dealignment is a common theme in discussions of the contemporary American electorate. See Nie, Verba, and Petrocik, *The Changing American Voter*, chaps. 4 and 19; and Everett C. Ladd and Charles D. Hadley, *Transformation of the Party System* (New York: W. W. Norton, 1975). The Ladd and Hadley book is an especially noteworthy discussion of this topic. Also see Ronald Inglehart and Avram Hochstein, "Alignment and Dealignment of the Electorate in France and the United States," *Comparative Political Studies* 5 (October 1972): 343–72.

8. Sundquist, *Dynamics of the Party System*, pp. 195.

9. Samuel Lubell, *The Future of American Politics* (New York: Doubleday Anchor Books, 1952), pp. 29 and 30. Samuel J. Elderveld's "The Influence of Metropolitan Party Pluralities in Presidential Elections since 1920," *American Political Science Review* 43 (December 1949): 1189–1205, is one of the first studies to show that prior to the late 1920s the major cities had only a small impact on the party pluralities, but that they have been instrumental in Democratic success since that date.

10. V. O. Key, "A Theory of Critical Elections," *Journal of Politics* 17 (February 1955): 3–18.

11. Angus Campbell et al., *The American Voter* (New York: John Wiley & Sons, 1960), pp. 153–54.

12. Walter Dean Burnham, "The Changing Shape of the American Political Universe," *American Political Science Review* 59 (March 1965): 7–28; David R. Cameron, "Stability and Change in Patterns of French Partisanship," *Public Opinion*

Quarterly 36 (Spring 1972): 19–31; Ronald Inglehart and Avram Hochstein, "Alignment and Dealignment of the Electorate in France and the United States," *Comparative Political Studies* 5 (October 1971): 343–71; Paul Allen Beck, "A Socialization Theory of Partisan Realignment," in *The Politics of Future Citizens,* ed. Richard G. Niemi et al. (San Francisco, Calif.: Jossey-Bass, 1974), pp. 199–220; Andersen, *The Creation of a Democratic Majority.*

13. Przeworski, "Institutionalization of Voting Patterns."

14. U.S. Department of Commerce, Bureau of the Census, *The Statistical Abstract of the United States: 1922* (Washington, D.C.: Government Printing Office, 1923.

15. Michael Kahn, "Immigration as a Political Event, with Special Attention to the Case of Australia" (1974).

16. See David Burner, *The Politics of Provincialism: The Democratic Party in Transition, 1918–1932* (New York: Alfred A. Knopf, 1968), and, for a contemporary perspective, see Charles E. Merriam and Harold F. Gosnell, *The American Party System* (New York: Macmillan, 1929), pp. 12 ff.

Chapter 4

1. Wilfred Binkley, *American Political Parties: Their Natural History* (New York: Alfred A. Knopf, 1958).

2. Again, Binkley is a good source for this kind of material. For its impact on the electorate, see Paul Kleppner, *The Cross of Culture* (New York: Free Press, 1970).

3. Nathan Glazer and Daniel P. Moynihan, *Beyond the Melting Pot* (Cambridge: MIT Press, 1963).

4. In addition to Binkley and Glazer and Moynihan, see Ronald P. Formisano, *The Birth of Mass Political Parties: Michigan, 1827–1861* (Princeton: Princeton University Press, 1971). Formisano's book is an especially good treatment of this topic.

5. Two good sources on the importance of these issues are Kleppner's *Cross of Culture* and Formisano's *The Birth of Mass Political Parties.* A general review of the literature dealing with these issues as they affect the parties is James Wright, "The Ethno-Cultural Model of Voting: A Behavioral and Historical Critique," *American Behavioral Scientist* 6 (May–June 1973): 653–74.

6. Richard Jensen, *Winning the Midwest: Social and Political Conflict, 1888–96* (Chicago: University of Chicago Press, 1971).

7. These data are reported in Formisano, *The Birth of Mass Political Parties.*

8. The following data are reported in Formisano, *The Birth of Mass Political Parties.*

9. These data are from the *Population of the United States: Eighth Census* (Washington, D.C.: Government Printing Office, 1864). The data are from the table titled Recapitulation, pp. 616–23.

10. Almost any discussion of the second party system includes this observation. For some data and analysis of this regionalism, see Walter Dean Burnham, *Presidential Ballots: 1836–1892* (Baltimore: Johns Hopkins University Press, 1975).

11. Donald Strong makes this point particularly well in his "Durable Republicanism in the South," which appears in *Change in the Contemporary South,* ed. Alan Sindler (Durham: Duke University Press, 1963), pp. 174–94.

12. Key is responsible for this demonstration of the relationship between support for secession in the Southern states and the degree of Democratic dominance over the Republican party; see *Southern Politics in State and Nation* (New York: Alfred A. Knopf, 1949).

13. There are several good histories of the parties that describe the "party poli-

tics" of the period. Wilfred Binkley's American Political Parties may be the best.

14. J. M. Allswang, A House for All Peoples: Chicago's Ethnic Groups and Their Politics, 1890–1936 (Lexington: University Press of Kentucky, 1971), presents data illustrating the Democratic preference of this population.

15. Data on migration and residence patterns for migrants can be found in many sources. One of the better collections of these data is Conrad Taeuber and Irene B. Taeuber, The Changing Population of the United States (New York: John Wiley, 1958).

16. Allswang, A House for All Peoples. Data supporting this can also be found in Samuel Lubell, The Future of American Politics, rev. ed. (New York: Vintage Press, 1955); Charles Sellers, "The Equilibrium Cycle in Two-Party Politics," Public Opinion Quarterly 29 (Spring 1965): 16–38; Angus Campbell et al., The American Voter (New York: John Wiley & Sons, 1960), chap. 7; Nie, Verba, and Petrocik, The Changing American Voter (Cambridge: Harvard University Press, 1976), chap. 5; Kristi Andersen, The Creation of a Democratic Majority (Chicago: University of Chicago Press, 1979).

17. Thomas P. Jahnige, in "Critical Elections and Social Change: Towards a Dynamic Explanation of National Party Competition in the United States," Polity 3 (Summer 1971): 465–500, makes this argument. James Bryce, The American Commonwealth, vol. 2 (New York: Commonwealth Publishing, 1908), and M. K. Ostrogorski, Democracy and the Party System in the United States, rev. ed. (New York: Macmillan, 1921) are two period pieces which talk about the "shameless" exploitation of the immigrants by the machines. Less tendentious social scientists also appreciated the ability of the machine parties to orchestrate the immigrant electorates. See E. M. Sait, American Parties and Elections (New York: Appleton Century, 1927), and Charles E. Merriam and Harold F. Gosnell, The American Party System (New York: Macmillan, 1929). A recent book that also addresses the bias of Progressive reforms is Willis Hawley, Non-Partisan Elections and the Case for Party Politics (New York: Wiley-Interscience, 1973). An analysis of this decline in the electorate was done for a seminar by Christopher Myers, "The Effect of Registration and immigration on Turnout in Pennsylvania, 1890–1918" (1977). Walter Dean Burnham, Jerrold Rusk, and Philip E. Converse have argued about the consequences of some of the institutional changes that took place around the turn of the century. Burnham's position is that the decline in turnout represented a demobilization of the electorate for reasons that have more to do with voter apathy and cynicism that with the elimination of corruption. See "The Changing Shape of the American Political Universe," American Political Science Review 59 (March 1965): 7–28. He makes the same points and attempts to refute critics in his major book of the subject, Critical Elections and the Mainsprings of American Politics (New York: W. W. Norton, 1970). The emphasis on the influence of institutional changes can be found in Jerrold G. Rusk, "The Effect of the Australian Ballot Reform on Split-Ticket Voting, 1876–1908," American Political Science Review 64 (December 1970): 1220–38; and Philip E. Converse, "Change in the American Electorate," in The Human Meaning of Social Change, ed. Angus Campbell and Philip E. Converse (New York: Russell Sage Foundation, 1972): 263–337. They continue the debate in Walter Dean Burnham, "Theory and Voting Research: Some Reflections on Converse's 'Change in the American Electorate,'" Philip E. Converse, "Comment on Burnham's 'Theory and Voting Research,'" and Jerrold G. Rusk, "Comment: The American Electoral Universe: Speculation and Evidence," all in American Political Science Review 68 (September 1974): 1002–1049. Although Jahnige does not get into this debate directly, his suggestion that the Progressives may have been responsible for the observed electoral changes of the turn of the century by their attempts to reform politics and especially urban poli-

tics is a start toward a better explanation of the causes of the phenomena Rusk, Burnham, and Converse debate.

18. There are no systematic studies of this possibility, but there are good reasons for believing that the machines were not the industrious mobilizers we imagine them to be. A sure vote is better than a large vote, and by the middle of the 1890s most urban machine parties had largely stabilized competition in their favor. Had they worked hard at mobilizing the late-wave immigrants, it seems unlikely that the New Deal mobilization would have been so heavily fueled by them. Harold Gosnell, *Getting out the Vote* (Chicago: University of Chicago Press, 1927).

19. Burner, *The Politics of Provincialism: The Democratic Party in Transition, 1918–1936.*

20. Any of the ethnocultural approaches to the history of the parties will deal with this in detail. The best book on the subject dealing with the New Deal realignment is David Burner, *The Politics of Provincialism.*

21. Ibid. For more on the hostility of the Bryan wing of the Democrats and the degree to which it was obvious to most of his contemporaries, see Henry M. Littlefield, "The Wizard of Oz: Parable on Populism,"*American Quarterly* 16 (Spring 1964): 47–58.

22. The counties are Cook (Chicago); Wayne (Detroit); St. Louis City; King, Queens, and New York (New York City); Cuyahoga (Cleveland); Allegheny (Pittsburg); Philadelphia; and Milwaukee. The data on the immigrant composition of the population and the vote are from the *Statistical Abstract of the United States: 1922* (Washington, D.C.: Government Printing Office, 1923). It should be noted that the pattern is virtually identical for each city. The average in fig. 4.3 does not cover any intercity variability which refutes the argument that is presented here as an account of the New Deal realignment. The following seminar papers have documented this pattern for various cities and states, for different periods of time: David Waterhouse, "Progressive and the New Deal Realignment in New York and Minnesota"; Kathy Langsam, "The New Deal Realignment in San Francisco, 1920–1940"; Mark S. Dzarnoski, "A Model of Voter Participation, 1880–1908"; Steven A. Olsen, "The New Deal Realignment: Ethnic Mobilization in New York." The impact of the mobilization of typically inactive ethnic groups is also a convenient explanation for the shift from Republican to Democratic dominance in Hawaii. This is documented in Ronnie Menor, "The Rise of the Democratic Party in Hawaii: The Role of Voter Mobilization in Party Realignment."

23. Allan J. Lichtman, in *Prejudice and the Old Politics* (Chapel Hill: University of North Carolina Press, 1979) disputes the importance of the cities and Al Smith's candidacy for the formation of the New Deal. His conclusions are probably faulty.

24. For more on this see the works by Burner, Allswang, and Lubell. See also James L. Sundquist, *Dynamics of the Party System: Alignment and Realignment of Political Parties in the United States* (Washington, D.C: Brookings Institution, 1973).

Chapter 5

1. The obvious shortcomings of such an analysis of the parties has not, however, stopped students of the party coalitions from attempting to make statements about the coalitions by examining the bivariate relationship between social traits and partisanship. See Arthur H. Miller, "The Majority Party Reunited? Comparison of the 1972 and 1976 Elections," in Jeff Fishel, *Parties and Elections in an Anti-Party Age* (Bloomington: Indiana University Press, 1978), pp. 127–40.

2. The average adjusted chi-square when the index of party identification (Democrat, Independent, Republican) is tabulated with the social characteristics is

about 170. The average adjusted chi-square between the social and demographic variables listed in table 5.1 is over 277.

3. Many studies have made this point, but two that are interesting if only because they are relatively recent and derive the social characteristics associated with party support in a manner similar to the one used here are David R. Segal and David Knoke, "Political Partisanship: Its Social and Economic Basis in the United States," *American Journal of Economics and Sociology* 29 (July 1970): 253–62, and Richard Rose, *Electoral Behavior* (New York: Free Press, 1974), chap. 1. A comparative study that is of interest in spite of deficiencies in its historical reasoning can be found in David Segal, "Classes, Strata, and Party in West Germany and the United States," *Comparative Studies in Society and History* 10 (October 1967): 66–84. A study that emphasizes religious aspects of party identification is R. Darcy and William Adams, "Who Wants What, When, How: Issue Politics in America, 1952–1972" (paper presented at the annual meeting of the Midwest Political Science Association, Chicago, May 1–3, 1975). A more recent study of the sociology of the parties is David Knocke, *Change and Continuity in American Politics: The Social Bases of Political Parties*, (Baltimore: Johns Hopkins University Press, 1976).

4. The statistical technique has been developed and described in John A. Sonquist and James N. Morgan, *The Detection of Interaction Effects* (Ann Arbor: Institute for Social Research, 1964). Applications can be found in several places, but see Richard Rose, *Electoral Behavior.*

5. The association is presented in table 5.1 not as a single correlation but as the percent of the variance in party identification correlated with the sociodemographic variables. The categories and scales of these variables are discussed in Appendix B.

6. The party bias of the electorate as a whole is 19 points pro-Democratic. While the party bias of German Catholics is 29 points pro-Democratic, this is markedly less than that of Catholics of other nationalities. See Samuel Lubell, *The Future of American Politics*, chap. 7 for some explanation of this greater Republican orientation among Americans of German descent.

7. This difference persists across their voting choices.

8. These estimates are from the survey data sets.

9. The regions include states according to the eight regions defined in the election studies of the Survey Research Center/Center for Political Studies.

10. Less than 10 percent of Southern whites are of German or Scandinavian ancestry. Non-German and non-Scandinavian Protestants appear more Democratic because of this regional bias in settlement patterns of the immigrants waves. It is interesting that these Southern German and Scandinavian nationalities are less Democratic than their Southern neighbors. It is possible that their more Republican sympathies reflect their mobilization into the electorate during the Civil War. Most German and Scandinavian Protestants, as was pointed out in the last chapter, would have been coming of age politically about the time of the rise of the Republican party and the start of the Civil War, some 15 to 20 years after they entered the United States in large numbers. Perhaps those who settled in the South were influenced like their northern coreligionists, notwithstanding the fact that they were in the Confederacy.

11. There is a 65 percentage point difference between the party bias of white Protestant Southerners and white Protestant Northerners. The Southerners are over 50 points Democratic in their party bias and the Northerners are about 14 points Republican. If the distribution of Protestant nationalities in the North is used to weight the Protestant nationality groups in the South (that is, if the South were given the same distribution of Protestant nationalities found in the North),

the party bias of the South would be 44 points Democratic. The adjusted difference between the North and the South is 58 points. This 7-point change (65 to 58) is an 11 percent change in the difference between the North and the South. If the party bias of the nationality groups is similarly adjusted for their regional distribution, the average 18-point difference between Scandinavian and German Protestants and other Protestants is reduced to only 5 percentage points.

12. For some of this debate, see Robert Dahl, *Who Governs?* (New Haven: Yale University Press, 1961); Raymond E. Wolfinger, "The Development and Persistence of Ethnic Voting," *American Political Science Review* 59 (December 1965): 896–908; Michael Parenti, "Ethnic Politics and the Persistence of Ethnic Identification," ibid. 61 (September 1967): 717–26; Scott Greer, "Catholic Voters and the Democratic Party," *Public Opinion Quarterly* 25 (Winter 1961): 611–25; Richard A. Gabriel, "A New Theory of Ethnic Voting," *Polity* 4 (Summer 1972): 405–28.

13. The principal reason for not being able to distinguish the partisanship of Catholics and Northern Protestants by social status is that they are not different. Northern Protestant and Catholics are almost identical in their relative SES scores.

14. Parenti, "Ethnic Politics and the Persistence of Ethnic Identification."

15. Lubell, in *The Future of American Politics,* argues that residents of the small towns in farm states are the Republicans, and not those engaged in farming (p. 179). These data refute that proposition. Clearly the small-town residents of farm states are more Republican in their party preference than the farmers, but the farmers are clearly biased toward the Republican party and in comparison with the national norm, they are quite Republican. This difference will not be analyzed here but perhaps it should come as no surprise. The Democratic party is more likely than the Republican party to promote schemes to aid the farmers, but there is no need for the farmers to identify as Democrats because of this. After all, the Democrats are more likely than Republicans to support a variety of schemes to aid business enterprises of all types, and small businessmen and corporate executives are not noted for reciprocating with their support for Democrats.

16. The use of the word "group" in this context does not correspond to the typical social science definition of the concept but to an ordinary language use of the word. A group is defined here as any collectivity, based on some permutation of characteristics, which can be distinguished from another collectivity identified by a given permutation of these same characteristics. The sociodemographic groups that are discussed here and in subsequent chapters are groups in the sense that all overweight males with less than a high school education are a group compared with all overweight males with advanced degrees. They are not groups in the sense of being organized around a task, or in the sense of having any measurable degree of self-awareness, or in the sense that the members have discernible patterns of interaction with one another. The groups defined here are not dependent on any members of these groups being self-conscious about such membership. The groups are, thus quite informal and are not self-perpetuating in any conscious fashion.

Having offered these disclaimers, I should point out that neither are the groups completely artificial. Some groups have more self-awareness than others. Jews and blacks are two prominent examples of groups in which membership is a very conscious thing. Yet, each of these groups are real sociological collectives since members share particular life-styles. The distinctive social characteristics that confer membership in the groups are associated with an entire milieu different from that experienced by those not marked by the characteristics of the group. Blacks, for example, have more to do with blacks than with other groups, and there is a subculture of values and a life-style that separates blacks from other segments of the society. Similarly, residential patterns separate the lives of the very high status from those who occupy lower rungs in the status hierarchy. Finally, there are patterns of family socialization which give the members of ethnic, racial, and class groups considerable differences from each other.

In short, while the groups in this chapter do not always meet all the tests of the social science use of the word, they are certainly not nongroups (in the social science sense) either. They are a bit of both; and if their status as "groups" is difficult to justify with sociological or social psychological theory, it is not correct to assert that the collectivities defined in this chapter are without differences that go beyond the social and economic characteristics used in their identification. Fundamentally, it is the existence of other, ultimately more significant, differences that explain the correlation of party preference with social, economic, racial, and religious distinctions.

17. The 1962 data are excluded because it is not possible to distinguish immigrant Southerners nor is it possible to identify nationality groups.

18. Two examples might be Andrew Greeley, "Ethnicity and Inequality" (paper presented at the 1975 meeting of the American Association for the Advancement of Science) and also "Political Participation among American Ethnic Groups in the United States: A Preliminary Reconnaisance," *American Journal of Sociology* 80 (1974): 170–204.

19. Two interesting books that comment directly on the representation of Polish and Irish Americans in the Democratic party, and the controversy in which they are usually the protagonists, are Len O'Connor, *Clout* (Chicago: Henry Regnery, 1975) and Milton Rakove, *Don't Make No Waves . . . Don't Back No Losers* (Bloomington: Indiana University Press, 1975).

Chapter 6

1. See the changes documented by Robert Axelrod in "Where the Votes Come from: An Analysis of Electoral Coalitions, 1952–1968," *American Political Science Review* 66 (March 1972): 11–20, and "Communications," ibid. 68 (June 1974): 717–20.

2. This theme is followed in Richard Scammon and Ben J. Wattenberg, *The Real Majority* (New York: Coward, McCann, & Geohegan, 1970); Mark R. Levy and Michael S. Kramer, *The Ethnic Factor: How America's Minorities Decide Elections* (New York: Simon & Schuster, 1972), and Nie, Verba, and Petrocik, *The Changing American Voter* (Cambridge: Harvard University Press, 1976), chaps. 13 and 14.

3. Burnham has presented this argument in several places. See the revised edition of *The American Party Systems: Stages of Political Development* (New York: Oxford University Press, 1975); also "Revitalization and Decay: Looking toward the Third Century of American Electoral Politics," *Journal of Politics* 38 (August 1976): 146–72. For a different approach, but the same conclusion, see Everett C. Ladd and Charles D. Hadley, *Transformations of the American Party System* (New York: W. W. Norton, 1975).

4. Kevin Phillips, *The Emerging Republican Majority* (New Rochelle: Arlington House, 1969). The reader should note that the opposite interpretation can be found in Lanny J. Davis, *The Emerging Democratic Majority: Lessons and Legacies from the New Politics* (New York: Stein & Day, 1974).

5. Levy and Kramer, *The Ethnic Factor*; and Scammon and Wattenberg, *The Real Majority*; James L. Sundquist, *Dynamics of the Party System: Alignment and Realignment of Political Parties in the United States* (Washington, D.C.: Brookings Institution, 1973).

6. It is quite possible that the kinds of voters who were responsible for the fluctuation in the party bias of the electorate prior to 1966 are the same kinds who fed the increase in nonpartisanship after that year. As unstable partisans their acknowledged party preference oscillated with short-term forces, and as the electorate came to a more baleful view of parties after the mid-1960s, they responded by describing themselves as Independents.

7. The first column which is labelled as the "change in party identification" is simply the change in the distribution of the index of party identification for the group. The following example will illustrate how the number is obtained. In the 1950s, the "silk-stocking" Protestant group was: 16 percent Democrat, 20 percent Independent, and 64 percent Republican. In the 1970s, the group was 18 percent Democrat, 33 percent Independent, and 50 percent Republican. For the "silk-stocking" group, there was a 14 percent redistribution of partisanship which can be seen in the 14 point decline in Republican identifiers, the 2 percent increase in Democrats and the 13 points increase in Independents. The general formula is

$$\text{Change in party identification} = 1/2 \ (\text{abs} \ [\%D'70s - \%D'50s]$$
$$+ \ \text{abs} \ [\%I'70s - \%I'50s] + \text{abs} \ [\%R70 - \%R'50s])$$

where "abs" is the abolute value of the difference and %D, %I, %R represent the percent Democratic, Independent, and Republican in the 1950s and the 1970s.

The second column is simply the arithmetic difference between the proportion of the group identified as Independent in the 1970s less the proportion identified as Independent in the 1950s. Most of the numbers in column B are positive, indicating that most groups have more Independents now than twenty years ago. The third column is the change in the party bias, which is defined as the change in the proportion of Democrats relative to the proportion of Republicans. See chap. 2, note 2 for more on this. A change in the party bias is defined as:

$$\text{Party bias change} = (\%D'70s - \%R'50s) - (\%D'50s - \%R'50s)$$

A positive number would indicate an increase in the proportion of Democrats relative to Republicans between the 1950s and 1970s. A negative number would indicate an increase in the relative proportion of Republicans.

8. Robert H. Somers, "A New Asymmetric Measure of Association for Ordinal Variables," *American Sociological Review* 27 (December 1961): 799–811; Jae-On Kim, "Predictive Measures of Ordinal Association," *American Journal of Sociology* 76 (March 1971): 891–907, and Herbert Weisberg, "Models of Statistical Relationship," *American Political Science Review* 68 (December 1974): 1638–55. Detailed year-by-year data which show the changing partisanship of the groups are in Nie, Verba, and Petrocik, *The Changing American Voter*.

9. A good contemporary analysis of this is John C. Topping, John R. Lazarek, and William H. Linder, *Southern Republicanism and the New South* (Cambridge, 1966).

10. See Angus Campbell, "Surge and Decline: A Study of Electoral Change," in Angus Campbell et al., *Elections and the Political Order* (New York: John Wiley & Sons, 1966), pp. 40–62, and a more recent study by Douglas Dobson and Douglas St. Angelo, "Party Identification and the Floating Vote: Some Dynamics," *American Political Science Review* 69 (June 1975): 481–90. The thesis of Dobson and St. Angelo's work is different from the point here but most of their analysis of the "change in party identification and the floating vote" (pp. 487–90) captures nothing more than the assertion of a party identification by voters who plan to vote for the presidential candidate of that party and confuse the matter of the vote with the issue of party identification.

11. See in particular W. Phillips Shively's analysis of the meaning of the *Literary Digest* polls in mispredicting the 1936 election, "A Reinterpretation of the New

Deal Realignment," *Public Opinion Quarterly* 35 (Winter 1971/72): 621–24, and Harold Gosnell and William Coleman, "Political Trends in Industrial America, Pennsylvania an Example," *Public Opinion Quarterly* 4 (September 1940): 473–86.

12. V. O. Key, *Southern Politics* (New York: Vintage Books, 1949), and Alfred Steinberg, *The Bosses* (New York: Macmillan, 1972), chaps. 4 and 5.

13. Philip E. Converse, "On the Possibility of a Major Political Realignment in the South," in *Elections and the Political Order*, ed. Angus Campbell et al. (New York: John Wiley & Sons, 1966), pp. 212–42.

14. For additional analyses which largely parallel these findings, see Paul Allen Beck, "Partisan Dealignment in the Postwar South," *American Political Science Review* 71 (June 1977): 477–96; Bruce Campbell, "Change in the Southern Electorate," *American Journal of Political Science* 21 (February 1977): 37–64; Bruce Campbell, "Patterns of Change in the Partisan Loyalties of Native Southerners: 1952–1972," *Journal of Politics* 39 (August 1977): 730–61.

15. Their concentration in large cities, the swing effect of the large cities, the electoral college, and the relative ease of campaigning in large cities all combine to make blacks an important group in most elections.

16. Allswang's book *A House for All Peoples: Chicago's Ethnic Groups and Their Politics, 1890–1936* (Lexington: University Press of Kentucky, 1971) is a good document for this change.

17. Blacks and Jews may be the infrequent instances of actual conversion. See Nie, Verba, and Petrocik, *The Changing American Voter*, chaps. 4 and 5; and Angus Campbell et al., *The American Voter* (New York: John Wiley & Sons, 1960), chap. 11.

18. Donald S. Strong, *Urban Republicanism in the South* (Birmingham: University of Alabama Press, 1956); John C. Topping, John R. Lazarek, and William H. Linder, *Southern Republicanism and the New South*; V. O. Key, *Southern Politics*, part five.

19. Strong, *Urban Republicanism*.

20. Topping, Lazarek, and Linder, *Southern Republicanism and the New South*, provide a particularly good narrative of this development.

21. The use of the word "ethnics" always implies a nationality that is typically Catholic in religion.

22. This possibility is derived solely from the theory of cognitive dissonance (Leon Festinger, *A Theory of Cognitive Dissonance* [New York: Harper & Row, 1957).

23. The 14.5 percent change is calculated by summing the absolute percentage differences between the proportionate size of the group in the parties in the 1950s with the proportionate size of the group in the parties, and dividing the sum by two to eliminate double counting. The contribution of any group or number of groups to the change is calculated the same way and is then divided by the overall 14.5 percent change.

24. See chapter 2, above, for the conceptual underpinnings of this judgment.

25. See note 7, above, for the technique used to get this estimate. The adjustment for population change is based upon corrections for the shifting size of the coalition groups in the electorate.

26. The reason for considering a change in the party coalitions that leaves each party representative of the groups in the electorate arises from the emphasis on "dealignment" in much of the party change literature. If the parties are dissolving (in some sense), one would expect their distinctive social base largely to evaporate. Using a change to proportionality as the likely future state of the parties, the

amount of change that has occurred can be estimated by comparing how nearly proportional the groups are in each party compared with how much different they were from proportional in the decade of the fifties. Of course, this exercise is largely heuristic. I am not presuming that the social-group coalitions that define the party clienteles are about to erode.

27. Opinion on the attractiveness of Carter to Southern whites is not unanimous. See "How Solid a South for Carter," *U.S. News and World Report*, 11 October 1976, pp. 18–20; D. A. Williams, "Not Quite Solid Southern Votes," *Newsweek*, 11 October 1976, p. 30.

28. A nice summary of popular thinking on the reasons for Carter's popularity among Southern blacks is in "Why Carter Wins the Black Vote," *Time*, 5 April 1976, p. 15. The "debt to blacks" theme was common during and after the election; see D. A. Williams, "Blacks and Politics '76," *Newsweek*, 20 September 1976, pp. 16–18; J. K. Obtala, "Black Constituency: How Carter Should Pay His Debt," *Nation*, 27 November 1976, pp. 550–52; V. E. Jordon, "Blacks Have a Claim on Carter," *Newsweek*, 22 November 1976, p. 15.

29. The need for Carter to deal with this coalition and some of the strains that resulted were commented upon by many; see S. M. Lipset, "Catholic Defection," *New Republic*, 2 October 1976, pp. 10–11; M. Greenfield, "Carter and the Once-Born: Jewish Voters," *Newsweek*, 2 August 1976, p. 80; Harold Williams, "The Reverse Bigotry against Carter: Liberals Urged to Overcome Suspicions of Southern Baptist Heritage," *Los Angeles Times*, 29 July 1976; Harriet Van Horne, "...But Uneasiness Persists in His Party," *Los Angeles Times*, 9 August 1976.

30. T. Nicholson and J. Doyle "Old Coalition," *Newsweek*, 15 November 1976, p. 29; Harry Bernstein, "Election Shows Labor's Return to Democrats," *Los Angeles Times*, 4 November 1976; William Schneider, "Democrats Got Their Act Going Again," *Los Angeles Times*, 7 November 1976. In commenting on the 1976 election Ladd and Hadley wrote that "American electoral politics can once again be understood in the framework made familiar during the Roosevelt era" (Everett C. Ladd with Charles D. Hadley, *Transformation of the American Party System*, rev. ed. [New York: W. W. Norton, 1978], p. xxv). The first results of the CPS/SRC election study are reported in Arthur H. Miller and Warren E. Miller, "Partisanship and Performance: 'Rational' Choice in the 1976 Presidential Election" (paper presented at the annual meeting of the American Political Science Association, Washington, D.C., September 1977). See also Arthur H. Miller, "The Majority Party Reunited?: A Summary Comparison of the 1972 and 1976 Elections," in *Political Parties and Elections in an Anti-Party Age*, ed. Jeffrey Fishel (Bloomington: Indiana University Press, 1978), pp. 127–40.

31. See Gerald Pomper et al, *The Election of 1976* (New York: McKay, 1977), esp. pp. 79–82, for a brief analysis of aggregate data which illustrate the divergence of the Carter vote from the one that characterized previous Democratic presidential coalitions.

32. Published studies of the 1948 election are scarce. The SRC study done in 1948 was small and could not support very extensive analyses of voting patterns; the data used to write *Voting* came from a single community. All of the analysis of the Truman vote and the 1948 election in this chapter rests upon the recalled 1948 vote which appears in the 1952 election study.

33. A more detailed presentation of these data can be found in the revised edition (1979) of Nie, Verba, and Petrocik, *The Changing American Voter*, pp. 382–85, and John Petrocik, "Contextual Sources of Voting Behavior: The Changeable American Voter," in *The Electorate Reconsidered*, ed. John C. Pierce and John L. Sullivan (Beverly Hills, Calif.: Sage Publications, 1980), pp. 257–78.

34. Chap. 9 represents an analysis of the impact of race issues on the party coalitions—Southern whites in particular—as an illustration of an issue whose partisan valence changed in recent years.

Chapter 7

1. These are estimates from survey data. The census data indicate that about 52 percent of the population would not have been eligible to vote before 1952. The year 1952 is a conservative estimate of the outer limit of time when one might suspect that the events of the Depression are still exerting influence. That year is picked because it permits the individual to have developed some political aware-ness during the last years of the FDR presidency.

2. See Nie, Verba, and Petrocik, *The Changing American Voter*, chap. 13.

3. This is done by simply excluding those under a certain age from the election surveys of 1968 through 1972. So, for the 1968 survey all those under 29 years of age are deleted from the analysis; in 1970 those under 31 are deleted; and in 1972 those under 33 are deleted. This eliminates the influence of the post-1960 cohort. It assumes that, had the post-1960 cohort been included, and had their partisanship not been so different, the differences between the two periods would reflect changes that are not related to cohort replacement except for the portion that results from the death of older groups. Another way to do this is simply to weigh the age distribution of the late 1960s and early 1970s with the party preference of the same groups in the 1950s. The results are virtually identical.

4. The method used to obtain these numbers is substantially similar to the one used for table 7.1, but with an additional level of complexity because the changes have been broken down into regional as well as cohort differences. Any differences between this and the preceding tables reflects the use of the 1976 data as the terminal point in table 7.2, while an average of the 1968 through 1972 data are used as the terminal point earlier. Since the trends have not changed, because the averaging tends to reduce the differences between the comparison points, and because the 1976 data represent the apogee of a developing pattern, it is used to get a handle on the drift of the South to the Republicans.

5. The 37 percent is simply the ratio of the 2 percent increase in Republicans compared with the 5.4 percent decline in Democrats.

6. The idea that led to this analysis arose out of a paper by Bruce Campbell, "Patterns of Change in the Partisan Loyalties of Native Southerners: 1952–1972" (presented at the annual meeting of the Midwest Political Science Association, Chicago, Illinois, May 1–3, 1975).

7. John C. Topping, John R. Lazarek, and William H. Linder, *Southern Republicanism and the New South* (Cambridge, 1966).

8. This turnout is considerably higher than that reported by the Bureau of the Census. An analysis of the discrepancy can be found in Aage R. Clausen, "Response Validity: Vote Report," *Public Opinion Quarterly 32* (Winter 1968/69: 588–606; and, for a less methodological treatment, in Stanley Kelley, Jr., and Thad W. Mirer, "The Simple Act of Voting," *American Political Science Review 68* (June 1974): 572–91.

9. See chaps. 3 and 4 for an extended discussion of the theory and associated data on which this is based.

10. The data are presented in Bruce Campbell, "Patterns of Change in the Partisan Loyalties of Native Southerners."

11. Chap. 3 cites this literature.

Chapter 8

1. Everett Carll Ladd is the person most closely associated with this approach to conceptualizing realignments. The initial statement is in *American Political Parties* (New York: W. W. Norton, 1970). He has extended this analysis of the relationship between party-system change and the agenda (with Charles D. Hadley) in *Transformations of the American Party System* (New York: W. W. Norton, 1975).

2. Ladd, *American Political Parties,* part 2.

3. *Transformations of the Party System.*

4. This has been the approach taken by historians who engage in narratives of American party history. Wilfred Binkley, *American Political Parties: Their Natural History* (New York: Alford A. Knopf, 1958) is an example of this. Discussions and even analyses of realignments by political scientists have used this explanation.

5. Paul Allen Beck, "A Socialization Theory of Partisan Realignment," in *The Politics of Future Citizens,* ed. Richard G. Niemi et al. (San Francisco: Jossey-Bass, 1974), pp. 199–220.

6. James L. Sundquist, *Dynamics of the Party System: Alignment and Realignment of Political Parties in the United States* (Washington, D.C.: Brookings Institution, 1973) chap. 2.

7. Answers that focus on the benefits that specific classes of voters will or will not receive from a party constitute the most frequent types of response. Over 40 percent of the population appear to evaluate the parties in terms of group benefits.

8. John E. Jackson, "Issues and Party Alignment," in *The Future of Political Parties,* ed. Louis Maisel and Paul M. Sacks (Beverly Hills, Calif.: Sage Publications, 1975). Also see John E. Jackson, "Issues, Parties, and Presidential Votes," *American Journal of Political Science* 19 (May 1975): 161–86.

9. Similar analysis appears in Herbert F. Weisberg and Jerrold G. Rusk, "Dimensions of Candidate Evaluation," *American Political Science Review* 64 (December 1970): 1167–85; Jerrold G. Rusk and Herbert F. Weisberg, "Perceptions of Political Candidates: Implications for Electoral Change," *Midwest Journal of Political Science* 16 (August 1972): 288–410.

Chapter 9

1. This is not a discovery. Any student of the American parties will appreciate the lack of enduring or large foreign policy cleavages between the Democrats and the Republicans. While trade and tariff matters have historically divided the parties (and still do), most other issues do not neatly separate the parties in government. Certainly, the kinds of issues that have concerned the electorate over the past two decades are weakly related to party identification. An early, but still useful study, of issue differences between the parties is in Julius Turner and Edward V. Schneier, *Party and Constituency: Pressures on Congress,* rev. ed (Baltimore: Johns Hopkins University Press, 1970).

2. The relatively low association between foreign policy preferences and party preference may be very important nonetheless. Since foreign policy has become a very important issue in recent years, the fact that it is largely unrelated to "normal" patterns of party identification may indicate that it is an issue capable of realigning the parties. As James L. Sundquist indicates in his *Dynamics of the Party System: Alignment and Realignment of Political Parties in the United States* (Washington, D.C., Brookings Institution, 1973), issues on which the parties are

not divided become the issues that precipitate realignment because they, for whatever reason, emerge as issues of political debate and they divide supporters of the same party from each other. That foreign policy questions may provide the central issues of a party realignment in this age is suggested by Herbert Weisberg and Jerrold Rusk in "Dimensions of Candidate Evaluation," *American Political Science Review* 64 (December 1970): 1167–85. The precipitous decline in the amount of attention given to foreign policy questions since the end of American involvement in the war in Vietnam and especially since the end of the war itself might also be taken as an indication that foreign policy issues will continue to be peripheral to the issue cleavages which support the party division.

3. As Appendix A indicates, the measures of political attitudes for the groups in this chapter cannot be used to make absolute comparisons. The percentage differences for each question have been standardized by removing the average percentage difference for the question in that year. A group that is described as more liberal in the seventies than it was in the fifties is, therefore, only more liberal relative to the population. The absolute proportion of the group providing a liberal response to a question may be constant in the two time periods but if the proportion of the population making the liberal response has declined, the group, by the measures used here, would appear to have become more liberal. This procedure for measuring political opinions can be justified from two perspectives. In the first place, by comparing the responses of the members of the group vis-à-vis the responses of the entire population, the confounding effects of changes in question wording are reduced. Taking out the population average assumes that the effects of question wording are constant for all groups, and that if a question is asked in 1974 on which it is easier to be liberal than a similar question asked in an earlier period, the proportionate increase in liberal responses is constant for all groups in the population. The second justification for comparing responses that have been standardized by removing the mean is that the substantive meaning of liberal and conservative can change even over a very short period of time. As a consequence the only meaning that we may be able to assign a question response in liberal and conservative terms is by reference to the way the population defined the question. By removing the mean percentage difference from the group we are permitting the population definition of liberal and conservative to characterize the group. Both of the reasons seem to be valid. For the one instance where it does not seem to apply see Nie, Verba, and Petrocik, *The Changing American Voter*, p. 252, n.3.

4. The reader is reminded that this description of liberal and conservative is always in a relative sense. See note 6 below and Appendix A.

5. Lower-status Catholics and native and border Southerners are principal examples. In the case of lower-status Catholics there has been more than the average change in their opinions on race and welfare matters but very little change in their party bias. Southerners, in contrast, have changed their party bias considerably but have changed their attitudes on race and economic welfare questions hardly at all.

6. The understanding of the notion of liberal and conservative that is assumed here corresponds to the ordinary language use of the words. A group would be considered liberal if, for example, the group strongly preferred a national medical care system, was very supportive of greater government regulation and control of the economy, and supportive of action by the government designed to benefit blacks especially. A conservative group would be less likely to support any of these.

7. By the 1976 election study the post-1960 cohort amounted to almost 42 percent of the electorate.

8. In figure 9.3 opinions on racial and economic welfare issues have been averaged together. The average covers some of the features of the issue changes that are so obvious in figs. 9.1 and 9.2. At the same time, this average does not distort the attitudinal predisposition of the groups. At a minimum, it is possible to order the groups in a liberal and conservative sense. Blacks and Jews, for example, come out as liberal groups and Southerners and upper-status white Northern Protestants come out as relatively conservative. Groups which are divided on the issues—liberal on one side, but conservative on the other—come out in the center, unless the members of the group are dramatically more liberal or conservative on one of the issues. Being able to order the groups on some issue continuum, however, does not resolve the problem that appears in Figs. 9.1 and 9.2. If a group's attitudes are changing in different directions on the two issues, it will not be possible to account for group changes in partisanship with the attitudes. Nothing is solved by considering the opinions together. At the same time nothing is distorted. If, on the one hand, the racial and economic welfare attitudes of the groups changed in a consistent direction and if that direction corresponds to the direction of any changes in partisanship, the summary attitude index will correlate at least as well with the party change as the individual attitudes. If, on the one hand, the attitude changes are contradictory, the summary index will show this by not correlating well with changes in partisanship. In short, a summary index will not explain anything that constituent items will not explain; it will only reflect the relationship between party change and change in the constituent issue items. A group with a party bias that is changing opposite to the direction of changes in issue attitudes will show up in this summary data as a group with party preference changes that cannot be explained by the changes in attitudes. Of course, if changes in partisanship were tied to specific attitudes, then the summary measure used in fig. 9.4 would be misleading, since it would find inconsistencies when, from the point of view of the model and the characteristics of the group, there were none. As the data in fig. 9.2 make abundantly clear, there is no specificity of attitudes for a group's change in partisanship. The summary attitude index used in fig. 9.3 does not distort the patterning of the data.

9. The equation that predicts changes in the party bias of a group from changes in the race and issue attitudes of the group is:

Change in the party bias − (−.01037* race attitude change)
+ (.7689* welfare attitude change) + .01673.

10. Probably the most famous is the study done of the 1968 New Hampshire primary which indicated that 60 percent of those who voted for Eugene McCarthy were "hawks" on the Vietnam issue. P. E. Converse et al., "Continuity and Change in American Politics: Parties and Issues in the 1968 Election," *American Political Science Review* 63 (December 1969): 1092.

11. For a full discussion of the meaning of the term *unifunctional* as a description of the American parties, see Theodore J. Lowi, "Party, Policy and Constitution in America," in *The American Party System: Stages of Development*, ed. Walter Dean Burnham (New York: Oxford University Press, 1967).

12. The equation that predicts changes in the party bias of the groups from changes in the issue connectedness scores of the group is:

(1.3696 * welfare connectedness changes)
+ (.09006 * race connectedness changes) + .02361.

13. The reader should be aware that the changes that are predicted from these equations are the changes in the party bias of the pre-1960 cohort. The post-1960 cohort is removed from the data. Since they were, by definition, not around in the

pre-1960 period, changes in their scores on these variables cannot be correlated. The regression equation that predicts changes in party bias from changes in issue opinion and issue connectedness is:

$$(2.75115 * \text{welfare connectedness changes})$$
$$+ (-.66184 * \text{race attitudes changes})$$
$$+ (-.28288 * \text{race connectedness changes})$$
$$+ (-.35121 * \text{welfare attitude changes}) -.00556.$$

14. See Nie, Verba, and Petrocik, *The Changing American Voter*, chap. 4.

15. The data, which are not shown, are from a study conducted early in 1974 by the National Opinion Research Center. A limited amount of the data were used in *The Changing American Voter*. The data in table 9.1 and fig. 9.11 are from the 1974 survey.

16. This explanation presumes that the younger cohorts, always sensitive to the prevailing political winds, have chosen to describe themselves as Independents because the short-term forces are not as friendly to parties now as they would be in a more "normal" period. There is no reason for the "immunization effect" to be asymmetrical. It is as reasonable to expect the young to dealign faster than the average for the same reasons that we expect them to align or realign their loyalties faster than the older cohorts. For the theory behind this, see chap. 4, above. Some data to this point can be found in Andrew Greeley, "Postscript" (National Opinion Research Center, 1975).

Chapter 10

1. Those who do not live in geologically active areas only dimly appreciate that "after shocks" are earthquakes whose magnitude often exceeds that of the first shock. The "pre-shock" that I am pointing to may be followed by a major after-shock with more severe consequences, but we will have been visited by an earthquake both times. The metaphor is only marginally appropriate, but it may help to keep this twist in mind if we are to continue to think in terms of re-alignments that can be followed by secular processes which also realign segments of the electorate.

2. This debate on "closet" Independents is quite extensive. For some references as well as data which call into question the propriety of thinking of the In-dependents as heavily infiltrated with partisans, see John Petrocik, "Contextual Sources of Voting Behavior: The Changeable American Voter," in *The Electorate Reconsidered*, ed. John C. Pierce and John L. Sullivan (Beverly Hills, Calif.: Sage Publications, 1980), pp. 257–78.

3. Andrew Greeley, "Postscript: Plus ca change; plus la meme chose" (National Opinion Research Center, 1975).

4. An example will make this clearer. Consider a group which is 24 percent Republican, 43 percent Independent, and 33 percent Democratic: If the Democratic vote of the group in 1976 followed the swing of the election, the group would have cast just less than 50 percent of their ballots for Carter ($.33 \times .83$) + ($.43 \times .45$) + ($.14 \times .24$) = .498). Any deviation from this expected vote represents either the effect of election-specific forces which have a special impact on the group in question or a level of partisan commitment in the group which is unlike that of other Democrats, Independents, and Republicans. Fig. 10.1 used the full 7 point index of party identification. The above illustration used the keep the example simple. The actual algorithm was ($.92 \times$ % strong Dem) + ($.75 \times$ % weak Dem) + ($.76 \times$ % leaning Dem) + ($.43 \times$ % Ind) + ($.14 \times$ % leaning Rep) + ($.22 \times$ % weak Rep) + ($.03 \times$ % strong Rep).

5. The data referred to are from a study done by Market Opinion Research in December of 1974.

6. Everett C. Ladd and Charles D. Hadley, *Transformations of the American Party System* (New York: W. W. Norton, 1975), and Richard M. Scammon and Ben J. Wattenberg, *The Real Majority* (New York: Coward, McCann, & Geoghegan, 1970).

7. For more speculation on this, see Samuel P. Huntington, "Postindustrial Politics: How Benign Will It Be?" *Comparative Politics* 6 (January, 1974): 163–92.

Bibliography

Allswang, J. M. A House for All Peoples: Ethnic Politics in Chicago, 1890–1936. Lexington: University Press of Kentucky, 1971.

Andersen, Kristi J. The Creation of a Democratic Majority, 1928–1936. Chicago: University of Chicago Press, 1979.

Axelrod, Robert. "Where the Votes Come From: An Analysis of Electoral Coalitions: 1952–1968." American Political Science Review 66 (March 1972):1121.

Beck, Paul Allen. "A Socialization Theory of Realignment." In The Politics of Future Citizens, ed. Richard G. Niemi et al. San Francisco: Jossey-Bass, 1974.

Benson, Lee. The Concept of Jacksonian Democracy. Princeton: Princeton University Press, 1962.

Berelson, Bernard; Lazarsfeld, Paul F.; and McPhee, William N. Voting. Chicago: University of Chicago Press, 1954.

Bernstein, Harry. "Election Shows Labor Returns to Democrats." Los Angeles Times, 4 November 1976.

Binkley, Wilfred. American Political Parties: Their Natural History. New York: Alfred A. Knopf, 1958.

Bryce, James. The American Commonwealth, vol. 2. New York: Commonwealth Publishing, 1908.

Burdick, Eugene, and Brodbeck, Arthur J., eds. American Voting Behavior. New York: Free Press, 1959.

Burner, David. The Politics of Provincialism: The Democratic Party in Transition, 1928–1932. New York: Alfred A. Knopf, 1968.

Burnham, Walter Dean. "American Politics in the 1970's: Beyond Party?" In The Future of Political Parties, ed. Louis Maisel and Paul M. Sacks. Beverly Hills: Sage Publications, 1975.

———. "The Changing Shape of the American Political Universe." American Political Science Review 59 (March 1965):7–28.

———. Critical Elections and the Mainsprings of American Politics. New York: W. W. Norton, 1970.

———. "Insulation and Political Responsiveness in Congressional Elections." Political Science Quarterly 90 (Fall 1970):411–36.

———. Presidential Ballots, 1838–1892. Baltimore: Johns Hopkins University Press, 1955.

———. "Rejoinder to 'Comments' by Philip Converse and Jerrold Rusk." American Political Science Review 68 (September 1974):1050–57.

———. "Revitalization and Decay: Looking toward the Third Century of American Electoral Politics." Journal of Politics 38 (August 1976):146–72.

———. "Theory and Voting Research: Some Reflections on Converse's "Change in the American Electorate.'" American Political Science Review 68 (September 1974):1002–23.

Butler, David, and Stokes, Donald. Political Change in Britain. New York: St. Martin's, 1969.

Cameron, David R. "Stability and Change in Patterns of French Partisanship." *Public Opinion Quarterly* 36 (Spring 1972):19–31.

Campbell, Angus. "Surge and Decline: A Study of Electoral Change." In Angus Campbell et al., *Elections and the Political Order*. New York: John Wiley & Sons, 1966.

Campbell, Angus; Gurin, Gerald; and Miller, Warren E. *The Voter Decides*. Evanston: Row-Peterson, 1954.

Campbell, Angus, and Kahn, Robert L. *The People Elect a President*. Ann Harbor: Institute for Social Research, 1952.

Campbell, Angus et al. *Elections and the Political Order*. New York: John Wiley & Sons, 1966.

———. *The American Voter*. New York: John Wiley & Sons, 1960.

Campbell, Bruce. "Change in the Southern Electorate." *American Political Science Review* 21 (February 1977):37–64.

———. "Patterns of Change in the Partisan Loyalties of Native Southerns, 1952–1972." *Journal of Politics* 39 (August 1977):730–61.

Clausen, Aage R. "Response Validity: Vote Report." *Public Opinion Quarterly* 32 (Winter 1968–69):588–606.

Converse, Philip E. "Change in the American Electorate," In *The Human Meaning of Social Change*, ed. Angus Campbell and Philip E. Converse. New York: Russell Sage Foundation, 1972.

———. "Comment on Burnham's Theory and Voting Research." *American Political Science Review* 68 (September 1974):1024–27.

———. "The Concept of Normal Vote." In Angus Campbell et al., *Elections and the Political Order*. New York: John Wiley & Sons, 1966.

———. "Information Flow and the Stability of Partisan Attitudes." In Angus Campbell et al., *Elections and the Political Order*. New York: John Wiley & Sons, 1966.

———. "On the Possibility of a Major Political Realignment in the South." In Angus Campbell et al., *Elections and the Political Order*. New York: John Wiley & Sons, 1966.

———. *The Dynamics of Party Support*. Beverly Hills: Sage Publications, 1975.

———. "The Nature of Belief Systems in Mass Publics." In *Ideology and Discontent*, ed. David Apter. New York: Free Press, 1964.

Converse, Philip E.; Clausen, Aage; and Miller, Warren E.; "Electoral Myth and Reality: The 1964 Election." *American Political Science Review* 59 (June 1965):321–36.

Converse, Philip E., et al. "Continuity and Change in American Politics: Parties and Issues in the 1968 Election." *American Political Science Review* 63 (December 1969):1092.

Costain, Anne N. "An Analysis of Voting in American National Nominating Conventions, 1940–1976." *American Politics Quarterly* 6 (January 1978): 375–94.

Dahl, Robert. *Who Governs?* New Haven: Yale University Press, 1961.

Davis, Lanny J. *The Emerging Democratic Majority: Lessons and Legacies from the New Politics*. New York: Stein & Day, 1974.

Dexter, Lewis A. "What Do Congressmen Hear: The Mail." *Public Opinion Quarterly* 20 (Spring 1956):16–17.

Dobson, Douglas, and St. Angelos, Douglas. "Party Identification and the Floating Vote: Some Dynamics." *American Political Science Review* 69 (June 1975):489–90.

Elazar, Daniel J. "Megalopolis and the New Sectionalism." *Public Interest* 11 (September 1968).

Eldersveld, Samuel J. "The Influence of Metropolitan Party Pluralities in Presidential Elections Since 1920." *American Political Science Review* 43 (December 1949):1189–1126.

Epstein, Leon D. *Political Parties in Western Democracies*. New York: Praeger, 1967.

———. "Political Parties." In *The Handbook of Political Science*, ed. Fred Greenstein and Nelson Polsby. Cambridge: Addison-Wesley, 1967.

Erikson, Robert S. "The Advantage of Incumbency in Congressional Elections." *Polity* 3 (Spring 1971):395–405.

———."Malapportionment, Gerrymandering and Party Fortunes in Congressional Elections." *American Political Science Review* 66 (December 1972):1234–45.

Ferejohn, John A. "On the Decline of Competition in Congressional Elections." *American Political Science Review* 71 (March 1977):166–76.

Festinger, Leon. *A Theory of Cognitive Dissonance*. New York: Harper & Row, 1957.

Fiorina, Morris P. "The Case of the Vanishing Marginals: The Bureaucracies Did It." *American Political Science Review* 71 (March 1977):177–81.

Flanigan, William H., and Zingale, Nancy. "The Measurement of Electoral Change." *Political Methodology* (Summer 1974):49–82.

Formisano, Ronald P. *The Birth of the Mass Political Parties: Michigan, 1827–1861*. Princeton: Princeton University Press, 1971.

Fuchs, Lawrence. *The Political Behavior of American Jews*. Glencoe: Free Press, 1956.

Funston, Richard. "The Supreme Court and Critical Elections." *American Political Science Review* 69 (September 1975):795–811.

Gabriel, Richard A. "A New Theory of Ethnic Voting." *Polity* 4 (Summer 1972):405–28.

Ginsberg, Benjamin. "Elections and Public Policy." *American Political Science Review* 70 (March 1976):41–49.

Glazer, Nathan, and Moynihan, Daniel P. *Beyond the Melting Pot*. Cambridge: MIT Press, 1963.

Gosnell, Harold, and Coleman, William. "Political Trends in Industrial America: Pennsylvania an Example." *Public Opinion Quarterly* 4 (September 1940):473–86.

Greeley, Andrew. "Political Participation among American Ethnic Groups in the United States: A Preliminary Reconnaissance." *American Journal of Sociology* 8 (July 1974):170–204.

Greenfield, M. "Carter and the Once Born: Jewish Voters." *Newsweek*, 2 August 1976, p. 80.

Greer, Scott. "Catholic Voters and the Democratic Party." *Public Opinion Quarterly* 25 (Winter 1961):611–15.

Hawley, Willis. *Non-Partisan Elections and the Case for Party Politics*. New York: Wiley-Interscience, 1973.

Hays, Samuel. "The Social Analysis of American Political History, 1180–1920." *Political Science Quarterly* 80 (1965):373–94.

———. "Political Parties and the Community-Society Continuum." In *the American Party Systems: Stages of Political Development*, ed. William Nesbit Chambers and Walter Dean Burnham. New York. Oxford University Press, 1967.

Hinckley, Barbara; Hofstetter, C. Richard; and Kessel, John H. "Information and the Vote: A Comparative Election Study." *American Politics Quarterly* 2 (1974):131–58.

Horne, Harriet Van. "But Uneasiness Persists in His Party." *Los Angeles Times* 9 August 1976.

"How Solid a South for Carter?" *U.S. News and World Report*, 11 October 1976, pp. 18–20.

Huntington, Samuel P. "Postindustrial Politics: How Benign Will It Be?" *Comparative Politics* 6 (January 1974):163–92.

Hutchinson, Richard G., III. "The Internal Effect of Incumbency and Two-Party Politics: Elections to the House of Representatives from the South, 1952–1974." *American Political Science Review* 60 (December 1975):1399–1401.

Inglehart, Ronald, and Hochstein, Avram. "Alignment and Dealignment of the Electorate in France and the United States." *Comparative Political Studies* 5 (October 1972):343–72.

Jackson, John E. "Issues and Party Alignment." In *The Future of Political Parties*, ed. Louis Maisel and Paul M. Sacks. Beverly Hills: Sage Publications, 1975.

———. "Issues, Parties and Presidential Votes." *American Journal of Politics* 19 (May 1975):161–86.

Jahnige, Thomas P. "Critical Elections and Social Change: Towards a Dynamic Explanation of Party Competition in the United States." *Polity* 3 (Summer 1971):466–500.

Jensen, Richard J. *Winning the Midwest: Social and Political Conflict, 1888–1896.* Chicago: University of Chicago Press, 1971.

Jordan, Vernon. "Blacks Have a Claim on Carter." *Newsweek*, 22 November 1976, p. 15.

Kahn, Michael. "Immigration as a Political Event, with Special Attention to the Case of Austrialia." Unpublished, 1974.

Knocke, David. *Change and Continuity in American Politics: The Social Basis of Political Parties.* Baltimore: Johns Hopkins University Press, 1976.

Kelley, Robert. *The Cultural Pattern in American Politics: The First Century.* New York: Alfred A. Knopf, 1979.

Kelley, Stanley, Jr., and Mirer, Thad W. "The Simple Act of Voting." *American Political Science Review* 68 (June 1974):572–91.

Kernell, Samuel. "Presidential Popularity and Negative Voting: An Alternative Explanation of the Midterm Congressional Decline of the President's Party." *American Political Science Review* 71 (March 1977):44–66.

Key, V. O. "A Theory of Critical Elections." *Journal of Politics* 17 (February 1955): 3–18.

———. *Southern Politics in State and Nation.* New York: Alfred A. Knopf, 1949.

———. "Secular Realignment and the Party System." *Journal of Politics* 21 (May 1959):198–210.

Kim-Jae-On. "Predictive Measures of Ordinal Association." *American Journal of Sociology* 76 (March 1971):891–907.

Kleppner, Paul M. *The Cross of Culture: A Social Analysis of Midwestern Politics, 1800–1900.* New York: Free Press, 1970.

Kostroski, Warren Lee. "Party and Incumbency in Postwar Senate Elections." *American Political Science Review* 67 (December 1973):1213–34.

Ladd, Everett C. *American Political Parties.* New York: W. W. Norton, 1970.

Ladd, Everett C., and Hadley, Charles D. *Political Parties and Political Issues: Patterns of Differentiation Since the New Deal.* Beverly Hills: Sage Publications, 1973.

———. *Transformations of the American Party System.* New York: W. W. Norton, 1975; rev. ed., 1978.

Lazarsfeld, Paul F.; Berelson, Bernard; and Gaudet, Hazel. *The People's Choice.* New York: Columbia University Press, 1948.

Levy, Mark B., and Kramer, Michael S. *The Ethnic Factor: How America's Minorities Decide Elections.* New York: Simon & Schuster, 1972.

Lichtman, Allan J. *Prejudice and the Old Politics: The Presidential Election of 1928.* Chapel Hill: University of North Carolina Press, 1979.

Western World: Falsified Predictions and Plausible Postdictions." In *Ethnic Conflict in the Western World*, ed. Milton J. Esman. Ithaca: Cornell University Press, 1977.

Lipset, Seymour M. "Catholic Defection." *New Republic*, 2 October 1976, pp. 10–11.

Lipset, Seymour M., and Rokkan, Stein. *Party Systems and Voter Alignments*. New York: Free Press, 1967.

Littlefield, Henry M. "The Wizard of Oz: Parable on Populism." *American Quarterly* 16 (Spring 1964):47–58.

Lowi, Theodore J. "Party, Policy, and Constitution in America." In *The American Party System: Stages of Development*, ed. William Nesbit Chambers and Walter Dean Burnham. New York: Oxford University Press, 1967.

Lubell, Samuel. *The Future of American Politics*. New York: Harper & Row, 1952.
———. *The Hidden Crisis in American Politics*. New York: W. W. Norton, 1970.

MacRae, Duncan, Jr., and Meldrum, James A. "Critical Elections in Illinois, 1888–1858." *American Political Science Review* 54 (September 1960):667–83.

McCloskey, Herbert. "Consensus and Ideology in American Politics." *American Political Science Review* 58 (June 1964):361–82.

McCloskey, Herbert; Hoffman, P. J.; and O'Hara, R. "Issue Conflict and Consensus among Party Leaders and Followers." *American Political Science Review* 54 (June 1960):406–29.

McPhee, William N., and Glaser, William A. *Public Opinion and Congressional Elections*. New York: Free Press, 1962.

Merriam, Charles E., and Gosnell, Harold F. *The American Party System*. New York: Macmillan, 1919.

Milbrath, Lester, and Goel, M. L. *Political Participation*. Chicago: Rand McNally, 1977.

Miller, Arthur H. "The Major Party Reunited? Comparison of the 1972 and 1976 Elections." In Jeff Fishel, *Parties and Elections in an Anti-Party Age*. Bloomington: Indiana University Press, 1978.

Miller, Warren E., and Strokes, Donald E. "Constituency Influence in Congress." *American Political Science Review* 57 (March 1963):45–56.

Miller, Warren, and Levitan, Teresa. *Leadership and Change: The New Politics and the American Electorate*. Cambridge: Winthrop Publishers, 1976.

More, David W., and Hofstetter, C. Richard. "The Representativeness of Primary Elections: Ohio, 1968. *Polity* 6 (Winter 1973):197–222.

Newman, Sigmund. *Modern Political Parties*. Chicago: University of Chicago Press, 1956.

Nexon, David. "Asymmetry in the Political System: Occasional Activists in the Republican and Democratic Parties, 1956–1964." *American Political Science Review* 65 (September 1971):716–30.

Nicholson, T., and Doyle, T. "Old Coalition." *Newsweek*, 15 November 1976, p. 29.

Nie, Norman; Verba, Sidney; and Petrocik, John R. *The Changing American Voter*. Cambridge: Harvard University Press, 1976; rev. ed. 1979.

Obtala, J. K. "Black Constituency: How Carter Should Pay His Debt." *Nation*, 27 November 1976, pp. 550–52.

O'Connor, Len. *Clout*. Chicago: Henry Regnery, 1974.

Ogburn, William F., and Talbot, Nell Snow. "A Measurement of the Factors in Presidential Election of 1928." *Social Forces* 8 (December 1922):75–183.

Parenti, Michael. "Ethnic Politics and the Persistence of Ethnic Identification." *American Political Science Review* 61 (September 1967):717–25.

Petrocik, John R. "Changing Party Coalitions and Attitudinal Basis of Realignment, 1952–1972." Ph.D. diss., University of Chicago, 1976.
———. "Contextual Sources of Voting Behavior: The Changeable American

Voter." In *The Electorate Reconsidered*, ed. John C. Pierce and John S. Sullivan. Beverly Hills: Sage Publications, 1980.

Phillips, Kevin. *The Emerging Republican Majority*. New Rochelle: Arlington House, 1969.

Pomper, Gerald. "Classification of Presidential Election." *Journal of Politics* 29 (August 1967):533–66.

Pomper, Gerald, et al. *The Election of 1976*. New York: David McKay, 1977.

Przeworski, Adam. "Institutionalization of Voting Patterns, or Is Mobilization the Source of Decay?" *American Political Science Review* 69 (March 1975):49–67.

Rakove, Milton. *Don't Make No Waves, Don't Back No Losers*. Bloomington: Indiana University Press, 1975.

Rose, Richard, ed. *Electoral Behavior*. New York: Free Press, 1974.

Rubin, Richard. *Party Dynamics*. New York: Oxford University Press, 1976.

Rusk, Jerrold G., and Weisberg, Herbert F. "Perceptions of Political Candidates: Implications for Electoral Changes." *Midwest Journal of Politicial Science* 16 (August 1972):388–410.

Rusk, Jerrold G. "Comment: The American Electoral Universe Speculation and Evidence." *American Political Science Review* 68 (September 1974):1028–49.

Sait, E. M. *American Parties and Elections*. New York: Appleton Century, 1972.

Scammon, Richard M., and Wattenberg, Ben. *The Real Majority*. New York: Coward, McCann & Geoghegan, 1970.

Schattschneider, E. E. *Party Government*. New York: Holt, Rinehart, 1942.

——. *The Semi-Sovereign People*. New York: Holt, Rinehart & Winston, 1960.

Schlesinger, Joseph A. "Political Party Organization." In *The Handbook of Organization*, ed. James G. March. Chicago: Rand McNally, 1965.

Schneider, William. "Democrats Got Their Act Going Again." *Los Angeles Times*, 7 November 1976.

Schneier, Edward V. *Party and Constituency: Pressures on Congress*. Rev. ed. Baltimore: Johns Hopkins University Press, 1970.

Segal, David. "Classes, Strata, and Party in West Germany and the United States." *Comparative Studies in Society and History* 10 (October 1967):66–84.

Segal, David R., and Knocke, David. "Political Partisanship: Its Social and Economic Basis in the United States." *American Journal of Economics and Sociology* 29 (July 1970):253–62.

Sellers, Charles. "The Equilibrium Cycle in Two-Party Politics." *Public Opinion Quarterly* 29 (Spring 1965):16–38.

Shively, W. Phillips. "A Reinterpretation of the New Deal Realignment." *Public Opinion Quarterly* 35 (Winter 1971):620–24.

Shover, John L. "Was 1928 a Critical Election in California?" *Pacific Northwest Quarterly* 58 (October 1967):196–204.

Sinclair, Barbara Deckard. "Party Realignment and the Transformation of the Political Agenda: The House of Representatives." *American Political Science Review* 71 (September 1977):940–53.

Somers, Robert H. "A New Asymmetric Measure of Association for Ordinal Variables." *American Sociological Review* 27 (December 1962):799–811.

Sorauf, Frank J. *Party Politics in America*. Boston: Little, Brown, 1972.

Steinberg, Alfred. *The Bosses*. New York: Macmillan Co., 1972.

Stokes, Donald E., and Miller, Warren. "Party Government and the Saliency of Congress." In *Elections and the Political Order*, ed. Angus Campbell et al. New York: John Wiley & Sons, 1966.

Strong, Donald. "Durable Republicanism in the South." In *Change in the Contemporary South*, ed. Alan Sinsler. Durham: Duke University Press, 1963.

————. *Urban Republicanism in the South.* Birmingham: University of Alabama Press, 1956.

Sonquist, John A., and Morgan, James N. *The Detection of Interaction Effects.* Ann Arbor: Institute for Social Research, 1964.

Sundquist, James L. *Dynamics of the Party System: Alignment and Realignment of Political Parties in the United States.* Washington, D.C.: Brookings Institution, 1973.

Taeuber, Conrad, and Taeuber, Irene. *The Changing Population of the United States.* New York: John Wiley & Sons, 1958.

Topping, John C.; Sazarek, John R.; and Linder, William H. *Southern Republicanism and the New South.* Cambridge, 1966.

Tufte, Edward. "Communications." *American Political Science Review* 68 (March 1974):212.

————."Determinants of the Outcome of Midterm Congressional Elections." *American Political Science Review* 69 (September 1975):812–26.

————. "The Relationship between Seats and Votes in Two Party Systems." *American Political Science Review* 67 (June 1973):540–54.

Turner, Julius, and Schneier, Edward V., Jr. *Party and Constituency: Pressures on Congress.* Rev. ed. Baltimore: Johns Hopkins Press, 1970.

U.S. Department of Commerce, Bureau of the Census. *The Statistical Abstract of the United States: 1922.* Washington, D.C.: Government Printing Office, 1923.

Verba, Sidney, and Nie, Norman. *Participation in America: Political Democracy and Social Equality.* New York: Harper & Row, 1972.

Weisberg, Herbert. "Models of Statistical Relationships." *American Political Science Review* 66 (December 1974):1638–55.

Weisberg, Herbert F., and Rusk, Jerrold G. "Dimensions of Candidate Evaluation." *American Political Science Review* 64 (December 1970):1167–85.

"Why Carter Wins the Black Vote." *Time Magazine,* 5 April 1976, p. 15.

Williams, D. A. "Blacks and Politics '76" *Newsweek,* 20 September 1976, pp. 16–18.

————. "Not Quite Solid Southern Votes." *Newsweek,* 11 October 1976, p. 15.

Williams, Harold. "The Reverse Biogtry against Carter: Liberals Urged to Overcome Suspicions of Southern Baptist Heritage." *Los Angeles Times,* 2 July 1976.

Wilson, James Q. *The Amateur Democrat.* Chicago: University of Chicago Perss, 1962.

Wolfinger, Raymond E. "Some Consequences of Ethnic Politics." In *The Electoral Process,* ed. M. Kent Jennings and L. Harmon Zeigler. Englewood Cliffs: Prentice-Hall, 1966.

————. "The Development and Persistence of Ethnic Voting." *American Political Science Review* 59 (December 1965):896–908.

Wright, James. "The Ethno-cultural Model of Voting: A Behavioral and Historical Critique." *American Behavioral Scientist* 6 (May–June 1973):653–74.

Index